VAN BUREN DISTRICT LIBRARY
DECATUR

W9-BND-287

DISCARDED

EMERGENCY
TELEPHONE NUMBERS

Ambulance (911 or local emergency medical dispatch number)

_____

Police department _____

Fire department _____

Local poison control center _____

Local health department _____

Hospital emergency department _____

Doctor _____

Doctor _____

Doctor _____

24-hour pharmacy _____

Other neighborhood pharmacy _____

Health insurance number _____

Work number _____

Work number _____

Dentist _____

Baby-sitter _____

School/Daycare center _____

Electric company _____

Gas company _____

Water company _____

Neighbor _____

Neighbor _____

Relative _____

Relative _____

Other _____

_____

_____

TAKE ACTION
IN AN EMERGENCY

FIRST RESPONSE
- Dial 911 or call out for someone to contact 911 or the local emergency medical dispatcher.
- Ask if an automated external defibrillator (AED) is available.

IMMEDIATE TREATMENT
- Look for signs of life. Check airway, breathing, and circulation (see pp. 35–39).
- Determine if the person's heart is beating; if not, use an AED if available (see p. 43). If no AED is available, begin chest compressions (see p. 38).
- Perform abdominal or chest thrusts for choking (see p. 46).
- Stop excessive bleeding by applying pressure (see p. 52).
- Treat severe allergic reaction with an "Epinephrine Auto-Injector" (see p. 58).

WHAT TO TELL THE DOCTOR, PARAMEDICS, OR 911 OPERATOR
- The person's noticeable injuries, symptoms, or signs
- When the incident occurred or the symptoms or signs began
- What medications the person has taken (if known)
- If poisoning has occurred, what has been swallowed, how much, and when
- The location of you and/or the sick or injured person
- The phone number of your location

WHAT TO TELL THE POISON CONTROL CENTER
The poison control center will ask a series of important questions when you call, so be prepared to answer the following:

- The poisoned person's name, phone number, age, and approximate weight
- The exact name of the ingested product and its ingredients and manufacturer (have the container or label at hand when you make the call)
- How much of the product was swallowed
- When the poisoning occurred or symptoms began
- The person's symptoms
- What first aid, if any, has been performed
- Medical history of the person and any current medications he or she is taking

AMERICAN
MEDICAL
ASSOCIATION

HANDBOOK
of FIRST AID
and
EMERGENCY
CARE

**ALSO AVAILABLE FROM
THE AMERICAN MEDICAL ASSOCIATION:**

American Medical Association Complete Medical Encyclopedia

American Medical Association Concise Medical Encyclopedia

AMERICAN
MEDICAL
ASSOCIATION

HANDBOOK
of FIRST AID
and
EMERGENCY
CARE

Italo Subbarao, DO, MBA
Medical Editor

Jim Lyznicki, MS, MPH
Medical Editor

James J. James, MD, DrPh, MHA
Medical Editor

**Random House
Reference**

NEW YORK   TORONTO   LONDON   SYDNEY   AUCKLAND

616.0252
Ame

The information, procedures, and recommendations in this book are not intended
as a substitute for the medical advice of trained health professionals. For specific
information concerning a medical condition, consult a physician. The names of
organizations or products appearing in this book are given for informational
purposes only. Their inclusion does not imply AMA endorsement, nor does the
omission of any organization or product indicate AMA disapproval.

Copyright © 2009 by American Medical Association

All rights reserved. Published in the United States by Random House Reference, an
imprint of The Random House Information Group, a division of Random House, Inc.,
New York, and in Canada by Random House of Canada Limited, Toronto.

RANDOM HOUSE is a registered trademark of Random House, Inc.

This is a revised and updated edition of a work originally published by
Random House, Inc., New York, in 1980.

Please address inquiries about electronic licensing of any products for use
on a network, in software, or on CD-ROM to the Subsidiary Rights Department,
Random House Information Group, fax 212-572-6003.

This book is available at special discounts for bulk purchases for sales promotions
or premiums. Special editions, including personalized covers, excerpts of existing
books, and corporate imprints, can be created in large quantities for special needs.
For more information, write to Random House, Inc., Special Markets/Premium Sales,
1745 Broadway, MD 6-2, New York, NY, 10019 or e-mail
specialmarkets@randomhouse.com.

Visit the Random House Web site: www.randomhouse.com

Library of Congress Cataloging-in-Publication Data

The American Medical Association handbook of first aid and emergency care /
Italo Subbarao, Jim Lyznicki, James J. James, Medical editor[s]. — [Rev. ed.].
    p. cm.
  ISBN 978-1-4000-0712-7
  1. First aid in illness and injury—Handbooks, manuals, etc. 2. Medical
emergencies—Handbooks, manuals, etc. I. Subbarao, Italo. II. Lyznicki, Jim.
III. James, James J. IV. American Medical Association. V. Title: Handbook of
first aid and emergency care.
  RC86.8.A426 2009
  616.02′52—dc22

                    2008050966

ISBN: 978-1-4000-0712-7

Printed in the United States of America

10 9 8 7 6 5 4 3 2 1

FOREWORD

If a disaster or other medical emergency were to strike you or a member of your family, would you be prepared to handle it? If a stranger collapsed in front of you, could you provide the necessary care at a moment's notice?

Of course, we hope that you never have to face an emergency situation. But when serious illness or injury does occur, providing first aid within the critical first few minutes can save a life. And when you perform first aid correctly, paramedics and doctors can provide their care more effectively.

When you have to deal with more minor occurrences—washing a scraped elbow or knee, or stopping a nosebleed—you will feel better knowing that you are handling the situation in the best way possible. And you will be better able to offer that all-important reassuring, kind word to the person who is hurt or sick.

Our purpose in publishing this edition of the American Medical Association Handbook of First Aid and Emergency Care is to help you and your family respond to major and minor emergencies. We hope that you take the time now to read through the information and procedures in this book so that you are better prepared to deal with and recover from emergencies and disaster situations. Please bear in mind that this book cannot take the place of formal training in lifesaving procedures such as cardiopulmonary resuscitation. We strongly encourage you to take a class from the American Red Cross, the American Heart Association, or your local hospital or fire department. Get trained, be prepared, and get involved.

The American Medical Association wishes you and your family healthy and safe lives.

Michael D. Maves, MD, MBA
Executive Vice President
Chief Executive Officer
American Medical Association

ABOUT THE MEDICAL EDITORS

ITALO SUBBARAO DO, MBA, is an emergency medicine physician and the director of the Public Health Readiness Office in the Center for Public Health Preparedness and Disaster Response at the American Medical Association. He serves as deputy editor of the journal *Disaster Medicine and Public Health Preparedness*, an official AMA publication.

JIM LYZNICKI MS, MPH, is the associate director of the Center for Public Health Preparedness and Disaster Response at the American Medical Association. He holds master's degrees in medical microbiology and in environmental and occupational health.

JAMES J. JAMES MD, DRPH, MHA, is a preventive medicine physician and the director of the Center for Public Health Preparedness and Disaster Response at the American Medical Association. He is the editor-in-chief of *Disaster Medicine and Public Health Preparedness*, an official AMA publication. Dr. James serves on the National Biodefense Science Board and the Defense Science Board.

This book is dedicated to our loving and supportive families.

AMERICAN MEDICAL ASSOCIATION

Michael D. Maves, MD, MBA
Executive Vice President, Chief Executive Officer

Robert A. Musacchio, PhD
Senior Vice President, Publishing and Business Services

Frank Krause
Vice President and General Manager of Publishing

Mary Lou S. White
Publisher, AMA Publications and Clinical Solutions

EDITORIAL STAFF

Italo Subbarao, DO, MBA
Editor in Chief

Jim Lyznicki, MS, MPH
Co-Editor in Chief

James J. James, MD, DrPH, MHA
Co-Editor in Chief

Suzanne Fraker
Senior Acquisitions Editor

Nancy Baker
Managing Editor

Elizabeth Kennedy
Developmental Editor

Mary Ann Albanese
Art Editor

CONTRIBUTORS AND REVIEWERS

JOHN ARMSTRONG, MD, Associate Professor, Division of Acute Surgery, University of Florida Health Science Center

GAVIN BARR, MD, Clinical Associate Professor of Emergency Medicine, Lehigh Valley Hospital, Allentown, Pennsylvania

FREDERICK M. BURKLE JR., MD, MPH, DTM, Senior Fellow, Harvard Humanitarian Initiative, Harvard School of Public Health

DAVID BURMEISTER, DO, Chairman Department of Emergency Medicine, Lehigh Valley Hospital, Allentown, Pennsylvania

AJ KIRK, MD, Clinical Fellow, Disaster Medicine and Homeland Security, University of Texas-Southwestern Medical Center at Dallas

THOMAS D. KIRSCH, MD, MPH, Director of Operations, Department of Emergency Medicine, Johns Hopkins University

DAVID MARKENSON, MD, EMT-P, Director, Center for Disaster Medicine, School of Public Health, New York Medical College

RON PIRILLO, MD, Professor of Emergency Medicine, Medical College of Wisconsin, Department of Emergency Medicine

RAYMOND E. SWIENTON, MD, Co-Director of EMS, Disaster Medicine and Homeland Security, University of Texas-Southwestern Medical Center at Dallas

ERNIE SULLIVENT, MD, Commander, U.S. Public Health Service, Medical Epidemiologist, Research Team, Division of Injury Response, National Center for Injury Prevention and Control, Centers for Disease Control and Prevention

CONTENTS

AMA
AMERICAN
MEDICAL
ASSOCIATION

HANDBOOK
of FIRST AID
and
EMERGENCY
CARE

HOW TO USE THIS BOOK

Medical emergencies and disasters can occur at any time and place, and frequently require the assistance of a skilled bystander. In serious life-threatening emergencies, knowledge of critical skills such as how to use an automated external defibrillator (AED) can save a person's life. In less serious situations, knowing what to do can save unnecessary visits to the doctor or emergency department. In fact, most medical emergencies can be prevented by taking personal responsibility for your health and safety and taking time to protect against commonly encountered dangers. Finally, the likelihood of experiencing some type of disaster affects everyone, and it is necessary to consider disaster preparedness in the context of personal health.

This book is intended to be a resource for any citizen concerned about personal and community health. It is divided into six sections to help you find information quickly on the prevention of diseases and injuries, as well as basic medical first aid for illnesses and injuries that occur commonly in everyday life. A comprehensive index at the back of the book helps you find the appropriate entry if your medical problem is not clearly listed.

The book is intended to be a supporting reference to existing accredited first aid courses and education and is not intended to replace these courses. All citizens are strongly encouraged to get additional hands-on training in basic life support skills such as cardiopulmonary resuscitation (CPR) from an accredited first aid course provider.

Part I

PREVENTION

PREVENTING ILLNESS AND INJURY

Preventing illness and injury is essential to living a healthy and fulfilling life. Unfortunately, such problems cannot be prevented completely. When an injury or illness does occur, affected persons may require medical treatment as well as the inner strength and willpower to help ensure a speedy recovery. To prevent illness and injury, everyone should take the necessary steps to achieve a healthy level of physical and mental health fitness. Such fitness is related directly to one's resilience, which is the ability to quickly rebound and adapt to physical and psychological stress. You can become more resilient by adopting healthy lifestyle behaviors and empowering yourself with knowledge of personal health risks and risk factors; the importance of medical screening; and the role of diet, exercise, sleep, and hygiene as essential for good health and well-being. Becoming resilient also involves taking steps to prevent and avoid predictable dangers to your health and safety, such as smoking, excessive drinking, and not wearing seat belts.

Injuries are a leading cause of preventable death and disability for all ages, regardless of gender, race, or income. For many people, injuries cause temporary pain and inconvenience; but for some, injuries lead to chronic pain, loss of function, and major changes in lifestyle. Common causes of injuries involve alcohol, fires, motor vehicle crashes, strenuous physical activity, firearms, fatigue, and inattention to your surroundings (for example, when listening to music on headphones or when talking or text-messaging on cell phones while walking or driving). Most injuries can be prevented by developing the situational awareness to recognize potential danger and take appropriate safety precautions.

Chronic diseases such as heart disease, cancer, and diabetes are among the most common and costly medical and public health problems. Cardiovascular diseases (for example, heart disease and stroke) are the leading cause of death and disability in the United States and are associated with preventable risk factors, notably high blood pressure, high cholesterol, and obesity. Behavioral and lifestyle risk factors such as unhealthy diets, physical inactivity, and tobacco use also

contribute to many chronic diseases. Like injuries, many dise
be prevented by taking responsibility for your health. Disease pre-
tion involves:

- Eliminating or controlling personal risk factors (quit smoking, control your weight, and avoid unhealthy foods)
- Recognizing early warning signs (such as a lump in the breast or bloody stool)
- Undergoing early detection screenings (for example, mammograms and colonoscopies)
- Guarding against potential risks in the environment (use seat belts, wear a helmet when riding a bicycle)

Talk with your doctor about the need for routine medical checkups and physicals, including cancer screening and prevention. Women should discuss the role of routine Pap smears and mammograms for the detection of cervical and breast cancer, respectively. Men should talk with their doctor about screening for prostate and testicular cancer. All men and women should discuss screening for skin cancer and colon cancer. Family history of a specific cancer can be a strong risk factor and may require your doctor to recommend earlier testing or additional screening procedures. Remember that obesity and smoking are important cancer risks.

Medical emergencies also commonly arise from infections that can be spread easily through personal contact. Various childhood and adult infections, such as chickenpox, measles, and influenza (or the "flu"), can be prevented with vaccines. Although there is no vaccine for the common cold, careful attention to proper hygiene, such as washing your hands and covering your mouth when coughing, can reduce the spread of viruses and other germs.

This section gives some basic guidance on measures to prevent injury and disease.

EAT A HEALTHY DIET

Eating healthier can help you prevent and control chronic diseases such as high blood pressure, heart disease, stroke, diabetes, cancer, and osteoporosis. An appropriate diet gives your body balanced nutrition and makes you less tired, gives you more energy, and stimulates weight loss. A healthy diet includes:

- Fruits, vegetables, whole grains, and fat-free or low-fat milk and milk products
- Proteins such as lean meats, poultry, fish, beans, eggs, and nuts (and remember it is better to bake it, broil it, or grill it than to fry it)
- Limited intake of saturated fats, trans fats, cholesterol, salt (sodium), and added sugars
- Appropriate hydration (drink plenty of water)

Adopting a healthier lifestyle includes reducing the amount of red meat and processed meats in your diet and replacing these with foods that are high in unsaturated fats such as fish and olive oil. This lifestyle change can reduce your risk for a heart attack, stroke, and cancer. A healthier lifestyle also includes minimizing excess carbohydrate intake from processed foods such as white bread or pasta and shifting your diet toward complex carbohydrates such as whole grain foods. It is important to minimize excess salt, caffeine, and alcohol intake. A high fiber diet that includes fruits and vegetables and drinking at least 8 cups of water for adults is vital to preventing gastrointestinal problems such as constipation. Most dietary authorities recommend a diet of 2,000 calories per day for adults, but you should always discuss your individual calorie needs with your physician or local dietician.

EXERCISE REGULARLY

Cardiovascular disease is linked to a sedentary lifestyle, so it is important to get regular exercise. Include aerobic activities such as walking, jogging, cycling, or swimming to improve circulation and strengthen your bones and muscles. Strength training (weight lifting) also should become part of your exercise routine. Consider taking up yoga or Pilates to improve flexibility and muscle tone. An optimal exercise program will include all three components: aerobic activities, strength training, and flexibility exercises. Prior to doing any physical

OBESITY

Excess weight is a result of consuming more calories than you expend through exercise and daily activities. As you consume excess calories, your body converts the energy into fat, which is stored throughout the body. Excess weight around the abdomen is particularly concerning because abdominal fat increases your risk of many serious medical conditions such as hypertension, diabetes, hyperlipidemia (high fats, high cholesterol), cardiovascular disease (heart attack and brain attack [stroke]), sleep apnea, and cancer, among others. In general, an adult woman's waist measurement should be less than 35 inches; an adult man's waist should measure less than 40 inches. These are rough cutoffs, but in general, the smaller the waist measurement the better.

The following factors—usually working in combination—can contribute to weight gain and obesity.

- **Poor diet.** High-fat foods such as fast food or fried foods contain a lot of calories. High-sugar products such as soft drinks, candy, and desserts are high in calories and promote weight gain.

- **Sedentary lifestyle.** People who do not get regular exercise are likely to gain weight because they don't burn calories through physical activity.

- **Medication effect.** Corticosteroids and tricyclic antidepressants, in particular, can lead to weight gain. Some high blood pressure and antipsychotic medications also may cause weight gain.

- **Medical problems.** Less commonly, obesity can be traced to a medical cause, such as low thyroid function or excess production of hormones by the adrenal glands (Cushing's syndrome). A low metabolic rate is unlikely to cause obesity. Some medical problems, such as arthritis, can lead to decreased activity, which may result in weight gain.

PREVENTION

Taking proactive responsibility and adopting a healthy lifestyle that includes daily exercise and a healthy diet are mainstays of prevention. It is important to monitor your weight regularly and be vigilant about caloric intake when buying food or eating out.

activity, it is important to "warm up" appropriately and have adequate water or other fluids available to drink (see Section IV, Sports First Aid). Consult your physician before beginning any exercise program and discuss your progress during follow-up medical visits.

To reduce the risk of chronic disease, average healthy adults should:

- Do moderate aerobic exercises for 30 minutes each day, 5 days a week; **or** do vigorous aerobic exercises for 20 minutes each day, 3 days a week. Moderate-intensity physical activity means working hard enough to raise your heart rate and break a sweat, yet still being able to carry on a conversation. It should be noted that to lose weight or maintain weight loss, 60 to 90 minutes of physical activity may be necessary 3 to 5 days a week.

- Both aerobic routines should be accompanied by 8 to 10 strength-training exercises twice a week, with 8 to 12 repetitions of each exercise.

AVOID TOBACCO USE

Tobacco use is the leading cause of preventable death in the United States. Tobacco use contributes to every chronic disease, including cancer, diabetes, asthma, chronic obstructive pulmonary disease, and heart problems. Smoking harms nearly every organ of the body, causing many diseases and reducing health in general. Exposure to secondhand smoke (also known as environmental tobacco smoke) causes heart disease and lung cancer in nonsmoking adults. In children, it is associated with increased respiratory conditions, middle ear infections, and behavioral problems. Breathing secondhand smoke has immediate harmful effects on the cardiovascular system that can increase the risk of heart attack. People with existing heart and lung diseases are at especially high risk.

Quitting smoking has immediate as well as long-term benefits, reducing risks for diseases caused by smoking and improving overall health. Numerous effective medications are available over the counter and by prescription to treat tobacco dependence. If you smoke, talk with your doctor about ways to quit and develop a treatment plan that is right for you. If you don't use tobacco, don't start. Make your home, workplace, and motor vehicle smoke-free environments.

GET ENOUGH SLEEP

Sleep is an essential aspect of illness and injury prevention. Many chronic diseases such as diabetes, cardiovascular disease, obesity, and depression are associated with insufficient sleep. Sleepiness and fatigue can put you at risk for a motor vehicle crash or mishap at work. How much sleep is enough? Sleep needs vary by age and person. Infants require the most sleep (15 to 18 hours per day). Children 5 to 12 years of age require 9 to 11 hours of sleep each day. Generally 8 hours of sleep is recommended for adults. Talk to your doctor about good sleep habits, especially if you are having difficulty sleeping.

PREVENT INFECTIONS

Many infectious diseases such as the common cold can be spread by coughing or sneezing or by unclean hands or surfaces. To help prevent the spread of germs and to avoid getting sick, it is important to adopt proper hygiene habits. This includes covering your mouth and nose with a tissue when you cough or sneeze. If you don't have a tissue, cough or sneeze into your upper sleeve, not your hands. Immediately clean your hands after coughing or sneezing and wash with soap and water for 20 seconds. If a bathroom is not nearby, use an alcohol-based hand cleaner. Hand sanitizers can significantly reduce the number of germs on the skin.

Many infectious diseases such as the flu can be prevented by vaccination. It is important to discuss the need for vaccines with your doctor.

AVOID HAZARDS

Driving to work, riding a bicycle, crossing a busy street, or walking near a construction site are examples of common everyday risks. It is important to take precautions when risks are known, such as wearing a seat belt while driving, wearing a helmet when riding a bicycle or motorcycle, or simply avoiding a potentially risky situation. It is also important to consider potential hazards when considering future activities. For example, if you plan to go on a hike in the woods, you need to take precautions such as notifying people when you leave and packing appropriate supplies (including flashlight, batteries, food, water, and cell phone).

BUILD RESILIENCE

Resilient people experience temporary disruptions in life when faced with challenges, but are able to continue with daily tasks and remain generally optimistic about life. People who are less resilient may obsess on problems, feel victimized and overwhelmed, and turn to unhealthy coping mechanisms, such as drugs or alcohol. They may even be more inclined to develop mental health problems.

The good news is that you can build resilience by taking personal responsibility for your physical and psychological health. Adoption of healthy lifestyle behaviors such as eating a well-balanced diet, getting regular exercise, and learning skills such as first aid and CPR actually help build personal resilience by enabling you to cope more effectively with potentially stressful physical or psychological situations (for example, the death of a loved one, job loss, or recent diagnosis of a serious illness). Building resilience also can help prevent mental health problems such as depression, anxiety, or post-traumatic stress disorder. Additional ways to strengthen your resilience include building healthy relationships (with family and friends and community groups), accepting and anticipating change, and taking action toward goals that can keep the mind focused.

SAFEGUARDING YOUR HOME AGAINST ACCIDENTS

Keeping your home safe for you and your family should be a top health priority. Injuries that occur in the home are an important cause of disability and death in the United States. Many of these injuries could have been prevented.

To ensure that your home is safe, take a few minutes to read over the information provided below, and review it each year. Create a safety checklist with the elements that apply to your home. The items listed are important to consider but are by no means all-inclusive. In addition to those listed below, other areas of the home to check regularly for safety hazards include closets, the attic, and additional storage areas such as garden sheds.

Reminder: **Smoke detectors, carbon monoxide detectors, and fire extinguishers are investments that can save lives**. Check them each month to ensure they are in working order. Change the batteries every year on an easy-to-remember date, such as your birthday.

> Kitchen

- Chemical cleaners and disinfectants: Tightly cap or close and properly store products (in their original container and with a label) out of the sight and reach of children and away from food. Never reuse these containers for storing food or other items.
- Knives: Properly store out of the sight and reach of children.
- Electric cords and outlets: Fix or replace cords and plugs if damaged; be sure all electric plugs and outlets are grounded properly.
- Oven and stove top: Clean regularly.
- Refrigerator and freezer: Clean and defrost regularly.
- Microwave oven: Clean regularly and be sure it is secured safely.
- Other electric appliances: Clean and properly store.
- Liquor: Properly store out of the sight and reach of children.
- All cabinets should have safety locks to prevent children from getting to items.

> Bathroom

- Glass containers: Remove or replace with plastic containers.
- Chemical cleaners: Tightly cap or close and properly store out of the sight and reach of children.
- Electric cords and outlets: Fix or replace cords and plugs if damaged; be sure all electrical plugs and outlets are grounded properly.
- Hair dryer, curling iron, electric shaver: Unplug and store properly.

- Rugs or mats: Tack down, hold in place with carpet tape, or remove.
- Tub and shower: Place adhesive grippers on floor of tub and install railing along wall to help prevent falls.
- All cabinets should have safety locks to prevent children from getting to items.

> Living and Sleeping Areas

- Walls and windowsills: Remove peeling paint. Note that many houses and apartments built before 1978 have paint that contain high levels of lead (called lead-based paint). Lead from paint, chips, and dust can pose serious health hazards if not taken care of properly. Take precautions to avoid exposure to lead dust when remodeling or renovating.
- Keep matches and lighters out of the sight and reach of children.
- Fireplace: Screen off fireplace.
- Furniture: Be sure that no metal springs are protruding.
- Electric cords and outlets: Fix or replace if damaged; be sure all electric plugs and outlets are grounded properly.
- Rugs or mats: Tack down, hold in place with carpet tape, or remove.
- Firearms and ammunition: If you choose to own a gun, you must take personal responsibility for securing it from unauthorized handling, whether by children, guests, neighbors, or criminals. Obtain firearm safety locks and store firearms under lock and key; store ammunition separately from firearms. If you choose to have a gun in your house, family members should be educated about firearms safety. No matter how they feel about firearms, it is important that children and other family members learn the basics of firearms safety. Even if a gun is never in your home, there may be one in the home of a friend, neighbor, or relative.

> Stairs

- Handrails: Verify the stability along the full length of the stairs at least on one side.
- Rugs or mats: Remove from top and bottom of stairs.
- Lighting: Adequately illuminate all steps.
- Safety gates: If there are young children in the house, they are a necessity.

> Garage or Basement

- Cleaners and chemicals such as insecticides and other pesticides (for example, rat poison), weed killers, antifreeze, paint, paint thinner, or charcoal lighter fluid: Tightly cap or close and properly store out of the sight and reach of children. Never reuse an empty container to store other items. Throw out old paint. Immediately clean up spills.

- Gasoline can: Tightly close and properly store out of the sight and reach of children. Immediately clean up spills.

- Saws, chisels, or other items with sharp blades: Properly store out of the sight and reach of children.

- Electric cords and outlets: Fix or replace if damaged; be sure all electrical plugs and outlets are grounded properly.

- Electric tools: Keep unplugged and with safety locks on.

- Old rags or newspapers: Discard.

- Loose cords or hoses: Properly roll up and store.

- Doors, windows, and screens: Properly store.

- Lighting: Adequately illuminate all areas, including corners.

- Buckets: Empty and properly store. Infants and young children can drown in fluid-filled buckets.

> Motor Vehicles

- Seat belts: Wear a lap-and-shoulder seat belt whenever you drive or ride in a car or truck, and make sure all passengers in your vehicle are secured properly. A rear seat is the safest place for all children to be secured.

- Child safety seats: All infants and children should be secured correctly in seat restraints that are appropriate for their age and size. Never place a rear-facing infant restraint in the front seat or allow children less than 12 years of age to sit in the front seat of a car that has a passenger-side air bag. Discuss the purchase and use of child safety seats with your child's doctor.

  > Infants should always ride in a rear-facing restraint until they are 1 year of age and weigh at least 20 pounds.

  > Children 1 year of age and at least 20 pounds can ride in a forward-facing safety seat.

  > Booster seats are available for older children who have outgrown their forward-facing safety seats. Children should

stay in a booster seat until the adult seat belts fit correctly (usually when a child reaches about 4 feet 9 inches in height and is between 8 and 12 years of age).

> Children who have outgrown their booster seats should ride in a lap-and-shoulder belt; they should ride in the back seat until 13 years of age.

• Alcohol and other drugs: Never drive after drinking alcohol or taking other drugs that could impair your judgment or concentration.

• Maintenance: Keep your car in good repair, especially the lights, brakes, and tires.

> Swimming Pool

• Perimeter: Fence and lock the area to prevent children from getting to the pool.

• Signs and markings: Clearly mark depths on the deck near the edge and along the sides of the pool. Place or paint "NO DIVING" signs on the deck near the shallow end.

• Floats and safety devices: Place floats across the width of the pool to mark where the deep end starts. Provide approved floating safety devices and ensure that they are not removed.

• Rules: Never allow running on the deck. Never allow diving in an above ground pool. Allow diving in an in-ground pool only if the water is more than 9 feet deep and there is sufficient distance between the diving board and the upward slope to the shallow end.

> Medications

• Store medications in a locked cabinet.

• Keep track of medications by writing them down in the chart on p. 386.

• When they are expired or no longer needed, it is important to dispose of prescription drugs and other medications properly to reduce the chance that they might harm others. When disposing of medications, federal authorities recommend that you:

> Take unused, unneeded, or expired prescription drugs and other medications out of their original containers and throw them in the trash. Drugs should be mixed with an undesirable substance, such as used coffee grounds or kitty litter, and put into closed, impermeable, nondescript containers, such as empty cans or sealable bags.

The U.S. Food and Drug Administration advises that the following drugs be flushed down the toilet instead of thrown in the trash:

Actiq (fentanyl citrate)	Meperidine HCl tablets
Avinza capsules (morphine sulfate)	OxyContin tablets (oxycodone)
Baraclude tablets (entecavir)	Percocet (oxycodone and acetaminophen)
Daytrana transdermal patch (methylphenidate)	Reyataz capsules (atazanavir sulfate)
Duragesic transdermal system (fentanyl)	Tequin tablets (gatifloxacin)
	Xyrem (sodium oxybate)
Fentora (fentanyl buccal tablet)	Zerit for oral solution (stavudine)

Note: Always refer to the printed material accompanying your medication for specific instructions.

Source: Office of National Drug Control Policy, February 2007.

> Flush prescription drugs down the toilet only if the label or accompanying patient information specifically instructs you to do so (see box above).

> Take advantage of community pharmaceutical take-back programs that allow you to bring unused drugs to a central location for proper disposal. Some communities have pharmaceutical take-back programs or community solid-waste programs that allow the public to bring unused drugs to a central location for proper disposal. Where these exist, they are a good way to dispose of unused pharmaceuticals.

Part II

BEING PREPARED FOR INJURIES AND EMERGENCIES

GETTING HELP IN AN EMERGENCY

Accessing medical help when faced with an emergency is a critical action. When faced with an emergency, immediately dial 911 or your local emergency medical dispatch number on any available phone and do not hang up until help arrives. This action will provide you, in most circumstances, with a person trained to assist you immediately in the next actions you should perform while you await the arrival of appropriate emergency medical personnel and vehicles at your location.

Staying on the phone gives you a person to talk with as you continue managing the situation until help arrives. If you become unable to speak, or must walk away from the phone to help the person, do not hang up the phone, as it may provide the operator a means to find your location while you are still connected.

If you are unable to access help by calling 911 or your local emergency medical dispatch number for whatever reason, and have attempted at least 3 times, you still have other options. These include directly calling a local hospital, ambulance company, or police or fire department. You can also contact the poison control center for your local area, especially if a poisoning, ingestion of an unknown substance, or possible chemical exposure is suspected.

Knowing the best routes to local hospitals or other urgent care facilities is an important part of being prepared. When driving to these facilities, one must exercise caution at all times, obey traffic rules and regulations, and avoid distractions in the vehicle. If the condition of the injured or ill person demands your attention, stop the vehicle safely in a secure, populated location (for example, a parking lot) to minimize the risk of a traffic crash and to get the attention of others who may be able to help.

PERSONAL AND FAMILY MEMBER MEDICAL INFORMATION

You should regularly update important medical information for yourself and family members. This information should be immediately accessible to you and your family at all times in the event of an emergency.

Medical information must include allergies; chronic illnesses or diseases; medications taken daily, including the dose; any implanted medical devices or other medical devices used regularly; and copies of important medical documents that you or family members have been advised to have immediately accessible. This includes health insurance information and documentation on organ donation and advanced directives (such as "living wills").

It is important for you to have quick access to the names and telephone numbers of doctors and other health care personnel who provide regular care to you and your family members. A list also should be maintained with contact information (complete names, addresses, and phone numbers) of family members, legal guardians, and others who have responsibility for making health care decisions in an emergency.

Page 386 of this handbook contains an example of a personal and family medical chart for your use. It is strongly advised that you complete this or a similar document. The chart lists medical information that you and the physicians or paramedics need in an emergency.

EMERGENCY MEDICAL IDENTIFICATION

Wearing an emergency ID bracelet or necklace or carrying an emergency information card could save the life of someone who is unable to speak after a serious accident or illness. This medical identification is particularly important for people with chronic conditions such as diabetes, epilepsy, glaucoma, or hemophilia, or those who may have a serious allergic reaction to certain medications (such as penicillin) or to insect stings. Talk with your doctor about the need to wear an emergency ID bracelet or necklace or carry an emergency information card, and discuss what information should be included to inform others about your health conditions and needs.

These bracelets, necklaces, and cards include such information as the individual's name, address, blood type, doctors, medications, person(s) you want contacted in an emergency with their address and

IN CASE OF EMERGENCY (ICE)

A new practice that has gained widespread recognition is to make an entry in your cell phone directory for ICE (In Case of Emergency) with the contact information for the person who should be called if you are ill or injured and cannot tell someone whom to call. Emergency medical and hospital personnel are now being taught to look for this information in cell phone directories. In addition, if there is a "note filed" capability in your cell phone, you can put key medical information in the ICE listing such as allergies, medications, and medical conditions.

phone number, and any serious conditions or allergies. These items are available through several manufacturers. Ask your doctor, hospital emergency department, or local medical association where you can order them.

MAKING AN EMERGENCY MEDICAL SUPPLIES KIT

Now is the time to assemble those basic items you may need when an injury occurs in your home or elsewhere. It is important that you clearly label all items in the emergency medical supply kit. If possible, keep all items in their original packaging as this will help keep them clean, reduce the chance of contamination, and help you identify the product expiration date. Store the kit in a safe location, out of the reach of small children or others not familiar with the proper use of the items. Check the supplies and medications regularly for damage such as ripped packaging, or signs of contamination such as discoloration, moisture, mold, or foul odors. Any expired items should be promptly replaced.

It is important that all family members of an appropriate age know where the kit is stored. You may want to prepare more than one emergency medical supply kit for use in your vehicle or boat or for recreational activities (camping, fishing, sports).

Categorizing items into groups may assist you in stocking and organizing your emergency medical supplies kit. One useful way is to have the items organized into 3 groups: health prevention and protection, medical supplies and equipment, and medications.

The following lists are suggestions of items that are useful in many illnesses and injuries.

Health Prevention and Protection

- Cell phone, charger, spare charged battery
- Gloves, disposable such as nitrile
- Sunscreen with a sun protection factor (SPF) of at least 15 or greater
- Insect repellant
- Bar of plain soap
- Flashlight and spare batteries
- Lightsticks, 12-hour duration, chemical powered
- Water, potable ("drinkable") for dehydration (1 gallon/person/day)
- Blankets for survival or rescue
- Poncho or other rain protection
- Face masks, appropriate for reducing infectious disease spread
- Dust masks
- Weather radio (NOAA stations), battery operated with spare batteries
- AM-FM radio, battery operated with spare batteries
- Knife in protective sheath or folding design
- Duct tape or equivalent product

Medical Supplies and Equipment

- Different sizes of sterile adhesive strips, Band-Aids, etc.
- Roll of gauze bandage (3 inches wide)
- Nonstick sterile gauze pads (4 inches x 4 inches) packaged separately in sealed wrappers
- Butterfly bandages and thin adhesive strips to hold skin edges together

- Roll of adhesive tape (1 inch wide)
- Scissors
- Elastic bandage (2 or 3 inches wide) for wrapping sprained ankles and wrists
- Package of cotton-tipped swabs
- Roll of absorbent cotton to pad a splint
- Thermometers
- Small jar or tube of petroleum jelly to use with rectal thermometer
- Tweezers without teeth
- Safety pins
- Water, potable ("drinkable") for wound irrigation to flush dirt and contamination
- Bottle of sterile saline solution or irrigation fluid to wash out eyes
- Spare batteries and other replaceable parts for equipment selected

Medications

- Pain control: acetaminophen, ibuprofen, or similar choices
- Fever control: acetaminophen
- Allergic reactions: antihistamine such as diphenhydramine; severe life-threatening allergies may require the use of an epinephrine auto-injector (see p. 58).
- Wound care: Potable ("drinkable") water or normal saline solution for rinsing and flushing the wound area. Other solutions may be useful such as household strength hydrogen peroxide (3%) or povidone-iodine solution (each of which should be diluted before use).
- Skin irritation or "itching" rash: tube of 1% hydrocortisone cream for topical use
- Regular medications: medications, prescription and nonprescription, which are taken regularly or based on chronic health conditions, as directed by your doctor

This list of health and medical supplies is a suggestion and your contents may vary. When selecting medications and supplies, you should consider the person's age (for example, children's doses) and route of administration of medications. It is important to keep all instructions for use such as "owner's manuals" and dosing instructions of medications with each product.

> Everyday Items That Can Be Used In an Emergency

Certain everyday items in your home can be used in an emergency situation when you are lacking the proper materials:

- For dressings, splint padding, and emergency childbirth: disposable or regular diapers, sanitary napkins, towels, sheets, or linens
- For securing bandages and slings: diaper or safety pins
- For conserving body heat: blankets
- For splints: rolled magazines and newspapers, umbrellas, or pillows
- For stretchers: doors
- For bandages and slings: large scarves or handkerchiefs

Keep in mind that adapting an item for a use it was not designed for can be dangerous, resulting in further illness or injury. Consider the potential risks before deciding to use them.

Medications should be used only as described in the package insert or instructions provided on the container label. You should not alter the intended use, change the dose, change the route of administration, or give the medication to a person not in the intended age range or to persons taking other medications because this could cause illness or death.

WHEN TO CALL YOUR LOCAL EMERGENCY MEDICAL DISPATCHER OR 911 CALL CENTER

If a problem appears to be a serious medical emergency, it is important to seek medical attention immediately and dial 911 or your local emergency medical dispatch number to summon help. The following are examples of medical emergencies:

- Chest pain or pressure with sweating and shortness of breath
- Loss of consciousness, fainting
- Difficulty breathing
- Eating, drinking, or breathing something that is poisonous
- Taking too much medication (drug overdose)
- Bleeding that does not stop
- Injuries from a fall or a collision
- Rape (sexual assault)
- Physical assault (being beaten by someone)
- Attempted suicide
- Seizures or convulsions
- A severe allergic reaction or a sudden asthma attack that does not stop
- Sudden numbness of or not being able to move (paralysis) an arm, leg, or one side of the body
- Sudden loss of vision, not being able to see
- A sudden severe headache, especially with neck pain or change in consciousness
- A change in mental ability, such as not knowing where you are or who your friends, family, or coworkers are
- Premature labor (when a woman starts to deliver a baby too soon)

In any of these situations, you can get medical help from the emergency medical system by calling 911 or the local emergency medical dispatch number. When speaking to the dispatch operator, remember to stay calm and speak slowly and clearly.

When calling the emergency medical dispatcher or speaking to a paramedic, it is very helpful to give him or her specific information about the person. Be prepared to provide the following information:

- What has happened
- The person's noticeable injuries, symptoms, or signs

- When the accident occurred or the symptoms or signs beg
- What medications the person has taken (if known)
- If poisoning has occurred, what has been swallowed, how much, and when
- Where you and/or the sick or injured person are located
- The phone number of your location

Above all—and especially in an emergency situation—try to remain calm and follow the medical professional's instructions. Ask what more you can do to help. Your first-aid measures could save valuable time and, possibly, the life of the person.

EMERGENCY MEDICAL SERVICES (AMBULANCE SERVICES)

Most communities have some type of ambulance service and specialized emergency medical personnel available. The most highly trained ambulance personnel are emergency medical technician (EMT) paramedics. They are trained to administer advanced life support techniques such as CPR, to take electrocardiographic (ECG) tracings that reveal the electrical activity of the heart, to start intravenous (IV) lines, and to give medication.

Other trained emergency medical personnel can provide CPR and perform medical procedures, such as splinting broken bones. Some can shock a person's heart with specialized equipment such as an AED if the heart has stopped beating. They cannot, however, administer medication or perform sophisticated medical procedures.

Many ambulances with paramedics have equipment hooked up to a local hospital to relay the ECG readings and other vital medical information. Instructions from hospital doctors can then be relayed via radio to help the paramedics treat the person.

If you have children, you should know that not all hospital emergency departments have personnel trained to handle childhood emergencies or equipment designed to treat children. Find out if there is a children's hospital in your area. If there is not a children's hospital, then call the emergency departments at the hospitals nearest your home and ask if they have pediatric capability. If you find a children's hospital or pediatric emergency department, keep the number and name near your phone so that you can take your child there or tell the ambulance personnel that is where you wish them to take your child in an emergency. Make sure you know the exact location in case you need to drive your child there.

Paramedics and other ambulance personnel are usually available through various community resources such as the fire department, police department, and volunteer associations. Check with the resources in your community before an emergency strikes so that you will know the type of service to call. Paramedics should not be called for minor illnesses or injuries such as sprained ankles, minor cuts, or colds; they need to be available to treat people who have more serious conditions. Often people with minor injuries can be driven to the hospital by a family member or friend. If you are taking someone to the hospital and there is time, call your doctor so that he or she can call the emergency department. This enables the staff to know what to expect, to prepare for the person's arrival, and to discuss the case with the doctor.

> Information to Give Emergency Department Personnel

Emergency department personnel treat the most serious and critical cases first. Any specific information you can give them about the person's condition will help them determine its seriousness. Describing specific complaints, such as severe crushing chest pain or sharp lower abdominal pain, is very helpful. Other useful information includes:

- When the symptoms began
- What makes the pain or condition better or worse and whether the pain has traveled to another part of the body
- What the person was doing when the injury or illness occurred
- What changes have occurred in the person since the onset of the illness or injury
- What medications the person has been taking
- What known allergies the person has

- The name of the person's primary care doctor
- If poisoning has occurred, what has been swallowed, how much, and when

If there is time before leaving for the hospital, gather insurance identification cards, Medicare or Medicaid cards, or any other record of medical benefits to which the person is entitled. Be prepared to give the person's name, age, address, a history of major injuries or illnesses, and known allergies. If the emergency department cannot handle a specific situation, it must arrange to send the person to another hospital that can handle the medical problem.

Emergency department treatment is generally more expensive than medical treatment received in a doctor's office. Most emergency departments must be staffed with doctors, nurses, and other personnel on a 24-hour basis, thus increasing their costs. Also, emergency departments must be equipped with costly equipment not usually found in a doctor's office. Most hospitals will process insurance forms. A number of hospitals are now also accepting major credit cards for payment.

FIRST AID TECHNIQUES TO LEARN AND PRACTICE

Dressings, bandages, slings, and splints are an important part of first aid care. It is a good idea to learn and practice their application

WARNING: BLOOD AND BODY FLUID EXPOSURE

Actions taken to assist an individual may raise your risk of exposure to blood and body secretions, thereby increasing your risk of exposure to human immunodeficiency virus (HIV), hepatitis B, and hepatitis C. These viruses can pass from an infected individual to a rescuer through broken skin or mucous membranes such as the eyes, nose, or mouth, or from open wounds. You can reduce your risk of exposure by wearing protective equipment such as face masks, eye shields, and gloves. With proper precautions, the risk of contracting these viruses through blood and body secretions is low.

before an emergency occurs. Knowing how to apply a dressing, bandage, or splint will enable you to do so calmly and expertly during a stressful situation. The best method to learn this is to take a formal course in first aid from the American Red Cross or other accredited provider.

DRESSINGS

A dressing, or compress, is a covering placed directly over a wound. Its purpose is to help control bleeding, absorb secretions from the wound, and prevent contamination by germs. Because the dressing is placed directly over the wound, it should be sterile. Sterile dressings such as gauze pads and bandages are individually wrapped and are available at most drugstores. If a sterile dressing is not available, a clean handkerchief, pillowcase, sheet, or other cloth can be used. Adhesive tape and fluffy materials such as absorbent cotton should never be applied directly to the wound because they can stick to the wound and be difficult to remove.

The dressing should be large enough to cover and go beyond all edges of the wound to prevent contamination of any part of the wound. To apply the dressing, hold it directly over the wound and lower it into place. Do not slide or drag the dressing over the skin; this contaminates the dressing. Discard any dressing that has slipped out of place before it has been bandaged.

BANDAGES

A bandage is a piece of material that holds a dressing or splint in place. It can also be a wrap, such as an elastic bandage, that is applied directly to an injured area to help decrease bleeding or swelling or give support to a joint or group of muscles. Bandages include gauze wraps, elastic wraps, and various adhesive tapes. Most bandages can be purchased at drugstores.

To function properly, a bandage must be applied snugly but not too tightly. A bandage applied too tightly can cut off circulation and cause serious tissue damage. Remember that an injured area may swell, causing a snug bandage to become too tight.

When applying a bandage to the arm, hand, leg, or foot, leave the fingertips or toes exposed so that danger signals such as swelling, bluish or pale color, or coldness can be observed or felt. If any of these signs appear or if the person complains of increased pain, numbness or tingling, loosen the bandage immediately.

COMMON ADHESIVE BANDAGES

RECTANGULAR BANDAGES
A rectangular bandage is used for simple cuts and scrapes and can be purchased at most drugstores. The rectangular bandage is a combination of dressing and adhesive bandage. To prevent contamination, do not touch the dressing while applying it over the wound.

BUTTERFLY BANDAGES AND NARROW ADHESIVE STRIPS
Butterfly bandages and narrow adhesive strips are thin pieces of tape that are used to hold the edges of a cut together, thus allowing the wound to heal. They are especially useful in treating small cuts. When applying the bandage, gently hold the edges of the cut together without touching inside the wound.

COMMON ADHESIVE BANDAGES

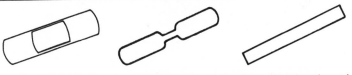

A rectangular bandage (left), a combination of both dressing and bandage, is used for simple cuts and scrapes. The butterfly bandage (center) and the narrow adhesive strip (right) are thin pieces of tape that are used to hold the edges of a cut together.

ROLLER GAUZE BANDAGES

The roller bandage comes in various widths and lengths and is usually made of gauze. It comes packaged in rolls and can be used on most parts of the body. If commercial roller bandages are not available, a bandage can be made from a clean strip of cloth. The most common uses of roller gauze are for circular (circumferential), figure-of-eight, and fingertip bandages.

CIRCULAR (CIRCUMFERENTIAL) BANDAGES

A circular bandage is the easiest to apply. It is used on areas that do not vary much in width, such as the wrist, toes, and fingers. To apply a circular bandage:

1. Anchor the bandage by placing the end of it at a slight angle over the affected part and making several circular wraps around the affected part to hold the end in place. Don't wrap the bandage too tightly.

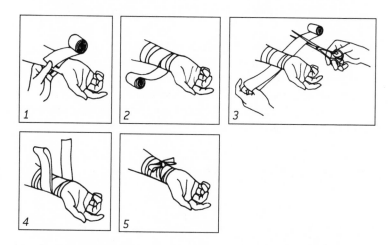

2. Make additional circular turns by overlapping the preceding strip by approximately ¾ of its width. Continue circling the bandage in the same direction until the dressing is completely covered.

3. To secure the bandage, cut the gauze with scissors or a knife and apply adhesive tape or a safety pin to the bandage. Or tie a loop knot by extending the rolled gauze out about 8 inches away from the part being bandaged. Then place your thumb or two fingers in the middle of the rolled-out gauze and pull that section of the gauze (from the fingers to the gauze roll) in the same direction as you did in applying the bandage. The remainder of the gauze and roll will be on the opposite side. If scissors are available, cut the gauze.

4. Check that the doubled gauze is on one side and the single gauze is on the other.

5. Tie a knot over the bandage.

6. Check to make sure the dressing is snug but not too tight. You should be able to slip 1 to 2 fingers underneath the bandage and the patient's skin color should be normal past the bandage and their sensation should be normal.

FIGURE-OF-EIGHT BANDAGES

A figure-of-eight bandage is particularly useful for the ankle, wrist, and hand. To apply a figure-of-eight bandage:

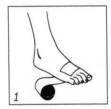
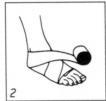

1. Anchor the bandage with one or two circular wraps around the affected part, being careful not to wrap the bandage too tightly.

2. To make the figure-of-eight, bring the bandage diagonally across the top of the foot, around the ankle, down across the top of the foot, and under the arch.

3. Continue these figure-of-eight turns, with each turn overlapping the preceding turn by about ¾ of its width. Bandage until the foot (not toes), ankle, and lower part of the leg are covered. Keep the toes exposed to check for circulation problems.

4. Secure the bandage with tape, clips, or safety pins, or tie off as described in the section on the circular bandage.

FINGERTIP BANDAGES

The fingertip bandage is particularly useful when the fingertip itself is injured. To apply a fingertip bandage:

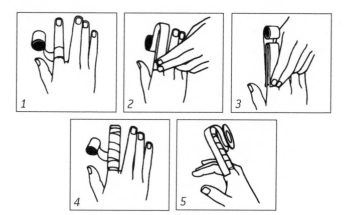

1. Anchor the bandage at the base of the finger with a few circular turns, being careful not to wrap the bandage too tightly.

2. With your index finger of one hand, hold the bandage down at the base of the finger where it is anchored. Bring the roll of bandage up the front of the finger you are bandaging, over the fingertip, and down the back side to the base of the finger.

3. With your thumb, hold down the bandage at the base and repeat the back-and-forth process of bandaging over the fingertip until several layers cover the finger.

4. Starting at the base of the finger, make circular turns up the finger and back to the base to hold the bandage in place.

5. To secure the bandage, apply a piece of tape approximately 6 inches long up the side of the finger, across the tip, and down the other side of the finger, or tie off as described in the section on the circular bandage.

TRIANGULAR BANDAGES

The triangular bandage has many uses in an emergency. It can serve as a covering for a large area such as the scalp or as a sling for a broken bone, or it can be folded into a rectangular scarf and used as a circular or figure-of-eight bandage. A triangular bandage is usually made of muslin, but other material can be used. A large bandana can be used or it can be easily made at home. To make a triangular bandage, cut a piece of cloth 36 to 40 inches square. Next, fold it diagonally or cut the fabric diagonally from corner to corner. Now you have two triangular bandages.

TRIANGULAR BANDAGE

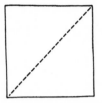

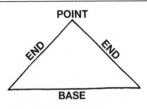

A triangular bandage can be used as a sling, as a head bandage, or as a (rectangular) figure-of-eight bandage. (See illustrations below and on pages 29 and 32.)

SLINGS

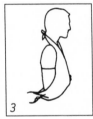

To make a sling:

1. Place one long end (point) of the triangular bandage over the uninjured shoulder so that the base and other end of the triangle hang down over the chest. Place the short point under the elbow of the injured arm.

2. Elevate the hand about 4 inches above the level of the elbow and lift the lower end of the bandage up over the other shoulder.

3. Tie the two ends together at the side of the neck.

4. Fold the point forward to the front of the sling and pin it to the outside of the sling. Leave the fingers exposed.

HEAD BANDAGES

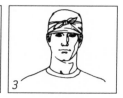
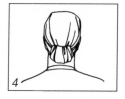

To make a head bandage:

1. Place the center of the base of the triangle across the forehead so that it lies just above the eyes, with the point of the bandage down the back of the head. Bring both ends above the ears and around to the back of the head.

2. Just below the lump at the back of the head, cross the two ends over each other snugly and continue to bring the ends back around to the center of the forehead.

3. Tie the ends in a knot.

4. Tuck the point hanging down the back of the head into the fold where the bandage crosses in the back.

SPLINTS

Splints are used to keep an injured body part from moving, thereby easing the pain and preventing further injury. Any smooth, rigid objects can be used for splinting. Examples include boards, straight sticks, brooms, pieces of corrugated cardboard bent to form a three-sided box, rolled newspapers or magazines, pillows, rolled blankets, oars, umbrellas, or tongue depressors (for finger injuries). The splint should extend above and below the joints that bracket the injured area in order to immobilize it.

Padding such as cloth, towels, or blankets should be placed between the splint and the skin of the injured part. Make sure that there are no knobs or projections that will be against the skin. Splints can be tied in place with neckties, strips of cloth torn from shirts, handkerchiefs, belts, string, rope, or other suitable material. Do not tie the splint so tightly that the ties interfere with circulation. Swelling or bluish discoloration in the fingers or toes may indicate that the ties are too tight and need to be loosened. Also loosen splint ties if the person experiences increased pain, numbness, or tingling, or if he or she cannot move the fingers or toes. Check the wrist or ankle for a pulse and loosen the ties if you can't feel a pulse.

To splint specific broken bones, see Broken Bones, p. 79.

EMERGENCY PROCEDURES TO KNOW

Knowing how to do CPR, use an AED, and perform the Heimlich maneuver can help you save a life. Accredited CPR and first aid courses are offered in most communities by the American Red Cross or the American Heart Association, a hospital, fire department, community center, school, or employer. Ask your doctor about classes in your area and sign up today. Once you learn basic life support techniques, practice them often so you will remember how to perform them in an emergency. The CPR techniques presented here are meant to refresh what you learn in a CPR class or to pique your interest in taking a CPR class; they are not a substitute for formal instruction in CPR.

CARDIOPULMONARY RESUSCITATION (CPR)

Cardiopulmonary resuscitation (CPR) is a basic life support technique used for a person who is not breathing and whose heart may have stopped beating. When the heart stops, the absence of oxygenated blood can cause permanent brain damage in only a few minutes. Functional recovery is rare after 5 minutes, and death will occur within 8 to 10 minutes.

Time is critical when you're helping an unconscious person who isn't breathing. The technique allows you to perform manually the involuntary actions of the heart and lungs that provide vital blood and oxygen to all parts of the body. Ideally, CPR involves two elements: chest compressions combined with rescue breathing. CPR involves opening and clearing the person's airway (by tilting the head backward and lifting the chin), restoring breathing (by mouth-to-mouth or mouth-to-nose resuscitation), and restoring blood circulation (by external chest compressions).* A complete description of how to do these procedures is provided in this section.

> To Perform CPR on an Adult or Child Over 8 Years of Age

BEFORE YOU BEGIN
Assess the situation before starting CPR:

- Is the person conscious or unconscious?

- If the person appears unconscious, tap or shake his or her shoulder and ask loudly, "Are you OK?"

- If the person does not respond and two people are available, one should call 911 or the local emergency medical dispatch number and the other should begin CPR. If you are alone and have immediate access to a telephone, call 911 before beginning CPR—unless you think the person has become unresponsive because of suffocation (such as from drowning). In this special case, begin CPR for one minute and then call 911 or the local emergency medical dispatch number.

- If an AED is immediately available, deliver one shock if advised by the device, then begin CPR. (See Use of AEDs with CPR, p. 43.)

THE ABCs OF CPR

A simple method to remember the order of actions to take if the person is not breathing or if his or her heart is not beating is the use of the term "ABCs." These letters stand for airway, breathing, and circulation, which represent the three basic steps in CPR: open and clear the person's airway, restore breathing, and restore blood circulation.

---

*Note: Actions taken to assist an individual may raise your risk of exposure to blood and body secretions, thereby increasing your risk of exposure to human immunodeficiency virus (HIV), hepatitis B, and hepatitis C. These viruses can pass from an infected individual to a rescuer through broken skin or mucous membranes such as the eyes, nose, or mouth, or from open wounds. It is extremely unlikely that you will contract these viruses from the blood or saliva of a person who requires rescue breathing or CPR. You can reduce your risk of exposure by wearing protective equipment such as face masks, eye shields, and gloves. With proper precautions, the risk of contracting these viruses through blood and body secretions is low.

Always think ABC—airway, breathing, and circulation—to remember the steps explained below. Move quickly through "airway" and "breathing" to begin chest compressions to restore "circulation."

AIRWAY: CLEAR THE AIRWAY

The person's airway must be clear and open in order to restore breathing. Clear the airway by doing the following:

1. Put the person on his or her back on a firm surface. If the person could have a head, neck, or back injury, gently roll the person with his or her head, neck, shoulders, and body in a straight line.

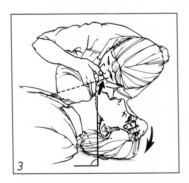

2. Quickly clear the mouth and airway of any visible foreign material with your fingers and remove any loose dentures.

3. Kneel next to the person and place your palm on the person's forehead, tilting the head back slightly. Place the fingers of your other hand under the bony part of the person's chin, lifting the chin.*

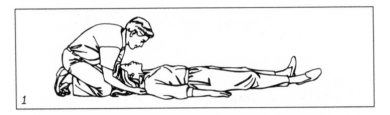

---

*If you suspect a head, neck, or back injury—especially if the person has fallen from a height, fallen from a motorcycle, been hit by a car, or been involved in a motor vehicle crash—and if the person is unconscious, do not move him or her. Exceptions to this rule apply only if you and the person are in imminent danger of death, such as in or near a fire, at an accident scene in which an explosion might occur, or near a collapsing building. (See Head, Neck, and Back Problems, p. 138.)

4. Check for normal breathing, taking no more than 5 or 10 seconds. With your head close to the person's head, look to see if his or her chest rises and falls, and feel for the person's breath on your cheek and ear. Listen for breathing sounds, gurgling, wheezing, or snoring (gasping is not considered to be normal breathing).

5a. If the person is not breathing normally and you are well-trained in CPR, and feel confident in your ability, proceed to "breathing" and "circulation."

5b. If the person is not breathing normally and you have not been trained in CPR or have previously received CPR training but are not confident in your abilities, skip "breathing" and proceed directly to chest compressions to restore circulation (see "circulation," page 38).

BREATHING: BREATHE FOR THE PERSON
Mouth-to-mouth breathing:

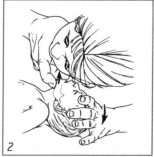

1. With the airway open, pinch the nostrils shut and cover the person's mouth with yours, making a seal. Place your open mouth tightly around the person's mouth and prepare to give 2 full breaths—so that air enters his or her lungs.

2. Give the first rescue breath, lasting 1 second. As you blow air into the person's mouth, watch closely to see when his or her chest rises, and stop blowing when you notice the chest expanding. Remove your mouth from the person's mouth and turn your head toward the person's chest so that your ear is over his or her mouth. Listen for air leaving the person's lungs and watch the chest fall. You may also feel air being exhaled from the person's nose and mouth.

> If the chest rises, remove your mouth, take a normal breath, and give another rescue breath after the person's chest has returned to normal position and you feel the air escape.

> If the chest does not rise, remove your mouth, take a normal breath, repeat the head-tilt, chin-lift maneuver, and then give another 1-second breath.

You will feel moderate resistance when you blow. If you encounter marked resistance and the chest does not rise, the airway is not clear and more airway opening is needed. Place your hands under the person's lower jaw and thrust the lower jaw up so that it juts out farther. For a child who does not have a head or neck injury, you may need to tilt the head back a little farther.

3. After giving 2 rescue breaths (even if the chest has not risen with either breath), begin chest compressions (see "circulation") and have someone attempt to locate an AED.

Mouth-to-nose breathing:

1. If the mouth is seriously injured or can't be opened, lift the lower jaw to close the mouth. Open your mouth wide and take a deep breath. Place your mouth tightly around the person's nose and blow into it. After your breath, remove your hand from the person's mouth to allow air to escape. Prepare to give 2 full breaths—so that air enters his or her lungs.

2. Give the first rescue breath, lasting 1 second. As you blow air into the person's nose, watch closely to see when his or her chest rises, and stop blowing when you notice the chest expanding. Remove your mouth from the person's nose and turn your head toward the person's chest so that your ear is over his or her mouth. Listen for air leaving the person's lungs and watch the chest fall. You may also feel air being exhaled from the person's nose and mouth.

> If the chest rises, remove your mouth, take a normal breath, and give another rescue breath after the person's chest has returned to normal position and you feel the air escape.

> If the chest does not rise, remove your mouth, take a normal breath, and then give another 1-second breath.

3. After giving 2 rescue breaths (even if the chest has not risen with either breath), begin chest compressions (see "circulation") and have someone attempt to locate an AED.

CIRCULATION: RESTORE BLOOD CIRCULATION WITH CHEST COMPRESSIONS

The procedure to restore blood circulation must be done in conjunction with artificial breathing. In emergency situations, restoring circulation for the person is essential for survival, and chest compressions, as outlined in this section, should be attempted. When performing chest compressions, it is important to limit interruptions because every time you stop chest compressions, the person's blood flow stops.

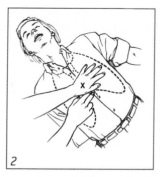
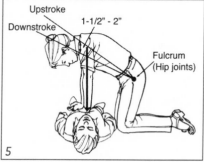

1. Make sure you are in a safe area, free from danger. If not, move the person to safety if possible (see page 35).

2. Kneel next to the person and find the correct hand position for chest compressions. Use your fingers to feel for the bottom of the person's breastbone, where the ribs come together in the middle of the chest. Place 2 fingers at the tip of the breastbone (sternum) and place the heel of the other hand directly next to the finger closest to the person's face.

3. Place the heel of one hand over the center of the person's chest. Place your other hand on top of the first hand. Lock the fingers of both hands together, and raise the fingers so they don't touch the person's chest.

4. Straighten your arms, lock your elbows, and center your shoulders directly over your hands.

5. Keep your elbows locked and press down forcefully in a steady rhythm, using your upper body weight (not just your arms). Each thrust should go straight down onto the sternum, compressing it 1½ to 2 inches (approximately 5 centimeters).

6. Push hard and push fast, at a rate of about 100 to 120 compressions per minute.

7. Count "1 and 2 and 3 and 4 and...," giving 1 downward thrust each time you say a number. Between thrusts, when you say "and," lift your weight, but not your hands, from the person's chest. Allow the person's chest to return to normal position after each compression but give equal time for compressions and relaxation.

8. Give 30 chest compressions.

9. Prepare to give 2 rescue breaths after every 30 compressions (see "breathing). If someone else is available, ask that person to give 2 breaths after you do 30 compressions.

10. Repeat the cycle of 30 chest compressions and 2 rescue breaths until an AED arrives; the person breathes, coughs, or moves; or emergency medical personnel take over. For children, use pediatric pads with the AED, as appropriate. If pediatric pads are not available, use adult pads. If an AED is not available, continue CPR until there are signs of movement or until emergency medical personnel take over.

HANDS-ONLY CPR

When an adult has a sudden cardiac arrest, his or her survival depends greatly on immediate medical assistance, including CPR. While concerned bystanders may be willing to help, they may be worried that they might do something wrong or make things worse. To alleviate such concern for persons who are not trained in CPR or are not confident in their abilities, the American Heart Association recommends two simple steps:

1. Call 911

2. Push hard and fast in the center of the chest.

> To Perform CPR on a Child Aged 1 Through 8

The procedure for giving CPR to a child age 1 through 8 is essentially the same as that for an adult, with the following differences:

- If you are alone, perform 5 cycles of chest compressions and rescue breaths on the child—this should take about two minutes—before calling 911 or your local emergency medical dispatch number or using an AED.

- Use the same compression/breath rate as used for adults: Push at a rate of about 100 to 120 compressions per minute, in a cycle of 30 compressions followed by 2 rescue breaths.

- Depending on the child's size, you can use the heel of 1 hand instead of 2 hands for chest compressions. The heel of your hands (or hand) should be positioned in the center of the lower half of the sternum at the nipple line (think of an imaginary line drawn from nipple to nipple). Press the sternum down one-third to one-half the depth of the child's chest. (Breathe more gently.)

> To Perform CPR on an Infant Younger Than 1 Year of Age

Most cardiac arrests in infants occur from lack of oxygen, such as from drowning or choking. If you know the infant has an airway obstruction, perform first aid for choking (see "Heimlich maneuver" on page 47). If you don't know why the infant is not breathing, perform CPR.

To begin, assess the situation. Stroke the baby and watch for a response, such as movement, but don't shake the child. If there's no response, follow the ABC procedures below. Time a call for help as follows:

- If you are the only rescuer and CPR is needed, do CPR for two minutes—about five cycles—before calling 911 or your local emergency number.

- If another person is available, have that person call for help immediately while you attend to the baby.

AIRWAY: CLEAR THE AIRWAY

1. Place the baby on his or her back on a firm, flat surface, such as a table. A hard surface may be your forearm and the palm of your hand. The floor or ground also will do.

2. Tilt the child's head back only slightly, or the airway could be closed off. Gently tip the head back by lifting the chin with one

hand and pushing down on the forehead with the other hand. To tilt the head back, place your index finger of one hand under the child's chin and the other hand at the top of the child's forehead and lift the chin up toward the top of the child's head. Do not close the child's mouth or press under his or her chin or you could close off the airway.

3. In no more than 10 seconds, put your ear near the baby's mouth and check for breathing: Look for chest motion, listen for breath sounds, and feel for breath on your cheek and ear.

4. If the infant isn't breathing, begin rescue breathing (mouth-to-mouth-and-nose) immediately.

BREATHING: BREATHE FOR THE INFANT

1. Cover the baby's mouth and nose with your mouth.

2. Prepare to give 2 rescue breaths. Use the strength of your cheeks to deliver gentle puffs of air (instead of deep breaths from your lungs) to slowly breathe into the baby's mouth one time, taking one second for the breath. Watch to see if the baby's chest rises. If it does, give a second rescue breath. If the chest does not rise, repeat the head-tilt, chin-lift maneuver and then give the second breath. Place your mouth tightly over the baby's mouth and nose and blow gently for 1 second. Avoid rapid or forceful breaths.

3. If the chest still doesn't rise, examine the mouth to make sure no foreign material is inside. If you see an object, sweep it out with your finger. If the airway seems blocked, perform first aid for a choking infant.

4. Begin chest compressions to restore circulation.

CIRCULATION: RESTORE BLOOD CIRCULATION

Repeat the cycle of 30 compressions and 2 rescue breaths until medical emergency responders arrive or until the person breathes, coughs, or moves.

1. Imagine a horizontal line drawn between the baby's nipples. Place 2 fingers of one hand on the infant's sternum, about 1 finger-width below the nipple line (think of an imaginary line drawn from nipple to nipple).

2. With the 2 fingers, gently compress the sternum down one-third to one-half the depth of the child's chest.

3. Count aloud as you pump in a fairly rapid rhythm. Push at a rate of about 100 to 120 compressions per minute, in a cycle of 30 compressions followed by 2 rescue breaths.

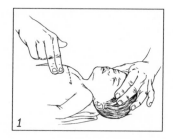

4. Give 2 rescue breaths (mouth-to-mouth-and-nose) after every 30 compressions.

5. Perform CPR for about two minutes before calling for help unless someone else can make the call while you attend to the baby.

6. Continue CPR until you see signs of life or until a professional relieves you.

> Glossary of CPR Terms

ABCs. A term that describes the three basic steps in CPR: maintain an open airway, restore breathing, and restore circulation, if necessary.

Brachial artery. One of the main arteries in the body, found on the inside of the upper arm, between the elbow and shoulder. A rescuer can feel for a pulse—primarily in infants under 1 year—by gently pressing on this artery.

Cardiac arrest. A critical medical condition in which the heart has stopped beating.

Carotid artery. One of the main arteries in the body, found on either side of the neck. A rescuer can feel for a pulse—primarily in children over 1 year and adults—by gently, but firmly, pressing on this artery.

Compressions. Downward thrusts on the chest with the hands. Compressing or pushing down on the chest, like pressing water out of a sponge, pushes blood out of the heart to all parts of the body. Releasing pressure on the chest allows the rib cage to expand and, again similar to the dynamics of a sponge, draws blood into the heart.

CPR. Cardiopulmonary resuscitation, which means, literally, heart and lung revival. The process of clearing the airway, restoring breathing, and restoring blood circulation.

Pulse. The "wave" of blood flowing through arteries and veins that is in rhythm with the beating of the heart. When a rescuer feels for a pulse in one of the main arteries in the body, he or she is determining if the heart is beating.

Respiration. The process of breathing.

Resuscitation. The attempt to restore breathing and, if necessary, blood circulation in a person. This is done by mouth-to-mouth, mouth-to-nose, or mouth-to-mouth-and-nose respirations and by chest compressions.

Ventilations. The process of breathing air into a person's lungs. This is done in mouth-to-mouth, mouth-to-nose, or mouth-to-mouth-and-nose resuscitation.

USE OF AUTOMATED EXTERNAL DEFIBRILLATORS (AEDS) WITH CPR

An AED can shock the heart from an abnormal rhythm back to a normal rhythm. AEDs are available in many public places, including airports, shopping malls, workplaces, and schools. They are intended

---

4 BASIC STEPS FOR USING AN AED

Consider using an AED if a person has signs of cardiac arrest such as being unresponsive, not breathing, and having no pulse or other signs of circulation. There are four basic steps involved in using an AED:

1. Power on the AED.

2. Attach the AED to the person's chest with the electrode pads. Stop CPR while attaching the electrodes.

3. Let the AED analyze the person's heart rhythm. Stop CPR, and do not touch the person while the AED analyzes the heart rhythm.

4. Deliver a shock if the machine indicates it is required. Stay clear of the person while the shock is being delivered.

---

to be used by anyone, even people who have not had prior training, although AED classes are available in most communities.

The devices come with written and audio instructions. If available, they are easier to use and more effective than CPR.

The AED first checks the person's heart rhythm to determine if a shock is needed; an AED will administer a shock (or a series of shocks at fixed or escalating doses) only if the person needs it. Some AEDs can accurately recognize shockable heart rhythms in children from ages 1 to 8, and some are equipped to deliver energy doses suitable for children. Use pediatric pads, if available, for children ages 1 to 8. Do not use an AED for infants younger than age 1. An AED will work even if the pads are not placed in the exact position recommended. If you are with someone who may be having or may have had a heart attack, always first ask if an AED is available and immediately call (or have someone call) 911 or your local emergency medical dispatch number.

STEPS FOR USING AN AED FOR

ADULTS OR CHILDREN OVER 8 YEARS OF AGE:

1. Remove any medication skin patches from the chest area and dry the area before attaching the AED. This is especially important with a nitroglycerin patch.

2. Deliver one shock to the person's chest as soon as possible.

3. Immediately start CPR, beginning with 30 chest compressions (see pages 34–39) followed by 2 rescue breaths.

4. Do 5 cycles of CPR (30 chest compressions and 2 rescue breaths), which will take about 2 minutes.

5. Use the AED to check the person's heart rhythm every 2 minutes. Some AEDs are programmed to signal when to check the rhythm.

STEPS FOR USING AN AED FOR CHILDREN AGES 1 TO 8:

1. If you have seen a child suddenly collapse, use an AED (with a pediatric dosing system, if possible) as soon as it is available.

2. If you have not seen the child collapse, first give 5 cycles of CPR (for about 2 minutes), starting with chest compressions (see pages 39–40).

3. If the AED does not have child pads or a way to deliver a smaller, children's dose, use a regular AED with adult pads.

4. Use the AED to check the person's heart rhythm every 2 minutes. Some AEDs are programmed to signal when to check the rhythm.

STEPS FOR USING AN AED

IF AN UNCONSCIOUS PERSON IS IN WATER:

1. Remove the person from the water and dry his or her chest.

2. Remove any medication skin patches from the chest area and dry the area before attaching the AED. This is especially important with a nitroglycerin patch.

3. Follow the steps above and on page 48, depending on the age of the person.

FIRST AID FOR CHOKING

Choking occurs when food, dentures, and other potential items become dislodged in the windpipe (trachea). The universal sign for choking is hands clutched to the throat. Additional signs include an inability to talk or cough forcefully; skin, lips, and nails turning blue; and potential loss of consciousness.

UNIVERSAL CHOKING SIGN

A person who is choking will involuntarily grasp his or her neck.

A "five and five" recommendation is given for dealing with choking. Begin by delivering 5 back blows—hitting the person forcefully and repeatedly between the shoulder blades with the palm of your hand; and then providing 5 abdominal thrusts (Heimlich maneuver). Alternate between these two procedures as necessary until the person coughs up the object or becomes unconscious. Look to see if the object appears in the person's mouth or at the top of the throat; if so, use your fingers to pull the object out.

> Heimlich Maneuver on an Adult or Child Over 1 Year:

If the person can speak, cough, or breathe:

This means that he or she is moving air through the airway. Do not interfere in any way with his or her efforts to cough out a swallowed or partially swallowed object.

If the person cannot breathe but can stand up:

1. Stand behind him or her and place your fist with the thumb side against his or her stomach slightly above the navel and below the ribs and breastbone. Be careful not to touch the breastbone.

2. Hold your fist with your other hand and give several quick, forceful upward thrusts. This maneuver increases pressure in the abdomen, which pushes up the diaphragm. This, in turn, increases the air pressure in the lungs and will often force out the object from the windpipe. Do not squeeze on the person's ribs with

your arms—use only your fist in the abdomen. It may be necessary to repeat the Heimlich maneuver 6 to 10 times.

If the person is lying down:

Turn the person on his or her back. Straddle the person and put the heel of your hand on his or her stomach, slightly above the navel and below the ribs. Put your free hand on top of your other hand to provide additional force. Keep your elbows straight. Give several quick, forceful downward and forward thrusts toward the person's head in an attempt to dislodge the object. Doing so will increase pressure in the abdomen, forcing pressure into the lungs to expel the object out of the windpipe and into the mouth. It may be necessary to repeat the procedure 6 to 10 times.

> Heimlich Maneuver on an Infant Under 1 Year of Age:

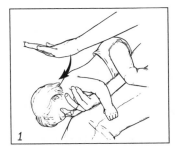 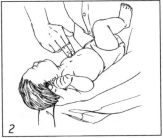

1. Place the infant face down across your forearm with his or her head slightly lower than the trunk. Support the head by firmly holding the infant's jaw. Rest your forearm on your thigh and give 5 forceful back blows with the heel of your hand between the infant's shoulder blades pressing downward and toward the child's head. The blows should be gentler than those for an adult.

2. If unsuccessful, turn the infant over onto his or her back, keeping the head lower than the trunk. Give 5 quick thrusts on the chest. To do this, place 2 fingers one finger-width below an imaginary line joining the nipples. Push downward. Thrusts should be gentler than those for an adult.

3. If necessary, repeat both procedures.

> Special Circumstances

If the choking person is unconscious or becomes unconscious:

1. Place the person on his or her back on a rigid surface, such as the ground.

2. Open the person's airway by extending the head backward. To do this, place the palm of your hand on the person's forehead and the fingers of your other hand under the bony part of the chin. Attempt to restore breathing with mouth-to-mouth resuscitation. (See pp. 36–37.)

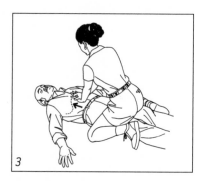

3. If still unsuccessful, and with the person on his or her back, begin the Heimlich maneuver by putting the heel of one hand on the person's stomach slightly above the navel and below the ribs. Put your free hand on top of your other hand to provide additional force. Keep your elbows straight. Give several quick, forceful, downward and forward thrusts toward the head.

4. If these procedures fail, grasp the person's lower jaw and tongue with one hand and lift up to remove the tongue from the back of the throat. Place the index finger of the other hand inside the person's mouth alongside the cheek. Slide your fingers down into the throat to the base of the person's tongue.

5. Carefully sweep your fingers along the back of the throat to dislodge the object. Bring your fingers out along the inside of the other cheek. Be careful not to push the object farther down the person's throat. If a foreign body comes within reach, grasp and remove it. Do not attempt to remove the foreign object with any type of instrument or forceps unless you are trained to do so.

6. Repeat all of the above steps until the object is dislodged or medical assistance arrives. Do not give up!

If the choking person is very overweight or pregnant:

1. Stand behind the person and place your fist on the middle of the breastbone in the chest, but not over the ribs. Put your other hand on top of it. Give several quick, forceful movements. Do not squeeze with your arms—use just your fist.

2. If this procedure does not work, stand behind the person and support his or her chest with one hand. With the heel of the other hand give several quick blows on the back between the person's shoulder blades.

If you are alone and choking:

1. Place your fist on your stomach slightly above your navel and below your breastbone. Place your other hand on top of your fist. Give yourself several quick, forceful upward abdominal thrusts.

2. If this procedure does not work, press your stomach forcefully over a chair, table, or railing.

BASIC LIFE SUPPORT AT A GLANCE

SYMPTOM, STEP, OR ACTION TO TAKE	IF THE PERSON IS 9 YEARS OR OLDER	IF THE PERSON IS BETWEEN AGES 1 AND 8 YEARS	IF THE PERSON IS YOUNGER THAN 1 YEAR
	Airway/Breathing		
Check for breathing:	Open the airway with the head tilt-chin lift method. Look to see if the person's chest rises and falls; listen for breathing sounds, gurgling, wheezing, or snoring; with your cheek near the person's mouth or nose, feel if air is moving out. Take no more than 5 or 10 seconds to do this.		
If the person is not breathing:	Give 2 rescue breaths, 1 second for each breath.		
	Chest Compressions		
If the person does not respond to rescue breaths by breathing, coughing, or moving, locate the site for chest compressions:	Move 2 fingers up the person's rib cage to where the ribs meet the breastbone at the center (sternum) and place your fingers on the tip of the sternum. Place the heel of your other hand directly next to your fingers toward the person's face. See illustration on page 38 [left].		One finger-width below an imaginary line drawn between the nipples, place 2 fingers on the child's sternum. See illustration on page 41.
Do chest compressions by pushing fast and hard with:	**2 hands** Heel of 1 hand on sternum, second hand on top of first hand, fingers of both hands interlaced. See illustration on page 38 [right]	**1 hand** Heel of 1 hand only on sternum **or** **2 hands** Same as for adults, depend-	2 fingers on the sternum just below the nipple line.

Compression depth	1½ to 2 inches	About ?/? to ?/? the depth of the child's chest	
Compression rate	About 100 chest compressions per minute		
Ratio of compressions to breathing	For every 30 compressions, give 2 rescue breaths.		
Choking			
If a conscious person is choking:	Use an alternating series of 5 back blows followed by 5 abdominal thrusts (Heimlich maneuver) to dislodge the object from the airway. See illustration on page 46.	Use alternating series of back slaps and chest thrusts to dislodge the object from the airway. See illustrations on page 47.	
If an unconscious person has choked:	Assess breathing, look in the person's mouth, if you see an object remove it, give 2 rescue breaths, give 30 chest compressions. Repeat sequence.		
Defibrillation			
If a person is not breathing or his or her heart has stopped, use an AED (automated external defibrillator) if available.	Follow the instructions on the AED. Use adult pads. Do *not* use child pads or a child energy dose.	Use AED after 5 cycles of CPR. Use child pads/child system for children ages 1 to 8 if available. If not available, use adult AED and pads.	Do not use an AED for infants younger than 1 year.

CONTROL OF EXTERNAL BLEEDING

Blood may flow from a vein or an artery or both. Blood from veins is dark red and flows steadily. Blood from arteries is bright red and usually spurts from the wound. Bleeding from an artery is more critical than bleeding from a vein because blood is being pumped out at a faster rate, leading to greater blood loss. Severe bleeding from an artery can be fatal. If you notice that blood is spurting from a wound, call 911 (or your local emergency medical dispatch number) or take the person to a hospital emergency department or doctor's office immediately.*

> What To Do

APPLY DIRECT PRESSURE TO THE WOUND
Direct pressure is the preferred treatment in bleeding injuries and, although it may cause some pain, constant pressure is usually all that is necessary to stop the bleeding. To apply direct pressure:

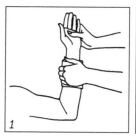 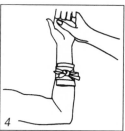

1. Place a thick clean compress (sterile gauze or a soft clean cloth such as a handkerchief, towel, undershirt, or strips from a sheet) directly over the entire wound and press firmly with the palm of your hand. (If cloth is not available, use bare hands or fingers, but they should be as clean as possible.)

2. Continue to apply steady pressure. A limb that is bleeding severely should be raised above the level of the person's heart.

---

*Note: Actions taken to assist an individual may raise your risk of exposure to blood and body secretions, thereby increasing your risk of exposure to human immunodeficiency virus (HIV), hepatitis B, and hepatitis C. These viruses can pass from an infected individual to a rescuer through broken skin or mucous membranes such as the eyes, nose, or mouth, or from open wounds. It is extremely unlikely that you will contract these viruses from the blood or saliva of a person who requires rescue breathing or CPR. You can reduce your risk of exposure by wearing protective equipment such as face masks, eye shields, and gloves. With proper precautions, the risk of contracting these viruses through blood and body secretions is low.

3. Do not disturb any blood clots that form on the compress. If blood soaks through the compress, leave the compress in place and apply another compress over it. Continue applying pressure, using firmer hand pressure over a wider area.

4. If bleeding stops or slows, apply a pressure bandage to hold the compress snugly in place. To apply a pressure bandage, place the center of the gauze, cloth strips, or a necktie directly over the compress. Pull steadily while wrapping both ends around the injury. Tie a knot over the compress. Do not wrap the bandage so tightly that it cuts off arterial circulation. (Arteries carry blood away from the heart to the extremities.) A pulse can be felt on an artery. You should feel a pulse below the bandage, meaning at a point on an artery that is farthest away from the trunk of the body.

5. Keep an injured limb elevated.

NOTE: You can stop bleeding in the mouth by placing a sterile gauze pad over the wound and applying pressure with your hand or by having the person bite on it, depending on where the bleeding is.

APPLY ARTERIAL PRESSURE

Applying pressure to pressure points (see illustration on p. 54) should be done only if bleeding does not stop after elevating an injured limb and applying direct pressure to the wound itself. This technique is used to press the artery supplying blood to the wound against the underlying bone and cut off circulation to the affected area. Applying pressure to pressure points is used in conjunction with applying direct pressure to a wound and elevating the wound above the heart. However, before using this technique, call 911 (or your local emergency medical dispatch number) for immediate medical help. Severe blood loss can be fatal.

To stop severe bleeding from an arm:

1. Grasp the person's arm bone midway between the armpit and the elbow with your thumb on the outside of the arm and the flat surface of your fingers on the inside of the arm, where you may actually feel the artery pulsating.

2. Squeeze your fingers firmly toward your thumb against the arm bone until the bleeding stops.

To stop severe bleeding from a leg:

1. Lay the person on his or her back, if possible.

2. Place the heel of your hand on the front center part of the person's thigh at the crease of the groin and press down firmly. Do not continue pressing any longer than necessary to stop the

PRESSURE POINTS ON THE BODY

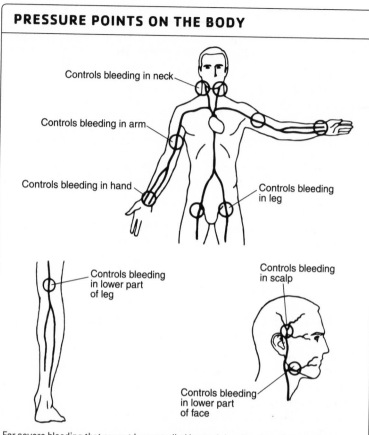

Controls bleeding in neck

Controls bleeding in arm

Controls bleeding in hand

Controls bleeding in leg

Controls bleeding in lower part of leg

Controls bleeding in scalp

Controls bleeding in lower part of face

For severe bleeding that cannot be controlled by applying direct pressure to the wound, pressing the artery that supplies blood to the wound firmly against the underlying bone can help. Apply pressure only until the bleeding stops. The circled areas on the arteries show the places to apply pressure to control bleeding in specific injured areas of the body. Each artery has a corresponding artery with a corresponding pressure point on the other side of the body.

bleeding. However, if bleeding recurs after you remove your hand, reapply pressure.

USE OF TOURNIQUETS
The use of a tourniquet should be reserved for injuries where a limb has been amputated and should be applied by someone qualified in its application. Improper use of tourniquets can result in increased tissue damage to the person.

Part III

ALPHABETICAL LISTING OF ILLNESSES, INJURIES, AND OTHER MEDICAL EMERGENCIES

ALLERGIC REACTIONS

HIVES

Hives are a common allergic reaction to various substances, including animal hairs, feathers, laundry detergents, plants, fabrics, dyes, medications, viral infections, and food (particularly chocolate, nuts, berries, and seafood), among other causes. Hives are caused when mast cells (immune system cells) release histamine and other chemicals into the blood stream, causing a localized inflammatory response.

> Symptoms

Hives are typically described as red, itchy, raised bumps or blisters of various sizes on your skin, which can burn and sting.

> What to Do

The standard treatment for hives is antihistamines, such as diphenhydramine, which block the symptom-producing release of histamine. Antihistamines may cause drowsiness, so you should not drive or perform any activities that require alertness while taking these drugs.

> Preventing Hives

To lower your likelihood of experiencing hives, avoid recognized triggers that may include certain foods or medications, or situations, such as temperature extremes, that have triggered past allergic attacks.

SEASONAL ALLERGIES

Seasonal allergies are a common medical complaint. The major culprit is the pollen that is generated in the springtime. Symptoms occur when the body's immune system is exposed to allergy-causing substances (or allergens) such as mold, pollen, dust, and pet dander.

> Symptoms

After exposure, allergy symptoms typically include:

- Runny nose
- Sneezing
- Coughing
- Nasal congestion
- Dry, scratchy eyes
- Possible skin reaction

> What To Do

Treatment for seasonal allergies is an over-the-counter antihistamine. Antihistamines can make you drowsy, but there are alternatives available that do not have this effect, such as loratidine. You should see your doctor if the symptoms do not improve with over-the-counter medications.

> Preventing Allergies

Monitor local TV, radio, and newspaper weather reports for pollen counts in the springtime. If levels are high, it is best to stay indoors. Avoid outdoor activities when pollen counts are high and remember that pollen clings to pet fur (so try to keep pets off furniture). Home air filters also can be considered.

SEVERE ALLERGIC REACTION

Some allergic reactions can proceed to tongue swelling and difficulty breathing and will require the need for an epinephrine auto-injector and trip to the emergency department. A severe allergic reaction can produce shock and life-threatening respiratory distress and circulatory collapse within minutes. Symptoms include:

- Tongue swelling
- Lip or eye swelling

- Difficulty breathing
- Bluish tinged lips
- Use of neck and shoulder muscles to assist with breathing
- Dizziness
- Mental confusion
- Nausea
- Abdominal cramping

> What to Do

1. Call 911 or your local emergency medical dispatch number.

2. Check for special medications that the person might be carrying to treat an allergic attack, such as an auto-injector of epinephrine. The use of an epinephrine pen is described below.

3. Have the person lie still on his or her back with the feet higher than the head.

4. Loosen tight clothing and cover the person with a blanket. Don't give anything else to drink.

5. If there is vomiting or bleeding from the mouth, turn the person on his or her side to prevent choking.

6. If there are no signs of circulation (breathing, coughing, or movement), begin CPR. (See pp. 33–45.)

See also: Bites and Stings, p. 177.

> Using an Epinephrine Pen

Here are the steps you should follow when using an epinephrine pen in an emergency. Also, check the package instructions.

1. Get the prescribed pen.

2. Take off the safety cap. Check the solution; do not administer the injection if the solution is brown or discolored (it should be clear) or if moisture or liquid is present on the pen.

3. Hold the pen in your fist, with your fist wrapped around the middle of the pen. Do not touch either end of the pen.

4. Press the pen tip hard against the side of the person's thigh, about halfway between the hip and the knee. It can be given through clothing. Do not give the injection into a vein or the buttocks.

5. Hold the pen in place for several seconds.

6. Rub the injection site for several seconds.

7. Dispose of the pen appropriately (see package instructions).

8. Stay with the person until medical help arrives.

AMPUTATIONS

SEVERED LIMBS

A severed limb is a serious emergency and requires prompt medical attention. A person who has a severed limb, such as a finger, hand, arm, or foot, may be bleeding profusely and have other problems that will need to be treated. With the loss of a limb, the first medical concern is saving the person's life. The second concern is successfully reattaching the severed limb. The leg is the most difficult to reattach successfully.

> What to Do

1. Call 911 (or your local emergency medical dispatch number). Maintain an open airway. Restore breathing and circulation if necessary. (See CPR, pp. 33–45.)

2. Treat for bleeding. (See pp. 52–54.)

3. If vomiting, turn the person on his or her side or turn the head sideways, only if you do not suspect a neck injury, so that he or she does not choke on the vomit.

To save the severed limb:

1. After you have cared for the person, rinse the limb with cool water (do not use soap). Place the limb in a clean plastic bag, garbage bag, or other suitable container to keep the limb from drying out and to prevent contamination.

2. Pack ice on the outside of the bag or container to keep the limb cold. The ice must not touch the limb directly and the limb should not soak in ice or water. If a second bag or container is available, the ice should be placed in this bag. Then place the bag with the limb in it in the bag of ice. Keeping the limb cold decreases its need for oxygen and can keep it viable for up to 18 hours.

3. If you are transporting the person to the hospital yourself, call the hospital to notify them of the severed limb. This will give the hospital time to prepare for the person's arrival. If the hospital is not equipped to perform surgical reattachment, the staff often can make arrangements and will direct you to a hospital that is able to perform this procedure.

AMPUTATION OF SMALLER BODY PARTS

Smaller body parts—especially a fingertip, nose, ear, or penis—are easier to save and reattach when amputated than larger body parts, such as limbs. To keep an amputated part viable, it must be kept adequately cool, at a temperature of about 38°F, until a doctor can reattach it. When kept at a low temperature, muscle can survive for up to 12 hours; bone and skin can survive for up to 24 hours.

> What to Do

1. Rinse the amputated body part with water or saline solution. Do not scrub it or use soap.

2. Wrap the amputated part in gauze or a clean cloth soaked in saline solution or water.

3. Place the part in a dry, plastic, waterproof bag.

4. Submerge the plastic bag and its contents in ice water, preferably in a polystyrene plastic container. Make sure that the ice does not come in direct contact with the amputated part.

5. Transport the injured person and the amputated part immediately to the nearest emergency department.

USE OF TOURNIQUETS

The use of tourniquets should be reserved for injuries where a limb has been amputated and should be applied by someone qualified in their application. Improper use of tourniquets can result in increased tissue damage to the person.

ANKLE, LEG, AND HIP PROBLEMS

ANKLE AND FOOT FRACTURES

Broken ankles and feet are common injuries caused by physical stress and trauma. Such injuries can involve any of the 26 bones that are in the foot, as well as the 3 ankle bones.

> Symptoms

Symptoms include:

- Immediate and significant pain with an associated inability to bear weight
- Swelling
- Tenderness
- Bruising
- Potential deformity with cuts or bone protrusion

Circulation in the foot or ankle also can be reduced causing the toenails to turn bluish in color with associated numbness.

> What To Do

Call 911 immediately if the toes turn blue, or if there is bone protruding through the skin. If the person does not have any of the above symptoms, follow the steps below for immobilizing the ankle before transporting him or her to a hospital emergency department or doctor's office:

1. Keep the person lying down.
2. Remove the person's shoe.

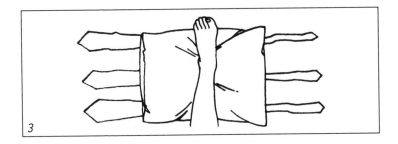

3

3. Place ties or strips under the leg. Place a pillow (preferably) or rolled blanket around the leg from the calf to well beyond the heel so that the pillow edges meet on top of the leg.

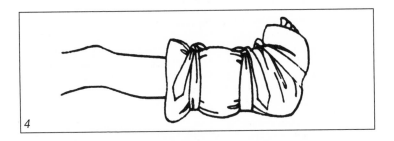

4

4. Fold the ends of the pillow that extend beyond the heel so that the pillow supports the foot and tie the pillow in place.

See also: Bone Injuries, pp. 79–83.

ANKLE SPRAIN

A sprained ankle occurs when a person steps down on the outside of the foot, causing the ligaments on the outside of the ankle to stretch or tear. The injury, which may involve one or both ligaments, can range from a tiny tear to complete severing of the ligaments. A sprained ankle can be more painful than a break in a bone and may take as long to heal. Once an ankle has been sprained, it may be susceptible to recurring sprains because of instability in the joint. Swelling and the development of bone spurs (small, spoke-like calcium growths) can make the ankle susceptible to arthritis.

> Symptoms

At the time of the injury, you may feel a flash of heat or a tearing sensation on the outside of the ankle or hear a popping sound. Pain, swelling, and bruising may develop on the outside of the ankle or the top of the foot, and you may not be able to walk on it. Your ankle may feel warm for several hours. Depending on the severity of the sprain, symptoms may appear immediately or 6 to 12 hours after the injury.

> What to Do

1. If the pain is severe or persistent or if your ankle is swollen, see your doctor to determine proper treatment. He or she can rule out a broken bone in the foot, ankle, or lower leg.

2. Stop the activity that caused the sprain. As soon as possible, elevate your ankle, preferably above the level of your heart, and place an ice pack on the ankle intermittently (20 minutes every hour while you're awake) for the first 24 hours after the injury. Cold treatments help stop internal bleeding and the accumulation of fluids in and around the injured area, thereby decreasing swelling.

3. Unless your doctor has prescribed another medication, take aspirin, ibuprofen, naproxen, or ketoprofen with food as directed to relieve pain and inflammation. (Acetaminophen relieves pain but has no effect against inflammation; ask your doctor or pharmacist for guidance.)

4. Do not engage in physical activity until the pain has subsided. Your physician may put a brace on the ankle to immobilize or restrict movement. Alternately, use of an elastic bandage on the ankle may aid stability. (If you have peripheral vascular disease or diabetes, consult your physician before using an elastic bandage.) Take aspirin, ibuprofen, naproxen, or ketoprofen as directed to relieve pain and inflammation.

5. See your physician if the pain and swelling continue.

6. Talk with your doctor about exercises to strengthen the muscles around the ankle and lower calf.

HIP FRACTURE

See Falls in the Elderly, (pp. 207–208.)

HIP POINTER

A hip pointer is a bruise or tear in a muscle that attaches to the top of the ilium bone at the waist. The injury is caused by a blow to or fall on the hip. With proper rest, hip pointers seldom have any long-term effects.

> Symptoms

A hip pointer causes pain and bruising in the hip. The pain may intensify several hours after the injury.

> What to Do

1. If the pain is severe or persistent, see your doctor to determine proper treatment.

2. Place an ice pack on the hip intermittently (20 minutes every hour while you're awake) for the first 24 hours after the injury. Cold treatments help stop internal bleeding and the accumulation of fluids in and around the injured area, thereby decreasing swelling.

3. After the swelling has stopped, place a heating pad on the hip at least once a day until the injury heals. Heat increases blood circulation in the area, providing vital nutrients to the injury and helping speed recovery. Do not apply heat before the swelling has subsided, or swelling in the injured area may increase.

4. Unless your doctor has prescribed another medication, take aspirin, ibuprofen, naproxen, or ketoprofen with food as directed to relieve pain and inflammation. (Acetaminophen relieves pain but has no effect against inflammation; ask your doctor or pharmacist for guidance.)

5. Avoid physical activity until the injury has had time to heal, or until the pain in the hip has gone. The length of time for the injury to heal depends on the severity of the tear and can range from 3 to 6 weeks or longer.

6. See your doctor if the pain continues or if the injury recurs.

7. After the injury has healed, talk with your doctor about exercises that can help stretch the muscles in your upper legs and waist.

See also: Hip Pointer, p. 263.

KNEECAP DISLOCATION

A dislocated kneecap can be extremely painful and is a common injury. Kneecap dislocations occur when the kneecap (or patella), which covers the front of the knee, slips out of place, usually to the outside of the knee. The dislocation is obvious, and the kneecap is likely to be moveable from side to side.

> Symptoms

Signs and symptoms of a dislocated kneecap include visible deformity, intense pain, swelling, and inability to straighten the knee or walk.

> What to Do

Call 911 and seek immediate medical care. Immobilize the affected leg.

1. Do not attempt to straighten the knee.

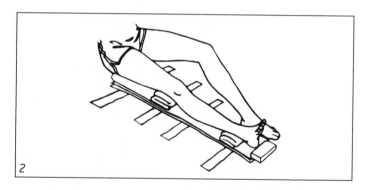

2. Place a padded board at least 4 inches wide underneath the injured leg. The board should be long enough to reach from the person's heel to the buttocks. Place extra padding under the ankle and knee.

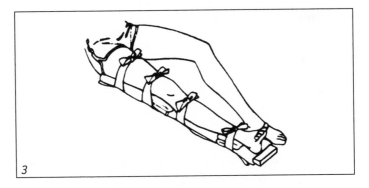

3

3. Tie the splint in place at the ankle, just below and above the knee, and at the thigh. Do not tie over the kneecap.

See also: Bone Injuries, pp. 79–83.

LOWER LEG FRACTURE

The shinbone (ortibia) is the most commonly broken bone in the body. It functions as the major weight-bearing bone in the lower leg. A person can break the shinbone across its length (shaft), or break the portion of the bone that attaches to the knee joint (tibial plateau) or ankle joint. The fibula is the bone that runs alongside the tibia below the knee and is commonly broken during ankle injuries.

> Symptoms

Symptoms include:

- Significant pain with an inability to bear weight
- Swelling
- Tenderness
- Bruising
- Obvious deformity
- Increased pain with activity

It is important to note that toddlers or young children with a broken leg may simply stop walking, even if they can't explain why.

> What to Do

Call 911 or the local emergency medical dispatch number immediately if the toes turn blue or if there is bone protruding through the skin. If the person does not have these symptoms, follow the steps below for immobilizing the lower leg before transporting to a hospital emergency department.

If splints are not available:

1. Carefully and slowly straighten the injured leg, if necessary.

2. Place padding, such as a folded blanket, between the person's legs.

3. Tie the legs together. (See Thigh Injury, below)

If splints are available:

1. Place a well-padded splint on each side of the injured leg. A third splint can be used underneath the leg. Splints should reach from above the knee to below the heel.

2. Tie the splints together in three or four places. Do not tie directly over the break.

To make a pillow splint:

1. Gently lift the injured leg and slide the pillow under the leg.

2. Bring the edges of the pillow to the top side of the leg. Pin the pillow together or tie the pillow around the leg in several places. For added support, place a rigid object such as a board or stick on each side of the pillow and fasten in place with ties above and below the suspected fracture site.

See also: Bone Injuries, pp. 79–83.

THIGH INJURY

An injury to the thigh can cause internal bleeding, which can be life threatening. If a person has had a severe blow to the thigh, or if you notice swelling or redness in the thigh, call 911 (or the local emergency medical dispatch number) or transport the person immediately to the nearest hospital emergency department.

> Symptoms

- Significant pain
- Swelling
- Bruising
- Potential pain with walking, limited mobility

> What to Do

Call 911 or the local emergency medical dispatch number immediately if the leg is numb below the level of the injury, if the person is unable to walk or extend the leg, if the skin under the toenails is blue, or if the person has an open wound.

If none of these symptoms are present, follow the steps below for immobilizing the leg before transporting the person to a hospital emergency department.

If board splints are not available:

1. Using traction (pull), carefully and slowly straighten the knee of the injured leg, if necessary.

2. Place padding, such as a folded blanket, between the person's legs.

3. Tie the injured leg to the uninjured leg. Legs should be tied together in several places, including around the ankles, above and below the knees, and around the thighs. Do not tie directly over the break.

If board splints are available:

1. Using traction (pull), carefully and slowly straighten the knee of the injured leg, if necessary.

2. Assemble about seven long bandages or cloth strips. Use a stick or small board to push each strip under the person's body at a hollow such as the ankle, knee, or small of the back and then slide each strip into place (at the ankle; above and below the knee; at the thigh, pelvis, and lower back; and just below the armpit).

3. Place two well-padded splints in parallel position. The outside splint should be long enough to reach from the person's armpit to below the heel. The inside splint should reach from the crotch to below the heel.

4. Tie the splints in place with knots at the outside splint.

ARM, HAND, AND SHOULDER PROBLEMS

COLLARBONE FRACTURE

Collarbone (clavicle) fractures are common traumatic injuries. The collarbone connects the upper part of the breastbone (sternum) to part of the shoulder blade (scapula). A fractured clavicle is usually a result of a direct blow to the bone.

> Symptoms

Symptoms include:

- Significant pain
- Swelling
- Tenderness
- Bruising
- Obvious deformity

> What to Do

Call 911 or the local emergency medical dispatch number immediately, if the person has difficulty breathing or pain when breathing, has an open wound in the chest, or has numbness in the adjacent arm.

If the person does not have any of the above symptoms, follow the steps described in the illustration on p. 71 for immobilizing the collarbone before transporting to a hospital emergency department.

See also: Bone Injuries, pp. 79–83.

ELBOW INJURY AND DISLOCATION

The elbow is a complex joint formed by the 3 long bones in the arm (humerus, radius, and ulna). Injuries resulting from direct trauma to

IMMOBILIZING THE COLLARBONE

Wrap an elastic bandage or other cloth (starting at the side of the neck) diagonally across the back, over the shoulder, under the arm, and again diagonally across the back, over the shoulder, and under the arm. Repeat a few times. You should be able to slide one finger snugly under the ties in front. Illustration shows front and back views.

the elbow can cause pain, swelling, and circulation problems to the lower arm. Seek medical help at once if an elbow injury is suspected.

A dislocated elbow is a common injury in toddlers and preschoolers that results from a weak ligament holding the tip of the radius permitting it to dislocate. It usually occurs when young children are lifted up or pulled strongly by their hands and forearms.

> Symptoms

Symptoms include:

- Significant pain
- Swelling
- Tenderness
- Bruising
- Obvious deformity, and increased pain with activity

> What to Do

1. Call 911 or the local emergency medical dispatch number immediately if the person has no pulse in the wrist, cannot move the fingers or hand, or has numbness in the hand or fingers.

2. If the person does not have any of the above symptoms, follow the steps below for immobilizing the elbow before transporting to a hospital emergency department.

If the elbow is bent:

1. Do not try to straighten the elbow.

2. Place the forearm in a sling and tie the sling around the person's neck, if possible.

3. If possible, bind the injured upper arm to the person's body by placing a towel or cloth around the upper arm, sling, and chest and tying it under the person's opposite arm.

If the elbow is straight:

1. Do not try to bend the elbow to apply a sling.

2. Place padding in the person's armpit.

3. Apply padded splints along one or both sides of the entire arm. If splints are not available, a pillow centered at the elbow and tied may be used.

See also: Bone Injuries, pp. 79–83.

HAND FRACTURE

Hand fractures occur commonly during sports activities. Each finger consists of one hand bone (metacarpal) and three finger bones (phalanges). Each thumb consists of one metacarpal bone and two phalanges. Any of these bones can break during a fall, a direct blow, or a crushing injury.

> Symptoms

Symptoms include:

- Significant pain
- Swelling
- Tenderness
- Bruising
- Obvious deformity, and increased pain with activity

> What to Do

Call 911 or the local emergency medical dispatch number immediately if the person cannot move the fingers, if the skin under the fingernails is blue, or if the fingers are numb.

If the person does not have any of the above symptoms, follow the steps below for immobilizing the hand before transporting to a hospital emergency department.

1. Bend the arm at the elbow.

2. Place a padded splint underneath the lower arm and hand and tie the splint in place.

3. Place the lower arm against the person's chest and put the lower arm into a sling and tie around the person's neck.

See also: Bone Injuries, pp. 79–83.

LOWER ARM OR WRIST FRACTURE

Forearm and wrist fractures are common injuries. The forearm is comprised of two bones (the radius and ulna), which mesh with eight small wrist bones (carpal bones). Fractures typically occur when someone falls on an outstretched hand.

> Symptoms

Symptoms include:

*   Significant pain
*   Swelling

- Tenderness
- Bruising
- Obvious deformity, and increased pain with activity.

It is important to note that toddlers or young children with a broken arm may simply stop using the injured arm or hand, even if they can't explain why.

> What to Do

Call 911 or the local emergency medical dispatch number immediately, if the person has a weak pulse in the wrist or cannot move the fingers, if they are numb, the skin under the fingernails is blue, or if any bone is protruding.

If the person does not have any of the above symptoms, follow the steps below for immobilizing the arm before transporting to hospital emergency department:

 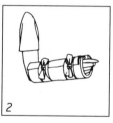 

1. Carefully place the lower arm at a right angle across the person's chest with the palm facing toward the chest and the thumb pointing upward.

2. Apply a padded splint on each side of the lower arm, or use folded, padded newspapers or magazines wrapped under and around both sides of the arm. The splint should reach from the elbow to well beyond the wrist. Tie the splint in place above and below the break.

3. Support the lower arm with a wide sling tied around the neck. The sling should be placed so that the fingers are slightly higher (3 to 4 inches) than the level of the elbow.

4. Have the person sit up while riding to the hospital.

See also: Bone Injuries, pp. 79–83.

SHOULDER DISLOCATION

In most cases of shoulder dislocation, the upper arm bone (humerus) pops out of the joint, usually toward the front. Ligaments, tendons, and other connective tissues are stretched or torn and may injure nerves and blood vessels in the shoulder region, sometimes causing numbness in the hand.

The injury can result from a traumatic event, such as a direct blow to or a fall on the shoulder or from falling on an outstretched hand or arm. Susceptibility to shoulder dislocation may also be genetic, particularly if the shoulder pops out often or easily. Members of the same family are often affected. In some cases, the shoulder can dislocate during sleep.

> Symptoms

A dislocated shoulder causes severe pain the moment the injury occurs. A person may experience limited movement in the shoulder area and swelling and bruising. The shoulder may look abnormal, with a large bump rising up under the skin on the front of the shoulder.

> What to Do

Do not move or try to put a dislocated bone back into its place. Unskilled handling can cause extensive damage to nerves and blood vessels.

Call 911 or the local emergency medical dispatch number if the person has a weak pulse in the wrist or if the shoulder injury was caused by a severe blow. A bone may be fractured and any movement may cause further tissue damage.

For other situations, follow the steps below for immobilizing the shoulder before transporting the person to a hospital emergency department or doctor's office:

1. If possible, on your way to the doctor's office or hospital, apply an ice pack to the shoulder area. Cold treatments help stop internal bleeding and the accumulation of fluids in and around the injured area, thereby decreasing swelling.

2. The shoulder may be put in a sling or wrapped to immobilize the area and aid recovery.

   > Place the person's injured forearm at a right angle to his or her chest.

   > Apply a sling and tie around the person's neck.

   > Bind the arm to the person's body by placing a towel or cloth around the upper arm and chest and tying it under the person's opposite arm.

3. Your doctor may recommend a nonsteroidal anti-inflammatory drug such as ibuprofen, naproxen, or ketoprofen to reduce swelling.

4. Do not participate in physical activity until your shoulder has had time to heal, which may take 3 to 6 weeks, depending on the extent of the injury.

5. With proper healing, the shoulder should regain its full range of motion. In some cases, especially after recurring dislocations, surgery may be recommended to help stabilize the shoulder.

6. Talk with your doctor about exercise to strengthen the muscles in the shoulder region.

   See also: Bone Injuries, pp. 79–83.

SHOULDER SEPARATION

A shoulder separation occurs when ligaments that hold the collarbone (clavicle) to the shoulder blade are torn. The collarbone also may be pushed out of alignment. A shoulder separation usually results from an injury, such as a direct blow to or fall on the shoulder area. It can also result from falling on an outstretched hand or arm. A shoulder separation usually has no lasting effects. Some people, however, may have pain, stiffness, or limitation of motion in their shoulder. In severe cases, surgery may be necessary; the surgery usually involves removing the outer ½-inch tip of the collarbone.

> Symptoms

A shoulder separation causes severe pain the moment the injury occurs. A person may experience swelling, bruising, and limited movement in the shoulder area. The shoulder may have an abnormal shape.

> What to Do

Call 911 or the local emergency medical dispatch number if the person has a diminished pulse in the wrist or if the shoulder injury was caused by a severe blow.

For other situations, follow the steps below for immobilizing the shoulder before transporting the person to a hospital emergency department or doctor's office:

1. If possible, on your way to the doctor's office or hospital, apply an ice pack to the shoulder area. Cold treatments help stop internal bleeding and the accumulation of fluids in and around the injured area, thereby decreasing swelling.

2. The shoulder may be put in a sling or wrapped to immobilize the area and aid recovery.

   > Place the person's injured forearm at a right angle to his or her chest.

   > Apply a sling and tie around the person's neck.

   > Bind the arm to the person's body by placing a towel or cloth around the upper arm and chest and tying it under the person's opposite arm.

3. Your doctor may recommend a nonsteroidal anti-inflammatory drug such as ibuprofen, naproxen, or ketoprofen to reduce the pain and swelling.

4. Do not participate in physical activity until the injury has healed, which may take 2 to 10 weeks, depending on the severity of the separation.

5. Talk with your doctor about exercises to strengthen the muscles in the shoulder region.

6. See your doctor if the pain and swelling reappear or if movement of the shoulder is limited.

UPPER ARM FRACTURE

An upper arm fracture refers specifically to a fracture of the humerus, which is the largest bone in the arm. The injury is usually caused by a direct blow to this bone.

> Symptoms

Symptoms include:

- Significant pain
- Swelling
- Tenderness
- Bruising
- Obvious deformity

It is important to note that toddlers or young children with a broken arm may simply stop using it, even if they can't explain why.

> What to Do

Call 911 or the local emergency medical dispatch number, if the person has a weak pulse in the wrist, cannot move the fingers or hand, cannot extend the wrist, if the fingers are numb, or if any bone is protruding.

If the person does not have any of the above symptoms, follow the steps below for immobilizing the arm and transport to a hospital emergency department:

1. Place some light padding in the person's armpit and gently place the arm at the person's side, with the lower part of the arm at a right angle across the person's chest.

2. Make a padded splint out of newspaper or other material and apply it to the outside of the upper arm. Tie it in place above and below the break. Support the lower arm with a narrow sling tied around the neck.

3. Bind the upper arm to the person's body by placing a large towel, bed sheet, or cloth around the splint and the person's chest and tying it under the opposite arm.

4. Have the person sit up while riding to the hospital.

See also: Bone Injuries, pp. 79–83.

BONE INJURIES (GENERAL CONSIDERATIONS)

BROKEN BONES

A break or crack in a bone is a fracture. A fracture may be closed or open. In a closed fracture, the broken bone does not come through the skin. Usually the skin is not broken near the fracture site.

In an open fracture, there is an open wound that extends down to the bone, or parts of the broken bone may stick out through the skin. An open break is usually more serious because of severe bleeding and the greater risk of infection.

Always suspect a broken neck or spinal injury if the person is unconscious or has a head injury, neck pain, tingling, or paralysis in the arms or legs.

Do not move the person, particularly if he or she has head, neck, or spine injuries (or if paramedics or other trained ambulance personnel are readily available), unless the person is in immediate danger from a fire, explosion, traffic, or other life-threatening situation. If the person must be moved, immobilize the injured part first. For example, tie the injured leg to the uninjured leg, if possible.

Do not lift a person with a suspected neck or spinal injury out of the water without a back support, such as a board. If the person must be dragged to safety, do not drag him or her sideways but pull by the armpits or legs in the direction of the length of the body, keeping the head in line with the body. Do not let the person's body bend or twist, particularly the neck or back. (See also: Head, Neck, and Back Problems, pp. 138–155.)

> Signs/Symptoms

Always suspect a broken bone under any of the following circumstances:

- The person felt or heard a bone snap.
- The site of the injury is painful or tender, particularly when touched or moved.

- The person has difficulty moving the injured part.
- The injured part moves abnormally or unnaturally.
- The person feels a grating sensation of bone ends rubbing together.
- The area of the injury is swollen.
- The injured part is deformed.
- The shape or length of a bone is different from the same bone on the other side of the body.
- The site of the injury shows a bluish discoloration.

For a closed break:

1. Call 911 or the local emergency medical dispatch number if the fracture is severe. Otherwise, immoblize the patient and transport the person to the nearest hospital emergency department.

2. Follow the steps on pp. 62–78 for immobilizing broken bones in specific parts of the body.

For an open break:

1. Call 911 or the local emergency medical dispatch number immediately.

2. Cut clothing away from the wound. Do not try to push back any part of the bone that is sticking out. Do not wash the wound or insert anything, including medication, into it.

3. Gently apply pressure with a large sterile or clean pad or cloth to stop the bleeding.

4. Cover the entire wound, including the protruding bone, with a bandage.

5. Apply splints if paramedics or other trained personnel are not readily available. Always splint the injured part by securing the splint above and below the injury before moving the person. (See Splinting and Other Procedures, below.)

6. Handle the person very gently. Rough handling often increases the severity of the injury.

7. Do not give the person anything to eat or drink.

> Splinting and Other Procedures

Splints are used to keep an injured part from moving, thereby easing pain and preventing the break from becoming worse. Objects that can be used for splinting include boards, straight sticks, brooms, pieces of corrugated cardboard bent to form a three-sided box, rolled newspapers or magazines, pillows, rolled blankets, skis or ski poles, oars, or umbrellas. Life jackets can be wrapped around knee or ankle injuries. If possible, the splint should extend beyond both the joint above and the joint below the broken bone. Padding, such as cloth, towels, or blankets, should be placed between the splint and the skin of the injured part.

Splints can be tied in place with neckties, strips of cloth torn from shirts, handkerchiefs, belts, string, rope, or other suitable material. Do not tie the splint so tightly that the ties interfere with circulation. Swelling or bluish discoloration of the fingers or toes may indicate that the ties are too tight and need to be loosened. Loosen splint ties if the person experiences numbness or tingling or if he or she cannot move the fingers or toes. Check for a pulse and loosen the ties if no pulse can be felt.

Instructions on how to splint and treat breaks of specific bones are on pages 62–80. Keep in mind, however, that any suspected fracture needs to be evaluated by a doctor. After immobilizing a broken bone, take the person immediately to a hospital emergency department or doctor's office.

BUMPS

Bumps are common injuries. Any bump on the head resulting from an injury may be serious and requires medical attention.

> What to Do

- As soon as the injury occurs, apply cold compresses or an ice pack to the affected area to decrease swelling and alleviate pain. Do not apply ice directly to the skin. Use a towel to protect the surface of the skin. Do not apply ice for any more than 20 minutes at any given time.

- *Head injury.* Seek medical attention promptly for a bump on the head if a person has bleeding from the ears, nose, or mouth; unconsciousness (brief or prolonged); a change in pulse; severe headache; difficulty breathing; seizures, fits, or convulsions;

severe vomiting; pupils of unequal size; slurred speech; a generally poor appearance; or a personality change. Check that the person is not unconscious by awakening him or her every half hour for the first 2 hours, and every 2 hours for the next 24 hours.

• Seek medical attention for any severe bump or bruise on any part of the body.

See also: Bone Injuries, p. 79; Bruises, p. 171, Eye Problems, p. 126; Head, Neck, and Back Problems, p. 138; Headaches, p. 139; Unconsciousness, p. 233.

DISLOCATIONS

A dislocation occurs when the end of a bone is displaced from its joint. It usually results from a fall or a blow to the bone. Common areas of dislocations include the shoulder, hip, elbow, fingers, thumb, and kneecap. One of the most frequent dislocations is a pulled elbow in children under 5 years. The dislocation usually occurs when a child's arm is pulled up by the wrist, causing one of the forearm bones to slip out of place.

> Symptoms

Dislocations may cause any or all of the following symptoms:

• Swelling

• Deformity

• Pain on moving the injured part or inability to move the part

• Discoloration

• Tenderness

• Numbness

> What to Do

1. Do not move or try to put a dislocated bone back into its place. Unskilled handling can cause extensive damage to nerves and blood vessels. The bone may be fractured and any movement may cause further tissue damage.

2. Place the person in a comfortable position.

3. Immobilize the injured part with a splint, pillow, or sling in the position in which it was found. (See Splints, p. 32.)

4. Seek medical attention promptly, preferably at the nearest hospital emergency department.

See also: Bone Injuries, p. 79; Sprains, p. 175; Wounds, p. 183; and Sports First Aid, pp. 235–290.

CHILD ABUSE

If you think a child is the subject of abuse, call a local child protective service agency, welfare department, public health department, or the police. (See p. 190.) You should suspect abuse if a child has any of the following:

- Fractures in the breastbone, back, skull, end of the collarbone, or ribs.
- Multiple fractures in different stages of healing.
- Fractures caused by twisting.
- Recurring fractures in the same part of the body.

BURNS

The objectives of first aid for burns are to stop the burning process, conserve body heat, relieve pain, and prevent or treat for shock. Burns caused by fire, sunlight, or hot substances are classified according to the degree of the injury. First-degree burns are the least dangerous. Third-degree burns are the most serious.

FIRST-DEGREE BURNS

A burn resulting in injury only to the outside layer of the skin is a first-degree burn. Sunburn and brief contact with hot objects, hot water, or steam are common causes of first-degree burns and cause no blistering of the burned areas. The goals are pain control and protection from further injury. First-degree burns usually heal within a week.

> Symptoms

First-degree burns can cause any or all of the following symptoms:

- Redness
- Mild swelling

CHILD ABUSE

If you think a child is the subject of abuse, call a local child protective service agency, welfare department, public health department, or the police. (See p. 190.) You should suspect abuse if a child has any of the following:

- A burn with a distinctive, recognizable pattern of an object such as a grid, hot plate, or light bulb
- Multiple circular burns from cigarettes
- A burn with the pattern of a glove or stocking on an arm or leg, or a clear-cut, sharp edge from being immersed in scalding water
- Multiple burns in various stages of healing.

- Pain
- Unbroken skin (no blisters)

> What to Do

1. Immediately put the localized burned area under cool running water or apply a cool-water compress (a clean towel, washcloth, or handkerchief soaked in cool water) until pain decreases.

2. Cover the burn with nonfluffy sterile or clean bandages. Do not apply butter or grease to a burn. Do not apply medications or home remedies without a doctor's recommendation.

TREATING A BURN

To lower the temperature of the burned area and stop further skin damage, immediately put the localized, first-degree burned area under cool running water or apply cool-water compresses until pain subsides.

SECOND-DEGREE BURNS

A burn that causes injury to the layers of skin beneath the surface of the body is a second-degree burn. Deep sunburn, hot liquids, and flash burns from gasoline and other substances are common causes of second-degree burns. Healing may take up to 3 weeks.

> Symptoms

Second-degree burns can cause any or all of the following symptoms:

- Redness, or a blotchy or streaky appearance
- Blisters
- Swelling that lasts for several days

- Moist, oozy appearance of the surface of the skin
- Pain

> ## What to Do

1. Stop the burning process. Do not soak extensive second-degree burns in water, as this will lead to rapid loss of body heat.
2. Gently pat the area dry with a clean towel or other soft material.
3. Remove any constricting jewelry.
4. Cover the burned area with a dry, nonfluffy sterile bandage or clean cloth to prevent infection. Do not attempt to break blisters or apply ointments, sprays, antiseptics, or home remedies.
5. Elevate burned arms or legs.
6. Seek medical attention. If the person has flash burns around the lips or nose or has singed nasal hairs, breathing problems may develop. Seek medical attention immediately, preferably at the nearest hospital emergency department.

WARNING

People who have inhaled smoke or other substances can develop lung damage and should seek immediate medical attention. Prompt medical attention is also required for burns that cover more than 20 percent of the body of an adult or 10 percent of the body of a child, or for burns on the face, hands, or feet. To determine the percentage of the burned area, the person's palm represents 1 percent of his or her body surface area.

THIRD-DEGREE BURNS

A burn that destroys all layers of the skin is a third-degree burn. Fire, prolonged contact with hot substances, and electrical burns are common causes of third-degree burns.

> ## Symptoms

Third-degree burns may cause any or all of the following symptoms:

- White or leathery skin at burn site
- Skin damage
- Little pain (because nerve endings have been destroyed)

WARNING

- Do not remove clothes that are stuck to the burn.

- Do not put ice or ice water on burns. This can intensify hypothermia (loss of body heat).

- Do not apply ointments, sprays, antiseptics, or home remedies to burns.

> What to Do

1. If the person is on fire, smother the flames with a blanket, bedspread, rug, or jacket.

2. Call 911 (or your local emergency medical dispatch number) or take the person to the nearest hospital emergency department. It is very important that persons with even small third-degree burns consult a doctor.

3. Check often to see if the person has trouble breathing and maintain an open airway if breathing becomes difficult. Breathing difficulties are common with burns, particularly with burns around the face, neck, and mouth, and with smoke inhalation.

4. Place a cool cloth or cool (not iced) water on burns of the face, hands, or feet to cool the burned areas.

5. Cover the burned area with thick, sterile, nonfluffy dressings. A clean sheet, pillowcase, or disposable diaper can be used. Use non-constricting bandages and be aware that circumferential burns (where the burn encircles an entire body part) can act as a tourniquet that reduces blood flow into an extremity.

6. Elevate burned hands higher than the person's heart, if possible.

7. Elevate burned legs or feet. Do not allow the person to walk.

8. If the person has face or neck burns, he or she should be propped up with pillows.

9. Watch for signs of shock, such as a fast and weak pulse and fast breathing. If the person is in shock, do the following while waiting for medical help to arrive:

   - Keep the person lying down unless the face or neck is burned.

   - Elevate the person's feet 8 to 12 inches unless the person is unconscious or has neck, spine, head, chest, or severe lower face or jaw injuries. A person who is unconscious or who has severe lower face or jaw injuries should be placed on his or her side (not facedown) with the head slightly extended to prevent choking on fluids or vomit. If the person is having trouble breathing, elevate his or her head and shoulders slightly.

- If pain increases, lower the feet again.

- Keep the person comfortably warm but not hot, covered with a blanket or coat. If possible, place a blanket beneath a person who is on the ground.

- Do not give fluids by mouth.

- Calm and reassure the person. Gentleness, kindness, and understanding play an important role in treating a person in shock. See also: Shock, p. 160.

ELEVATE A BURN

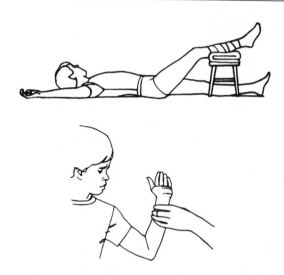

Cover the burn with a nonfluffy sterile or clean bandage to prevent infection. Elevate a foot or leg (above) with second- or third-degree burns higher than the person's heart. Elevate a hand or arm (below) with second- or third-degree burns higher than the person's heart.

CHEMICAL BURNS

> What to Do

1. Quickly flush the burned area with large quantities of running water for 5 to 10 minutes. Speed and quantity of water are both important in minimizing the extent of the injury. Use a garden hose, buckets of water, a shower, or a tub. Do not use a strong stream of water if it can be avoided.

2. Continue to flush with water while removing clothing from the burned area.

3. After flushing, follow the instructions on the label of the chemical that caused the burn, if available.

4. Cover the burn with a nonfluffy clean bandage or clean cloth. Do not apply ointments, sprays, antiseptics, or home remedies. Cool, wet dressings are best for pain.

5. Seek immediate medical attention.

    See also: Chemical Burns to the Eyes, page 127.

ELECTRICAL BURNS

Electrical burns may appear slight on the surface of the skin, but can be extremely severe in the underlying tissue. Exposure to ordinary household electrical current seldom causes serious problems, but exposure to high-voltage wires is usually fatal.

If you are the first person to arrive at the scene to offer first aid, it is extremely important not to risk electrocuting yourself. Do not touch the person directly until the electric current is turned off or the person is no longer in contact with it. Persons who have been struck by lightning may be touched immediately because they are not connected to a continuous supply of electricity.

All electrical burns, no matter how minor they may seem, require immediate medical attention.

> Symptoms

Electrical burns can cause one or both of the following symptoms:

- Slight redness at the site of the burn
- Muscle spasm

> What to Do

1. If possible, turn off the electric current by removing the fuse or by pulling the main switch. If this is not possible, or if the person is outside, have someone call the electric company to cut off the electricity. Try to stay at least 60 feet away from a high-voltage line.

2. If it is necessary to remove the person from a live wire, be extremely careful. Stand on something dry, such as a newspaper, board, blanket, rubber mat, or cloth, and, if possible, wear dry gloves. Push the person away from the wire with a dry board, stick, broom handle, or well-insulated wooden tool, or pull the

REMOVING SOMEONE FROM A LIVE WIRE

Be extremely careful to avoid being electrocuted yourself. Stand on something dry, wear dry gloves if possible, and push the person away from the wire with a dry board, stick, or tool—or pull the person away with a dry rope looped around the person's arm or leg.

person away with a dry rope looped around the person's arm or leg. Never use anything metallic, wet, or damp. Do not touch the person until he or she is free from the wire.

3. If the person is not breathing, call 911 (or your local emergency medical dispatch number). Maintain an open airway. Restore breathing and circulation, if necessary. (See CPR, pp. 33–45.)

4. Cover the burn with a clean, dry dressing. Be careful not to break any blisters.

5. Look for signs of broken bones or neck injuries from a fall.

6. Seek immediate medical attention, no matter how minor the burn may seem.

SUNBURN

See p. 351. See p. 351.

TAR AND ASPHALT BURNS

The large pots in which workers mix tar and asphalt at the back of roofing trucks maintain temperatures of up to 500°F. Spills or contact with tar or asphalt directly from the pot can cause severe third-degree burns. When spread on a roof, the material is somewhat cooler but is still hot enough to cause second-degree burns.

> What to Do

1. Apply cold water to the burned area to harden the tar.

2. Spread petroleum jelly on gauze or a soft cloth and wipe it over the area to remove the tar. Do not use gasoline, acetone, or kerosene to clean the burn.

3. Seek immediate medical attention.

See Also: Heat-Related Problems, p. 330; Seizures, p. 150; Shock, p. 160.

DENTAL PROBLEMS

KNOCKED-OUT TOOTH

A tooth that has been knocked out can be successfully reimplanted in the gum within 30 minutes of the injury. You can purchase a tooth-preservation kit at most drugstores to keep on hand; bring it along whenever you or your children are participating in sports activities.

> What to Do

1. Rinse the tooth gently in cool water (don't use soap), and hold it in place in the socket with a clean washcloth or piece of gauze, or put it in a clean container with some milk or saliva, which will keep the tooth alive until the dentist reimplants it. Do not put the tooth in tap water. The minerals in water may cause further harm. Saline (salt) water may be used, however.

2. If bleeding is present, fold a clean piece of gauze, handkerchief, or tissue into a pad and place it over the wound. Close teeth tightly to apply firm pressure to the bleeding area. Maintain pressure for 20 to 30 minutes. Repeat the procedure if necessary.

3. Immediately take the person and the tooth to the dentist or, if it is after business hours, to the hospital emergency department.

TOOTHACHE

Cavities and infections often cause toothaches. Home treatment offers only temporary relief from pain but is often helpful if a toothache occurs in the middle of the night or before you can seek professional attention. A trip to the dentist is necessary to find the exact cause of a toothache and to treat it effectively.

> What to Do

1. Give the person acetaminophen, naproxen, or ibuprofen.

2. Place cold compresses or ice packs on the face over the affected area. For some people, warm compresses may be more comforting. This varies with each individual.

3. Seek dental attention.

TOOTH EXTRACTION

Pain, slight swelling, and bleeding often occur after a tooth has been pulled. If these problems become severe or persistent, consult your dentist.

> What to Do

1. As soon as possible after the tooth has been pulled, place a cold compress or ice bag on the face on the affected area to relieve swelling. The compress should remain in place for 15 minutes out of each hour. Repeat the procedure for several hours.

2. If bleeding is present, fold a clean piece of gauze, handkerchief, or tissue into a pad and place it over the wound. Close teeth tightly to apply firm pressure to the bleeding area. Maintain pressure for 20 to 30 minutes. Repeat the procedure if necessary.

3. If the dentist did not prescribe medication for pain, acetaminophen, naproxen, or ibuprofen may be taken. Aspirin should not be taken because it can increase bleeding.

See also: Head, Neck, and Back Injuries, p. 138.

DIABETES-RELATED EMERGENCIES

DIABETIC COMA

Diabetic coma is a life-threatening condition that can occur in people who have diabetes when the level of the sugar-regulating hormone insulin in the blood is too low and blood sugar levels become dangerously too high. Insulin levels can go down to dangerous levels in people with diabetes if their bodies are not using the hormone properly—usually because they are not taking their medications or have missed a number of insulin doses, are not eating properly, or have an underlying infection.

> Symptoms

A diabetic coma can cause any or all of the following symptoms (which usually come on gradually):

- Extreme thirst
- Warm, red, dry skin
- Drowsiness
- Fruity-smelling breath
- Deep, rapid breathing
- Dry mouth and tongue
- Nausea with upper abdominal discomfort
- Vomiting
- Frequent urination
- Fast heart rate

> What to Do

1. Call 911 or the local emergency medical dispatch number. The individual needs immediate medical attention.

2. Maintain an open airway and support breathing and circulation. (See CPR, pp. 33–49.)

See Also: Unconsciousness, p. 233; Nausea and Vomiting, p. 113.

HYPOGLYCEMIA (LOW BLOOD SUGAR)

Hypoglycemia can occur in individuals who have diabetes when there is not enough blood glucose (sugar) in the blood to support the function of the vital organs. The condition arises when the person takes too much insulin or eats too little food after taking insulin or other diabetic medications.

> Symptoms

Insulin shock, which can come on suddenly, can cause any or all of the following symptoms:

- Hunger
- Pale and sweaty skin
- Excited and/or sometimes belligerent behavior
- Shallow breathing
- Confusion
- Slurred speech

> What to Do

If the person is conscious:

1. Give the person food containing sugar, such as fruit juice, sweetened drinks, honey, or just sugar in water.
2. Seek medical attention immediately.

If the person is unconscious:

Call 911 or the local emergency medical dispatch operator to seek medical attention at the nearest hospital emergency department. Maintain an open airway and support breathing and circulation.

DIGESTIVE PROBLEMS

ABDOMINAL PAIN

Abdominal pain is a common complaint in both adults and children. Episodes often stem from indigestion, overeating, or time-limited gastroenteritis. There are many causes of abdominal pain, but only some of these indicate serious medical problems that require immediate medical care. Abdominal pain can refer from one anatomical area to another. The navel or belly button divides the abdomen into quadrants (into an upper abdomen and lower abdomen as well as right and left).

Upper mid abdominal pain can be associated with heartburn, peptic ulcer disease, or gall bladder pain. Right upper quadrant pain can be caused by gallstones or by inflammation of the gallbladder or liver. Gall bladder pain is associated with eating fried or fatty foods. Pain is usually associated with nausea and vomiting. Right lower quadrant pain can be caused by appendicitis (inflammation of the appendix) or inflammatory bowel disease. Left upper quadrant pain can be associated with injury to the spleen. Left lower quadrant pain can be caused by inflammation of colon or rectum.

Abdominal pain in children is common and is usually not serious unless it lasts longer than an hour or is accompanied by other symptoms. But severe abdominal pain in infants and young children can indicate a serious medical disorder that requires immediate medical attention.

For both adults and children, if symptoms are severe or persist, seek medical attention promptly. A person with severe abdominal pain should never be given an enema, a laxative, medication, food, or liquids (including water) without a doctor's advice because doing so may aggravate the problem or cause a complication.

> What to Do

Treatment for mild abdominal pain and discomfort in adults:

For mild abdominal pain caused by something you ate, it may help to sip water or suck on ice chips. When you feel better, try small amounts of bland foods, such as toast, applesauce, or bananas. If stomach acid is an issue, an antacid may help.

When to seek immediate medical care:

An adult who has abdominal pain under any of the following conditions requires immediate medical attention and should be taken to a hospital emergency department:

- Pain accompanied by shortness of breath, chest pain, dizziness, bleeding, vomiting, or a high fever
- Pain associated with an inability to tolerate liquids
- Recent abdominal surgery or endoscopy (a procedure to diagnose or treat digestive disorders through a viewing tube called an endoscope)
- Pain that is focused in one specific area of the abdomen
- Pain that begins intermittently in a general area around the navel and later moves to the lower right part of the abdomen
- Pain that travels to the back or shoulder area
- Pain that is accompanied by fever, sweating, blood in stool, black stool, or blood in urine
- Pain that becomes suddenly severe and intolerable or that wakes a person from sleep
- Severe pain in the side or back that radiates to the groin
- Pain during pregnancy or with abnormal vaginal bleeding
- Pain that is accompanied by dry mouth, sunken eyes, lightheaded feeling when standing, fainting or decreased urination (symptoms of dehydration)
- Pain that is accompanied by difficulty breathing
- Pain that is associated with an injury to the abdomen
- Pain that is accompanied by vomiting blood or a greenish-brown fluid
- Abdominal swelling and tenderness

Abdominal pain in infants and young children up to age 5:

An infant with abdominal pain will usually cry loudly, bending the legs and drawing the knees toward his or her chest.

When to call 911 or the local emergency medical dispatch number:

A young child should be taken to a hospital emergency department if he or she has abdominal pain under any of the following conditions:

- Forceful vomiting right after feedings in a very young infant (usually between 3 and 6 weeks old)
- Pain that occurs suddenly, subsides, and then recurs without warning
- Pain that is accompanied by red or purple jellylike stool; blood in stool; or mucus in stool
- Pain that is accompanied by greenish-brown vomit
- Swollen abdomen that feels hard to the touch
- A hard lump in the scrotum, groin, or lower abdomen
- Pain associated with fever
- Pain in the groin or right side of the abdomen
- Persistent vomiting

See Also: Diarrhea, p. 102; Food-Related Illness, p. 104; Miscarriage, p. 230; Pregnancy Danger Signs, p. 231; Nausea and Vomiting, p. 113; Wounds (Abdominal Wounds), p. 184.

BLOODY STOOL

Bloody stool can be caused by many diseases in the upper (esophagus, stomach, small intestine) or lower (large colon, rectum) gastrointestinal tract. Bright red blood is most commonly due to hemorrhoids. Hemorrhoids can have associated rectal pain, itching, burning, and bloody mucus streaking of your stool. Hemorrhoids are commonly noticed after one wipes after a bowel movement.

> What to Do

For hemorrhoids, applying a topical over-the-counter steroid cream, such as hydrocortisone 1% cream, can help reduce the pain and swelling. Tucks pads can be used after each bowel movement to keep the area clean. Any bleeding should be reported to your physician.

When to seek immediate medical care:

Abdominal pain, weakness, and bleeding could indicate active internal bleeding and medical attention should be sought immediately. In such situations, call 911 or your local emergency medical dispatcher.

CONSTIPATION

Constipation is a common complaint and is usually due to inadequate fluid intake or diets low in fiber. Constipation can also be associated with hemorrhoids.

> Symptoms

- Straining to pass stool
- Infrequent bowel movements
- Passing hard stools

> What to Do

- Seek immediate medical care by calling 911 or the local medical emergency dispatch number if you have intense abdominal pain, are unable to pass any gas, or have blood in your stool (see Abdominal Pain, p. 96).

- Contact your doctor if you have a sudden change in bowel habits that is unrelieved by diet or exercise, if you have unexplained weight loss or thin pencil-like stools, or rectal pain, which might indicate a more serious health condition.

- Over-the-counter laxatives can be taken but avoid excess use. Stool softeners, such as docusate (Colace), can also be used to soften stool so that it passes through your intestines more easily. Do not use stool softeners on a regular basis because they can cause other problems.

- If symptoms persist, it is best to discuss your symptoms with your doctor, who may recommend an enema and further testing.

> Preventing Constipation

Avoiding or alleviating constipation includes getting more exercise, eating high-fiber foods, and drinking plenty of water. Changes in your lifestyle may be the safest way to manage constipation. Fiber supplements may also be considered, such as wheat bran or other over-the-counter products (for example, Metamucil or Citrucel). These natural supplements help make stools softer and are safe to use every day. Also be sure to drink plenty of water or other fluids every day. Oat bran, while helpful for lowering high blood cholesterol, does not improve bowel function.

DARK TARRY STOOL

Maroon or tarry-colored stools could indicate chronic bleeding due to ulcers or other causes. You should always report these symptoms to your family doctor, who will prescribe appropriate medications and refer you to gastroenterologist for further testing. Beets, Pepto-Bismol, and iron pills can commonly cause darker stools.

Symptoms include heartburn, belching, increased gas, nausea, abdominal bloating and pain.

> What to Do

1. Contact your doctor immediately with symptoms.

2. Further testing by a medical specialist (a gastroenterologist) may be indicated.

3. Do not give the person anything to drink.

4. Calm and reassure the person.

When to seek immediate medical care:

Abdominal pain, weakness, and bleeding could indicate active internal bleeding and medical attention should be sought immediately. In such situations, call 911 or your local emergency medical dispatch number.

See also: Amputations, p. 60; Pregnancy Danger Signs, p. 231; Shock, p. 160; Wounds, p. 183.

DEHYDRATION

Dehydration is a lack of adequate water in the body. Severe dehydration can occur with vomiting, excessive heat and sweating, diarrhea, or lack of food or fluid intake. Dehydration is a medical emergency and can be fatal. The condition is common in the elderly and can occur rapidly in infants and young children. Each year nearly 500 American children under 4 years old die of dehydration resulting from diarrhea.

> Symptoms

Dehydration may cause any or all of the following symptoms:

- Extreme thirst (that the person may not be able to quench)
- Tiredness
- Light-headedness
- Headache
- Abdominal or muscle cramping
- Restlessness
- Decreased urine output/frequency

> What to Do

1. Move the person into the shade or a cool area.

2. Replace lost fluids and body chemicals by giving the person water, a commercially available electrolyte rehydration drink, or clear broth. Avoid high-sodium and caffeinated beverages.

3. Seek medical attention if symptoms persist or if complications arise.

When to seek immediate medical care:

Call 911 (or your local emergency medical dispatch number) or take the person to the nearest emergency department if you notice any or all of the following signs of severe dehydration:

- Three or four loose, watery bowel movements every 4 to 6 hours
- Decreased urination in both frequency and amount
- Vomiting

- Seizures
- Fast, weak pulse
- Fast breathing
- Sunken eyes
- Lack of tears
- Dry mouth
- Tired or listless appearance
- Weak cry (in children)
- Pale skin
- Passing out
- Severe or prolonged stomach cramps
- Black, tarry stool
- Blood or mucous in stool

See Also: Diarrhea, below; Heat-Related Problems, p. 330; Seizures, p. 150; Nausea and Vomiting, p. 113.

DIARRHEA

Diarrhea—frequent loose, watery bowel movements—has many causes. The most common include food poisoning, certain medications, emotional stress, excessive drinking, and viral and bacterial infections.

If diarrhea is not severe and the individual can and will drink liquids, the body can replace lost fluids. If the individual can't or won't drink liquids or is vomiting, replacement of fluids orally will be impossible and dehydration can occur rapidly. Hospitalization may be necessary for intravenous fluid replacement.

▪ DIARRHEA IN ADULTS

> Symptoms

Diarrhea is characterized by any or all of the following symptoms:

- Frequent loose and watery stools (stools may vary from light tan to green)

- Stomach cramping
- Tiredness (due to loss of potassium)
- Thirst (due to loss of fluid)
- Blood streaks in or on stools

> What to Do

1. A liquid diet is recommended to replace lost fluids and some body chemicals. Drink clear broth, a commercially available electrolyte replacement drink, flavored gelatin (in liquid form), or carbonated beverages that have been allowed to go flat. Water alone may pass right through the body. Drink at least 8 ounces of liquids every hour. Do not eat solid foods for about 24 hours, and avoid milk and dairy products for several days.

2. If diarrhea persists longer than a day or two, or if urine decreases in both frequency and amount, seek medical attention immediately because fatal dehydration may occur.

■ DIARRHEA IN CHILDREN

Common causes of diarrhea in infants and children are infection, spoiled food, food allergies or intolerance, foods with laxative effects, and poisoning.

If diarrhea is not severe and the child can and will drink liquids, the body can replace lost fluids. If the child can't or won't drink liquids or is vomiting, replacement of fluids will be impossible and dehydration can occur rapidly, especially in children under 5. Hospitalization may be necessary.

> Symptoms

Frequent loose, watery bowel movements, which may or may not have a bad odor.

> What to Do

1. Give the child liquids to replace lost fluids and some body chemicals. Do not give fruit juice or milk, however, because they can make the condition worse. Have the child drink clear broth, flavored gelatin (in liquid form), or carbonated beverages that have been allowed

to go flat. Water alone may pass right through the body. Call the doctor before giving an electrolyte replacement drink or a sugar and salt solution (see below) to ask how much to give.

2. Do not give the child solid foods for 24 hours.

Sugar and Salt Solution

1 quart of water

1 tablespoon of sugar

4 teaspoons of cream of tartar

1 teaspoon of salt

½ teaspoon of baking soda

Mix the ingredients. If cream of tartar and baking soda are not available, use just water, sugar, and salt.

▪ TRAVELER'S DIARRHEA

See pages 109–110 and Food-Related Illness, below.

See Also: Dehydration, p. 101; Enteric Food Poisoning, p. 106; Nausea and Vomiting, p. 113.

FOOD-RELATED ILLNESS

Food-related illness (food poisoning) occurs when eating food that has been improperly handled, undercooked (meat, poultry, or chicken), or inadequately stored. Food poisoning can occur soon after eating the contaminated food and can be caused by bacteria, virus, parasite, or toxin. Symptoms include nausea, vomiting, and diarrhea.

Food poisoning is usually mild and lasts 24 to 48 hours. It typically requires only fluid replacement such as electrolyte fluids (Gatorade) or broth. Children, pregnant women, and the elderly are vulnerable and can become dehydrated if they are unwilling to take fluids by mouth. You should seek medical attention if the individual is unable to tolerate liquids or has severe abdominal pain or fever and bloody diarrhea.

Suspect food poisoning if several people become ill with similar symptoms at approximately the same time after eating the same food. Also suspect food poisoning if one person becomes ill after eating food no one else has eaten.

Food poisoning can be prevented by proper handling of foods, which includes hand washing, and by cooking foods at an appropriate temperature. Raw foods should not be mixed with cooked foods. Eating raw foods can increase the risk of food poisoning. The following are specific examples of food poisoning.

■ BOTULISM

Botulism is a very serious form of food poisoning that is often fatal. It is a medical emergency. Botulism most often occurs after eating improperly home-canned foods, but some cases have occurred after eating commercially prepared frozen foods, including pot pies, asparagus, green beans, peppers, and onions sautéed with margarine. Botulism has also been associated with eating some seafood, including salmon or seal, walrus, or whale meat.

In infants, honey can cause a rare and serious form of botulism. Honey is a known source of spores that produce the bacteria that cause botulism. When infants eat the spores, the bacteria can grow in the infant's digestive system and make the toxin that causes this disease. For this reason, infants under 12 months of age should never be fed honey. Honey is safe for persons 1 year of age and older.

> Symptoms

Botulism can cause any or all of the following symptoms, which usually appear within 6 to 72 hours:

- Dry mouth
- Dizziness
- Headache
- Blurred and/or double vision
- Muscle weakness

- Difficulty swallowing
- Difficulty talking
- Difficulty breathing
- Hoarseness
- Lack of coordination

> What to Do

Seek medical attention immediately, preferably at the nearest hospital emergency department.

> Preventing Botulism

Here are some steps you can take to avoid botulism:

- Do not keep cooked foods at room temperature (or higher than 40°F) for longer than 2 hours.

- Freeze foods for long-term storage.

- Discard cans that have defects such as swelling.

- When preserving foods, boil them for at least 10 minutes at a temperature higher than 212°F. (Dry-heating methods such as smoking do not kill the botulism toxin.) Use proper preserving techniques such as high acidity or nitrate preservatives.

▪ ENTERIC (GASTROINTESTINAL) FOOD POISONING

Food poisoning caused by coccidian parasites (for example, *Cryptosporidium parvum*) and enteric bacteria such as campylobacter, *Escherichia coli* (E. coli), salmonella, staphylococci, and shigella continues to occur commonly. General risks include undercooked poultry, fish, and beef, unpasteurized milk and juices, contaminated water, and unwashed fruits and vegetables. The summer months pose particular risks with picnics and an abundance of fresh fruits and vegetables.

A dangerous form of *E. coli*, called *E. coli* O157:H7, can cause severe bloody diarrhea that can be fatal. Infections with this bacterium have been associated primarily with eating contaminated ground beef.

Staphylococcus poisoning occurs most often by eating foods that have not been properly refrigerated. The most common foods affected include meats, poultry, eggs, milk, cream-filled bakery goods, salami, sausage, ham, tongue, and tuna and potato salad.

> Symptoms

- Diarrhea (sometimes with blood)
- Abdominal cramps
- Nausea and vomiting
- Headache
- Fever
- Body aches

> What to Do

1. Keep the person lying down and comfortably warm.

2. If vomiting occurs, keep the person on his or her side, preferably with the head lower than the rest of the body to reduce the risk of choking on the vomit.

3. After the person has stopped vomiting, give him or her fluids such as an electrolyte replacement drink (such as Gatorade or Powerade) or broth.

4. Seek medical attention promptly.

> Preventing *E. coli* Infections

Here are some steps you can take to avoid infection with E. coli:

- Always wash your hands before preparing food, and wash all foods you are going to eat raw.

- After handling raw meat, wash your hands, cutting boards, and any plates, bowls, or utensils the meat came into contact with. Cook all meat and poultry thoroughly.

- Peel fruits and vegetables such as apples and potatoes. Remove the outer layers of leafy vegetables such as lettuce. Rinse fruits and vegetables thoroughly under running water for a minute or two.

- When eating out, do not order rare meat—especially hamburgers and beef.

- Avoid unpasteurized milk products and fruit juices.

- Don't drink unchlorinated water.

- Don't allow a child in diapers to go in a swimming pool and don't allow a child with diarrhea to swim in a pool.
- Avoid swallowing lake water while swimming.

> Preventing Food Poisoning From Eggs

Here are some steps you can take to avoid food poisoning from eggs (usually caused by salmonella or staphylococcal bacteria):

- Eat only pasteurized eggs.
- Keep eggs refrigerated until you cook them.
- Never eat raw eggs.
- Boil eggs for at least 7 minutes.
- Poach eggs for at least 5 minutes.
- Fry eggs on each side for 3 minutes.
- Do not keep incompletely cooked eggs at room temperature for longer than 2 hours.
- Rinse hard-boiled eggs in water that is warmer than the egg itself.

■ MUSHROOM POISONING

Mushroom poisoning occurs after eating poisonous mushrooms found growing wild.

> Symptoms

Mushroom poisoning can cause any or all of the following symptoms, which appear within minutes to 24 hours, depending on the type and amount of mushroom eaten (symptoms may also vary according to the type of mushroom eaten):

- Abdominal pain
- Diarrhea (may contain blood)
- Vomiting (may contain blood)
- Difficulty breathing

- Sweating
- Salivation
- Tears
- Dizziness
- Hallucinations
- Seizures
- Muscle spasms

> What to Do

1. Call 911 or your local emergency medical dispatch number.
2. Keep the person resting in a quiet place.
3. If vomiting occurs, keep the person on his or her side, preferably with the head lower than the rest of the body to reduce the risk of choking on the vomit.
4. Seek medical attention immediately.

▪ TRAVELER'S DIARRHEA

Traveler's diarrhea is a form of food poisoning that can result from exposure to one of several different bacteria (usually E. *coli*, salmonella, or shigella), viruses, or parasites. The infection occurs most often during the rainy summer months in tropical regions of Africa, Latin America, the Caribbean, southern Asia, and Mediterranean countries.

> Symptoms

Traveler's diarrhea can cause any or all of the following symptoms, which usually appear quickly after eating the contaminated food and last up to 3 days:

- Abdominal cramps
- Fever
- Nausea and vomiting
- Watery diarrhea (2 to 4 bowel movements a day)

> What to Do

1. Keep the person lying down and comfortably warm.

2. When the person has stopped vomiting, give him or her warm, mild fluids such as electrolyte water (Gatorade) or broth.

3. If the diarrhea is mild and the person does not have a fever, or if the person has had only vomiting, give 2 tablespoons or two tablets of bismuth subsalicylate every 30 minutes (for an adult)— up to a total of eight doses in all. The medication should not be taken for more than 2 days. Another over-the-counter medication called loperamide can also be taken if symptoms are particularly troubling; up to 8 milligrams of loperamide may be taken a day for no more than 2 days. Talk to your doctor before giving any medication to a child.

4. If the symptoms last longer than 3 days or get worse, seek medical attention.

> Preventing Traveler's Diarrhea

Here are some steps you can take to avoid traveler's diarrhea:

- Avoid drinking tap water or ice made from untreated water. Limit your beverages to bottled water, carbonated drinks, beer, or wine.

- Avoid unpasteurized or unrefrigerated milk products or fruit juices.

- Avoid raw vegetables, salads, seafood, and meat.

- Peel all fruits and cook all food to steaming hot. (Dry foods such as bread are probably safe to eat.)

- Ask your doctor about taking medication to prevent traveler's diarrhea. He or she may recommend taking two tablets of bismuth subsalicylate four times a day, starting the day before you leave for your trip and every day during the trip. Bismuth subsalicylate should not be given to children under 5 or to people who are allergic to aspirin.

See also: Dehydration, p. 101; Diarrhea, p. 102; Unconsciousness, p. 233; Nausea and Vomiting, p. 113.

■ VIRAL GASTROENTERITIS

Gastroenteritis is common problem that is caused by a virus and typically resolves in 24 hours. The virus causes an inflammation of your stomach and intestines and symptoms include persistent nausea, vomiting, abdominal bloating, and diarrhea. A low-grade fever can accompany the symptoms. Children, pregnant women, and the elderly can be susceptible to dehydration.

> What to Do

1. Treatment includes fluid replacement such as electrolyte fluid (Gatorade) or broth.

2. Seek medical attention if your symptoms persist. Go to the emergency department if you notice signs of severe dehydration (see p. 102) or are unable to tolerate any liquids by mouth or have bloody vomit, bloody diarrhea, or mental confusion.

> Preventing Viral Gastroenteritis

Hand washing is the single most important step for preventing the spread of gastroenteritis. Avoid contact with sick people if possible. Avoid sharing food utensils with those who are sick.

HEARTBURN

Heartburn is caused by a regurgitation of stomach (gastric) acid into the esophagus. Heartburn usually occurs after eating.

> Symptoms

Heartburn is commonly described as an uncomfortable, burning sensation felt in the middle of the chest. Heartburn is also associated with:

- Nausea
- Belching
- Bitter aftertaste in your mouth

> What to Do

1. Antacids can be used to immediately improve symptoms, but you should not exceed labeled dosage per hour.

2. Over-the-counter medications that reduce stomach acid can be considered for treatment.

3. Proton pump inhibitors (for example, Omeprazole) are best reserved for those with chronic symptoms and do not have an immediate effect.

> Preventing Heartburn

1. Avoid foods that increase symptoms such as spicy or fried fatty foods. Caffeine, alcohol, smoking, and excess salt also can cause symptoms.

2. Development of frequent episodes more than 3 times a week, chronic belching, or difficulty swallowing foods should prompt an increased awareness and evaluation by your doctor.

INTERNAL BLEEDING

Internal bleeding is not always obvious. You may suspect internal bleeding if the person has been in an accident, fallen, or received a severe body blow. Internal bleeding in the chest, abdomen, or thigh can be life threatening.

> Symptoms

Internal bleeding can cause any or all of the following symptoms:

- Vomit that resembles coffee grounds or is red
- Coughed-up blood that is bright red and/or frothy (bubbly)
- Stools that are black or contain bright red blood
- Paleness
- Cold, clammy skin
- Rapid and weak pulse
- Light-headedness
- Distended (swollen) abdomen
- Restlessness
- Thirst

- Apprehension
- Mental confusion

> What to Do

1. Call 911 (or the local emergency medical dispatch number) or transport the person immediately to the nearest hospital emergency department.

2. If the person is not breathing, maintain an open airway. Restore breathing and circulation if necessary. (See CPR, pp. 33–49.)

3. Do not give the person anything to drink.

4. Calm and reassure the person.

NAUSEA AND VOMITING

Nausea is a queasy or sick feeling in the stomach and is often accompanied by the feeling that you are going to vomit. Vomiting is the forceful ejection of the stomach contents through the mouth. Muscles in the abdominal wall contract vigorously to create the pressure necessary for vomiting (retching). Nausea is a common symptom associated with many conditions including, but not limited to, pregnancy, indigestion, overeating or excessive drinking, drug withdrawal, reactions to medications, motion sickness, food poisoning, fainting, vertigo, or an infection. It may also be associated with more serious illnesses such as heart attack, appendicitis, or a bowel obstruction. Understanding the circumstances of what preceded the onset of nausea and vomiting can sometime help your doctor determine the cause.

Vomiting may last for 24 hours. Any vomiting, however, that is severe or lasts longer than a day or two needs medical attention because dehydration (loss of body fluids) or a chemical imbalance (loss of body chemicals) can occur—especially in infants, the elderly, or people who have a chronic illness.

Vomiting can indicate a serious problem. Always seek medical attention promptly if vomiting occurs with severe stomach pain or after a recent head injury or if the vomit contains blood that looks like coffee grounds. Pregnancy can also be a cause of vomiting.

> What to Do

1. To treat vomiting, replace lost fluids by frequently sipping water or water with electrolytes, for example, a sports drink, an hour after the last vomiting episode. After vomiting has stopped, avoid solid food. Work slowly back to a regular diet over the next 24 hours.

2. Call 911 or the local emergency medical dispatch number immediately if you are vomiting blood or a "coffee ground" substance. You need to be evaluated immediately.

3. Call 911 or the local emergency medical dispatch number immediately if a person is unconscious and vomiting. The dispatch operator may give you additional instructions on how to position the sick or injured person.*

▪ VOMITING IN INFANTS AND YOUNG CHILDREN

Vomiting in infants and children is common. Some of the most frequent causes include allergy, viral infections (flu), poisoning, carsickness, intestinal obstructions, pneumonia, colic, or head injuries. In newborns and infants, spitting up food after eating is common and is not the same as vomiting. It is usually not serious as long as the infant is not choking.

You should always talk to the doctor any time a child under 2 is vomiting. Vomiting in infants can be quite serious, particularly if vomited material is expelled with such force that it shoots out of the infant's mouth 1 or 2 feet across the room (projectile vomiting). This type of vomiting always needs prompt medical attention. It could represent a partially or completely obstructed intestine.

Prolonged vomiting or vomiting with diarrhea can lead to dehydration (loss of body fluids) and also needs prompt medical attention. Other possibly serious symptoms to watch for in infants and small children include vomit that contains blood and vomiting with fever, headache, or stomach pain.

---

*A person with a head injury should have his or her head turned to the side to prevent choking. Do this very carefully by rolling the person over as a unit, keeping his or her head in the same line with the rest of the body as you found it in case there is a neck injury (see p. 35).

> What to Do

To treat simple vomiting that accompanies intestinal upsets, give the child fluids and at first avoid solid foods, but then if liquids are tolerated, you can try solid foods again. Give small sips (approximately 1 teaspoon) of a pediatric rehydrating solution or water every 10 to 20 minutes. Gradually increase the amount if the child is keeping the fluids down. Slowly work back to a regular diet once the child's stomach is settled.

See also: Abdominal Pain, p. 96; Bites and Stings, p. 177; Cold-Related Problems, p. 318; Diarrhea, p. 102; Drug and Alcohol Problems, p. 198; Enteric Food Poisoning, p. 106; Heat-Related Problems, p. 330.

EAR, NOSE, AND THROAT PROBLEMS

· ·

CHOKING

Choking occurs when food, dentures, and other potential items become dislodged in the windpipe (trachea). A "five and five" recommendation is given for dealing with choking. Begin by delivering five back blows—hitting the person forcefully and repeatedly between the shoulder blades with the palm of your hand; and then providing five abdominal thrusts (Heimlich maneuver). Alternate between these two procedures as necessary until the person coughs up the object or becomes unconscious.

> Symptoms

Follow the steps on pp. 45–49 (First Aid for Choking) if you are with someone who has any or all of the following symptoms:

- Gasping or breathing noisily and/or coughing
- Grasping the throat
- Inability to talk or cough forcefully
- Skin, lips, and nails turning pale or blue
- Loss of consciousness
- Breathing stops

To prepare yourself for these situations, learn the Heimlich maneuver and CPR in a certified first aid training course.

See also: CPR, pp. 33–49, Unconsciousness, p. 233.

COMMON COLD

The common cold is a viral infection of the upper respiratory tract, namely the nose and throat.

> Symptoms

- Runny nose
- Sore throat
- Cough
- Congestion
- Mild body aches
- Mild headache
- Sneezing
- Watery eyes
- Fever (up to 102°F)
- Mild fatigue

> What to Do

There's no cure for the common cold. Antibiotics are of no use against cold viruses. Over-the-counter cold preparations won't cure a common cold or make it go away any sooner, and most have side effects. The Centers for Disease Control and Prevention warns against giving cough and cold medicines to children younger than age 2.

> Preventing the Common Cold

No effective vaccine has been developed for the common cold, which can be caused by many different viruses. But you can take some commonsense precautions to slow the spread of cold viruses:

Hand washing and proper cough etiquette are recommended (see Prevent Infections, p. 7). Clean your hands thoroughly and often, and teach your children the importance of hand washing. Carry a bottle of alcohol-based hand rub containing at least 60 percent alcohol for times when soap and water are not available.

EARACHES

Earaches are very common medical problems for both children and adults. The two most common conditions that cause earaches are infection of the outer ear (otitis externa) and infection of the middle ear (otitis media). Occasionally, ear pain is caused by a medical problem elsewhere in the body, such as a sore throat or temporomandibular joint dysfunction (a condition in which the ligaments, muscles, and joints of the jaw are out of alignment).

Outer ear problems are usually caused by a minor injury or infection to the skin of the ear or ear canal (such as a fingernail scratch).

Middle ear problems often follow respiratory infections when germs in the nose and throat move through the Eustachian tube to the middle ear. Children are particularly susceptible to middle ear infections because their Eustachian tubes are shorter and more horizontal than those of adults. Infected tonsils may also cause a middle ear infection. Common causes of middle ear problems include:

- Colds and upper respiratory tract infections
- Moisture trapped in the ear canal (this condition, commonly called swimmer's ear, can occur after swimming or bathing or sometimes just from hot humid weather, see p. 119).
- Minor injuries or scrapes to the skin of ear canal, which usually happens during attempts to clean the ear with objects, such as a cotton-tipped swab
- Allergies
- Exposure to tobacco smoke

> Symptoms

- Pain in the ear (most common symptom); mild cases may have more of an itch than pain
- Hearing loss
- Touching or pulling on the ear worsens the pain
- Ringing or buzzing sounds in the ear
- Full or "plugged" sensation in the ear

- Fever

- Swelling of the ear

- Thick drainage from the ear (such as when the eardrum ruptures and infected fluid drains out)

Other symptoms that may be seen in infants:

- Vomiting or diarrhea

- Irritability; infants with an ear infection cry loudly, particularly when lying down, and pull or bat at their ear or turn the head from side to side.

- Poor feeding

- Poor sleeping

> What to Do

1. Ear infections rarely need to be treated in the hospital. A doctor can safely handle most ear infections in an office setting.

2. Call a doctor about any severe earache that lasts more than a few hours, or even a mild earache that persists for more than a day should receive medical attention. An ear infection responds much better to treatment if therapy is started early, rather than waiting until it is severe.

GO TO THE NEAREST EMERGENCY DEPARTMENT FOR:

- Illness in an infant under 3 months

- Illness in an infant who is becoming weak or running a very high fever (104°F or higher). See Fever, p. 208)

- Severe headache, stiffness of the neck, or swelling in the neck may represent a complication of an ear infection and may require immediate attention

NOTE: Never put cotton-tipped swabs, hairpins, matches, or anything else in the ear for an earache.

■ SWIMMER'S EAR

Swimming in contaminated water can cause "swimmer's ear."

> Symptoms

Symptoms of swimmer's ear may include:

- Mild pain (particularly when the ear is pulled)
- Itching, and discharge of water (which has remained in the ear after swimming) from the ear

> What to Do

Call your doctor. This condition requires medical attention.

> Preventing Swimmer's Ear

Here are some steps you can take to avoid swimmer's ear:

- Do not swim in pools that don't have chlorine.
- After swimming, try to get the water out of your ears by tilting your head to the side and jumping up and down several times. Do this for both ears. If that doesn't work, dry each ear by blowing a hair dryer into it. Be sure to set the dryer at the lowest setting and hold it several inches away from the ear as you gently pull down on the ear lobe with your other hand.
- When surfing or windsurfing, wear a properly fitted swimming cap or wet suit hood.
- Use silicone earplugs (not wax ear plugs) when swimming.
- Ask your doctor about using eardrops or flushing out your ears with an ear syringe and warm water or vinegar after swimming.

If earwax tends to build up in your ears, you may be susceptible to swimmer's ear; ask your doctor about the best way to keep earwax under control.

EAR INJURIES

The eardrum can be ruptured by a loud blast, infection, diving, water-skiing falls, objects poked into the ear, or a head injury (such as a slap on the ear). Blood or other fluids coming from the ear canal may indicate a serious head injury. All ear injuries should be considered serious and require medical attention because of the possibility of hearing loss.

> Symptoms

An ear injury can cause any or all of the following symptoms:

- Bleeding from inside the ear canal
- Pain
- Hearing loss
- Dizziness

> What to Do

1. Call 911 or the local medical emergency dispatch number. If bleeding is due to a head injury with a possible skull fracture, treat the head injury first. The person should not be moved if a serious head, neck, or back injury is suspected unless his or her life is in danger. (See Head, Neck, and Back Problems, p. 138.)

2. Loosely cover the outside of the ear with a bandage or cloth to catch the flow of blood. Do not try to stop the flow of blood from the ear canal. Do not put anything into the ear.

3. Place the person on his or her injured side with the affected ear down, allowing blood to drain.

EPIGLOTTITIS

Epiglottitis is a life-threatening medical condition in which the epiglottis—the flap of tissue at the back of the throat that closes off the windpipe (trachea) during swallowing—becomes infected, inflamed, and swollen, partially closing off the airway. It usually occurs in children between the ages of 3 and 6. Symptoms may appear after the child has had a severe sore throat or cold.

> Symptoms

For a child with any of these symptoms, immediately call 911 or the emergency medical dispatcher:

- Difficulty swallowing
- Drooling

- Little or no voice
- Sits straight up with jaw thrust forward in an attempt to keep the airway open

> What to Do

- Call 911 (or your local emergency medical dispatch number). Keep the child in a sitting position.
- Do not place a spoon or other object in the child's mouth. This will not aid breathing and may cause airway obstruction.
- Do not agitate the child.

FOREIGN OBJECTS INSIDE THE EAR

Children often put objects—such as peas, beans, beads, paper, and cotton balls—in their ears. Insects may also get trapped inside the ear. Most foreign objects lodge in the outer portion of the ear.

> What to Do

1. All small objects trapped inside the ear need medical attention for removal. The only possible exception is paper or cotton if it is clearly visible outside the ear canal. In this instance, you may attempt to remove the object carefully with tweezers. A doctor should be seen, however, to make sure all of it is removed.

2. Do not put water or oil into the ear to attempt to flush out the object, unless the object is a live insect (see below). Putting a liquid into the ear could cause the object to swell and make removal more difficult.

3. If an insect inside the ear is alive and buzzing, put several drops of warm oil (such as baby, mineral, or olive oil) into the ear to kill the insect. This is the only time putting oil into the ear is justified. Seek medical attention for removal of the insect.

FROSTBITTEN EARS

See Cold-Related Problems, p. 318.

MONONUCLEOSIS

Mononucleosis (mono) is a viral illness associated with a sore throat and severe fatigue and is usually seen in teenage and young adults. It is nicknamed the "kissing disease" because it is spread through saliva.

> Symptoms

- Painful sore throat
- Swollen lymph nodes
- Swollen tonsils
- Headache
- Loss of appetite
- Enlarged spleen and liver
- Treatment

> What to Do

1. See your doctor if symptoms are consistent with mono. Fluids and rest are mainstays of therapy. Symptoms of mono usually last 10 days, but it can take weeks to recover one's strength.

2. Your doctor may do further testing. If mono is suspected, it is best to avoid close contact with others.

3. The spleen may enlarge with mono. Avoid contact sports until cleared by your doctor.

4. There is no specific therapy to treat infectious mononucleosis. Because mono is caused by a virus, antibiotics are not effective. Treatment mainly involves bed rest and adequate fluid intake.

NOSEBLEEDS

A nosebleed can be caused by a blow to the nose, scratching the nose, picking the nose, repeated nose blowing that irritates the mucous membranes, dry air, or an infection. Most nosebleeds that occur in children are not serious and usually stop within a few minutes. Those that occur in the elderly, however, may be serious and may require treatment at a hospital emergency department. Recurring nosebleeds may indicate an underlying medical problem and should be evaluated by a doctor.

> What to Do

1. Have the person sit down and lean forward, keeping the mouth open so that blood or clots will not obstruct the airway.

2. Squeeze the sides of the nose together for approximately 20 minutes. (Squeeze the nose below the bone, not on the top of the nose.) It is important not to discontinue squeezing the nose during these 20 minutes.

3. Release slowly. Do not allow the person to blow or touch the nose.

4. If bleeding continues, squeeze the nose closed again for 20 minutes. Be sure that the person is not swallowing blood.

5. Place a cold cloth or ice in a cloth over the bridge of the person's nose and face to help constrict blood vessels.

6. Seek medical attention if bleeding continues, an injury is involved, you suspect a broken nose, the person complains of dizziness or light-headedness, the person is pale or has a fast heart rate, or the person is taking blood thinners (Coumadin or Clopidogrel).

7. Do not let the person irritate or blow the nose for several hours after bleeding stops.

SNORING

See Sleep-Related Problems, p. 232.

SORE THROAT

Sore throats are a common complaint for doctor visits. Yet most of those visits are not necessary because sore throats typically go away on their own in about a week. Most sore throats are caused by viruses and only a small percentage of them require medical care. Bacterial infections that cause sore throats are sometimes treated with antibiotics (antibiotics aren't effective against viruses). Sore throats can also be a sign of the flu, common cold, or mononucleosis in teenagers or younger adults.

> Symptoms

- Dry scratchy throat

- Hoarseness

- Painful swallowing

> What to Do

1. Rest and fluids are the mainstays of treatment. You can gargle with salt water. Acetaminophen can be given to ease the pain of throat discomfort.

2. See your doctor if you begin to have symptoms of fatigue, weakness, or fever of 101° F or higher.

3. Call 911 or the local medical emergency dispatch number if you are having difficulty breathing, cannot tolerate liquids, or are unable to swallow your drool (see epiglottitis, p 121). Children are vulnerable to dehydration.

VERTIGO

See Dizziness, p. 197.

EYE PROBLEMS

BLOW TO THE EYE

Any injury resulting from a hard, direct blow to the eye, such as from a moving ball or a fist, needs medical attention by an ophthalmologist even though the injury may not look serious. There may be internal damage to the eye.

A black eye (shiner) is a common injury and is caused by bleeding beneath the skin around the eye. It is usually caused by direct trauma to the eye socket. Although most black eye injuries aren't serious, bleeding within the eye is serious and can reduce vision and cause damage. A black eye usually takes 2 to 3 weeks to clear up.

> What to Do

1. Seek immediate medical treatment: for bruising around both eyes (raccoon eyes), loss of consciousness, or if one experiences vision problems (double vision, blurring), severe pain, or bleeding in the eye or from the nose.

2. If the person is wearing contact lenses, do not remove them; a physician should remove them as soon as possible.

3. Using gentle pressure, apply a cold pack or a cloth filled with ice to the area around the eye. Take care not to press on the eye itself. Apply ice as soon as possible after the injury to reduce swelling, and continue using ice or cold packs for 24 to 48 hours.

4. If possible, keep the person lying down with eyes closed and head elevated.

> Sudden Eye Pain or Blurred Vision

Any sudden pain in the eyes without recent injury or a sudden blurring or loss of vision requires immediate medical attention.

CHEMICAL BURNS

Chemical burns of the eye are very serious and may lead to blindness if immediate action is not taken. Acids, drain cleaner, bleach, and other cleaning solutions are some chemical agents that can burn the eye. Speed in removing a chemical agent is vital. Damage can occur in 1 to 5 minutes.

> What to Do

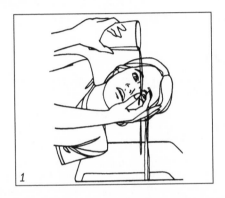

1. Before calling a doctor, have the person quickly remove his or her contact lenses and then immediately flush the eye with large quantities of cool, running water for at least 10 minutes to rinse out the chemical agent. Use milk if water is not available. Hold the person's head under a faucet (or shower, hose, or pitcher of water), with the eyelids held open, and allow the water to run from the inside corner (next to the nose) outward so that the water flows over the entire eye and so that the chemical does not get in the unaffected eye. If both eyes are affected, let water flow over both or quickly alternate between one eye and the other. Be sure to lift and separate the eyelids so the water reaches all parts of the eye. Flushing is the most important initial treatment.

2. Another method is to place the top of the person's face in a bowl or sink filled with water with the eyes in the water, and have the person move the eyelids up and down.

3. If the person is lying down, pour large quantities of water from a container from the inside corner of the eye outward, keeping the eyelids open. Keep repeating this procedure.

4. After following one of the above steps, cover the injured eye or eyes with a pad of sterile gauze or a clean folded handkerchief, and tape it in place with the eyelids closed.

5. Do not allow the person to rub his or her eyes.

6. Seek medical attention immediately, preferably at the nearest hospital emergency department.

CUTS

Any cut to the eye, including the eyelid, can be very serious and could lead to blindness if immediate action is not taken.

> What to Do

1. If the person is wearing contact lenses, do not remove them; a doctor should remove them as soon as possible.

2. Gently cover both eyes (because when one moves, so does the other) with a sterile pad or gauze or a clean folded cloth and tape it lightly in place without applying any pressure.

3. Seek medical attention immediately, preferably from an eye specialist (such as an ophthalmologist) or at the nearest hospital emergency department. Transport the person lying down flat on his or her back if possible.

EYE INFECTIONS
▪ CONJUNCTIVITIS

Conjunctivitis (sometimes referred to as pinkeye) is an infection of the eye that is usually caused by allergies, viruses, bacteria, or chemicals. The infection may affect one or both eyes. Certain forms of conjunctivitis can be very contagious for several days.

> Symptoms

Conjunctivitis can cause any or all of the following symptoms:

- Redness of the white portion of the eye
- Watery or sticky, yellow, green, or brown discharge from the eye

- Sticky upper and lower eyelashes, particularly in the morning
- Sensation of something in the eye

> What to Do

1. Have the person remove his or her contact lenses.
2. Consult a doctor.
3. Place an ice cube in a plastic bag and hold it over the eyelid for temporary relief of pain.
4. Wash your hands (and towels and washcloths) after any contact with the infected eye or surrounding area.

▪ STYE (CHALAZION)

A stye is an inflammation of the glands of the edge of the eyelid.

> Symptoms

A stye can cause any or all of the following symptoms:

- Tender, red, pimple-like bumps near the edge of the eyelid
- Itching or tearing

> What to Do

1. Have the person remove his or her contact lenses.
2. Apply warm water compresses to the affected area several times a day. Do not try to "pop" the stye.
3. If the stye persists for several days or recurs, seek medical attention.

FOREIGN OBJECTS IN THE EYE

Never attempt to remove any particle that is sticking out of the eyeball. Seek immediate medical attention for such injuries. Particles such as eyelashes, cinders, or specks that are resting or floating on the eyeball or inside the eyelid may be carefully removed.

> Symptoms

A foreign object in the eye can cause any or all of the following symptoms:

- Pain
- Burning sensation
- Tearing
- Redness of the eye
- Sensitivity to light

> What to Do

If the foreign object is embedded in the eye:

1. Wash your hands with soap and water before carefully examining the person's eyes. Do not allow the person to rub his or her eyes or to remove his or her contact lenses.

2. If you can see that the foreign object is embedded in the eyeball, do not attempt to remove the object.

3. Gently cover both eyes (because when one moves, so does the other) with a sterile compress and tape it lightly in place without applying any pressure. If bandages are not available, use a scarf, a large cloth napkin, or other suitable material and tie it around the head. Disposable cups work well too and can be taped in place over the eye.

4. Seek medical attention promptly, preferably from an ophthalmologist or at the nearest hospital emergency department. Keep the person lying down on his or her back while riding to the hospital. Use a stretcher if possible.

If the foreign object is resting or floating on the eye or inside the eyelid:

1. Wash your hands with soap and water before carefully examining the person's eyes. Do not allow the person to rub his or her eyes or to remove his or her contact lenses.

2. Gently pull the upper eyelid down over the lower eyelid and hold for a moment. This causes tears to flow, which may wash out the particle.

3. If the particle has not been removed, fill a medicine dropper with warm water and squeeze water over the eye to flush out the parti-

REMOVING A PARTICLE FROM THE EYE

To remove a particle resting on the inside of the upper lid, have the person look down as you hold the lashes of the upper eyelid and pull the eyelid upward.

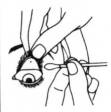

While holding the eyelid, place a cotton-tipped swab across the back of the lid and flip the eyelid backward over it.

Carefully remove the particle with a moistened, clean cloth or tissue.

cle. If a medicine dropper is not available, hold the person's head under a gentle stream of running water, or use a glass of water, to flush out the particle.

4. If still unsuccessful, gently pull the lower eyelid down. If the foreign object can be seen on the inside of the lower lid, carefully lift the particle out with a moistened, clean cloth or tissue.

5. If the speck is not visible on the lower lid, check the inside of the upper lid by holding the lashes of the upper eyelid and pulling downward. The person must look down during the entire procedure. While holding the eyelid down, place a cotton-tipped swab across the back of the lid and flip the eyelid backward over it. (The person can help by holding the swab.) Carefully remove the particle with a moistened, clean cloth or tissue.

6. If the particle still remains, gently cover the eye with a sterile or clean compress and seek medical attention promptly.

GLUE ON THE EYELIDS

When working with glue, people sometimes transfer glue from their hands to their eyelids, causing the eyelids to stick together.

> What to Do

- If the eyelids are completely stuck together, never try to pull them apart. Seek medical attention promptly.
- If the eyelids are partially stuck together, rinse them with water to loosen the glue. Seek medical attention promptly.

SUNBURN OF THE EYE

See Sunburn, p. 352.

GENITAL AND URINARY PROBLEMS

BLOOD IN URINE

Blood in the urine is a medical symptom that is associated with many causes including urinary tract infection and kidney stones, as well as strenuous exercise and some common drugs such as aspirin. Most cases are not serious, but urinary bleeding can also indicate a serious disorder such as cancer. Therefore, it is important for you to seek medical attention to determine the reason for the bleeding.

> Symptoms

Pink-, red-, or cola-colored urine

> What to Do

See your doctor, who will attempt to identify the underlying cause (for example, a urinary tract infection or kidney stone). If you are on a blood thinning medication such as warfarin, seek immediate medical attention at your local hospital emergency department.

FLANK PAIN/KIDNEY STONES

Sudden excruciating pain in the flank can be caused by a kidney stone. Kidney stones are deposits of mineral and acid salts that can crystallize in the urinary tract and cause pain or blockage (usually in the ureter, the tube that connects the kidney to the bladder). The pain typically starts in your side or back, just below your ribs, and radiates to your lower abdomen and groin. The pain can also fluctuate in intensity.

> Symptoms

- Blood in urine
- One-sided severe flank pain
- Pain with urination
- Nausea
- Vomiting
- Persistent urge to urinate

> What to Do

1. You should seek immediate medical care if you develop these symptoms.

2. Fluids and pain management are usual mainstays of treatment. Antibiotics may be indicated if there is evidence of infection.

3. Your doctor may also want to do further testing.

> Preventing Kidney Stones

Keeping hydrated (drinking plenty of water) is an important way to minimize formation of stones.

SEXUALLY TRANSMITTED DISEASES

Sexually transmitted diseases (STDs) are caused by viruses, bacteria, parasites, and fungi that are spread from person to person primarily through sexual contact with someone who has an infection. STDs can be painful, irritating, debilitating, and life threatening. More than 20 sexually transmitted diseases have been identified. Complications of STD infection include pelvic inflammatory disease (PID) and inflammation of the cervix (cervicitis) in women, inflammation of the urethra (urethritis) and inflammation of the prostate (prostatitis) in men, and fertility and reproductive system problems in both sexes. STDs are usually passed by having vaginal intercourse, but they can also be passed through anal sex, oral sex, or skin-to-skin contact. Common viruses that cause STDs include herpes, human papilloma virus (HPV), and human immunodeficiency virus (HIV). STDs caused by bacteria include chlamydia, gonorrhea, and syphilis.

> Symptoms

Common symptoms of STDs include:

- Itching around the vagina and/or discharge from the vagina
- Discharge from the penis
- Pain during sex or when urinating
- Pain in the pelvic (hip) area
- Sore throats in people who have oral sex
- Pain in or around the anus for people who have anal sex
- Chancre sores (painless red sores) on the genital area, anus, tongue, and/or throat
- A scaly rash on the palms of your hands and the soles of your feet
- Dark urine, loose, light-colored stools, and yellow eyes and skin
- Small blisters that turn into scabs on the genital area
- Swollen glands, fever, and body aches
- Unusual infections, unexplained fatigue, night sweats, and weight loss
- Soft, flesh-colored warts around the genital area

> What to Do

1. If you suspect you have an STD, see your doctor immediately.

2. As these diseases are spread sexually, it is recommended that you notify your partner of the infection and that he or she gets tested.

3. It is important to get tested for HIV because it can also be transmitted through sexual activity.

4. Viral STDs, such as genital herpes, HPV, and HIV, cannot be cured, but symptoms can be managed with medication.

5. Bacterial STDs, such as gonorrhea and chlamydia, can be cured with antibiotics.

6. Fungal (for example, vaginal yeast infection) and parasitic (for example, trichomoniasis) diseases can be cured with antifungal and antihelminthic agents, respectively. Early diagnosis and treatment increase the chances for cure.

> Preventing STDs

Although condoms when correctly and consistently used are highly effective for reducing transmission of STDs, no method (other than abstinence) is 100 percent effective. This is particularly true with certain STDs, such as genital warts and genital herpes. Birth control pills do not provide any protection against the transmission of STDs. The only sure way to avoid becoming infected with an STD is monogamy with an uninfected partner. It is important for partners to discuss their sexual and STD history before having sex and to consider getting tested. Prevention is possible only if sexually active individuals understand STDs and how they are spread.

URINARY TRACT INFECTION

A urinary tract infection is an infection of the urinary system that begins in the lower urinary tract—the urethra and the bladder. Due to anatomical reasons, women are at greater risk of developing urinary tract infections than men. A urinary tract infection can be painful and annoying. However, serious consequences can occur if a urinary tract infection spreads to your kidneys. Antibiotics are necessary to treat infection.

> Symptoms

- Burning sensation when urinating
- Strong persistent urge to urinate
- Passing frequent small amounts of urine, blood, or cloudy urine
- Strong-smelling urine

> What to Do

You should notify your doctor if you have a urinary tract infection because it should be treated with antibiotics. Your doctor also may prescribe a pain medication (analgesic) that numbs your bladder and urethra to relieve burning while urinating. One common side effect of urinary tract analgesics is discolored urine—bright blue or orange.

Seek immediate medical attention if you develop fever greater than 101°F, flank pain, nausea, and vomiting, which could indicate a more serious infection.

> Preventing Urinary Tract Infections

1. Drink plenty of liquids, especially water. Cranberry juice may have infection-fighting properties. However, do not take cranberry juice if you are on a blood thinner (for example, warfarin).

2. Females should always remember to wipe from front to back. Doing so after urinating and after a bowel movement helps prevent bacteria in the anal region from spreading to the vagina and urethra.

3. Empty your bladder as soon as possible after intercourse.

4. Using deodorant sprays or other feminine hygiene products such as douches and powders in the genital area can irritate the urethra.

HEAD, NECK, AND BACK PROBLEMS

BACK INJURIES

Never move a person with a suspected back injury without trained medical assistance unless the person is in immediate danger from fire, an explosion, or any other life-threatening situation. Any movement of the head, neck, or back may result in paralysis or death. With a severe back or neck injury, the person may not be able to move the arms, hands, fingers, legs, feet, or toes. The person may also have tingling, numbness, or pain in the neck or back that could radiate down the arms or legs.

> Symptoms

Severe back injuries can cause any or all of the following symptoms and require immediate medical attention:

- Inability to move the arms, fingers, legs, feet, or toes
- Tingling, numbness, or pain in the neck, back, or down the arms or legs
- Loss of bowel or bladder function

> What to Do

1. Call 911 (or your local emergency medical dispatch number).
2. Place folded blankets, towels, or clothing at the person's sides, head, and neck to keep him or her from rotating or moving from side to side.
3. Keep the person comfortably warm while waiting for medical help to arrive.

If the person must be removed from an automobile or from water:

1. Immobilize the back and neck with a reasonably short, wide board. The board should reach down to the person's buttocks.

2. Place the board behind the person's head, neck, and back, keeping these body parts in alignment.

3. Tie the person to the board at the forehead, under the armpits, around the lower abdomen, and around the lower legs.

4. Do not let the person's body bend or twist. Move the person very gently and slowly.

If the person is not breathing:

- Grasp the back of the jaw and push the jaw forward to open the airway. Do not twist or rotate the head.

If the person is facedown:

1. Get adequate help so that every part of the body can be turned over together as a unit in the same location in which it was found.

2. Restore breathing, if necessary. (See CPR, pp. 33–49.)

If the person must be taken to the hospital by someone other than trained medical personnel:

- When you are unsure whether the injury is to the neck or the back, treat it as if it were a neck injury. Always assume that an unconscious person has a neck injury. (See above.)

See also: Bone Injuries, p. 79; Ear, Nose, and Throat Problems, p. 116; Eye Problems, p. 126; Seizures, p. 150; Dental Problems, p. 92; Unconsciousness, p. 233.

HEADACHES

Headaches are a very common complaint and are usually caused by muscle tightening under the scalp. Most headaches are triggered by stress. Mild headaches are usually described as hurting on both sides of your head with a tightening or pressure sensation and may include mild nausea and sensitivity to light.

Severe headaches that come on suddenly and are accompanied by other symptoms, such as fever, vomiting, a stiff neck, or visual disturbances (such as loss of vision, double vision, or blurred vision), require immediate medical attention. A severe headache may be symptomatic of meningitis, encephalitis, high blood pressure, stroke, or a tumor. Such headaches also can be danger signals during pregnancy.

> What to Do

1. Seek immediate medical attention:

   - If the headache is associated with stiff neck, fever, rash, confusion or seizure, double vision, weakness, numbness, or difficulty speaking.

   - Follows a head injury, fall, or bump.

   - If the headache is so severe that it can be described as the "worst headache of your life."

2. Notify your doctor if:

   - You usually have three or more headaches a week.

   - You take a pain reliever for your headaches every day or almost every day.

   - You need more than the recommended dose of over-the-counter pain remedies to relieve your headaches.

   - Your headache pattern changes.

   - Your headaches are getting worse.

3. Headaches can usually be relieved by taking acetaminophen, aspirin, or a nonsteroidal anti-inflammatory medication (such as ibuprofen or naproxen), and resting.

4. Applying heat to the back of the neck and sitting or lying down in a dark room or massaging the neck muscles and the scalp may also help relieve headache pain. Any severe or persistent headache requires medical attention.

> Preventing Headaches

Exercise and stress relief should be considered to prevent headaches.

HEAD INJURY AND CONCUSSION

All head injuries must be taken seriously because they can result in brain or spinal cord damage or even death. Any person who is found unconscious must be assumed to have a head injury until medical personnel determine otherwise. Most head injuries are caused by a fall, a blow to the head, a collision, or stopping suddenly, as in an automobile collision. Anyone with a head injury may also have a neck injury.

> Symptoms

Head injuries may involve any or all of the following symptoms, some of which may not occur immediately:

- Cut, bruise, lump, or depression in the scalp
- Unconsciousness, confusion, or drowsiness
- Bleeding from the nose, ear, or mouth
- Clear or bloody fluid from the nose or ears
- Pale or reddish face
- Headache
- Vomiting
- Convulsions
- Pupils of unequal size
- Difficulty speaking
- Restlessness or confused behavior
- Change in pulse rate

> What to Do

1. Call 911 or the local emergency medical dispatch number if the individual experienced a loss of consciousness, is leaking clear or bloody fluid from ear or nose, appears confused, experiences vomiting, seizures, or obvious bleeding,

2. Maintain an open airway. Be very careful because there may be a possibility of a broken neck. Be prepared to provide CPR if necessary. (See CPR, pp. 33–49.)

3. Keep the person lying down, quiet, and comfortably warm. If you must move the person, handle him or her very carefully.

4. Do not give the person anything by mouth.

5. Control serious bleeding. (See External Bleeding, p. 52.) Gently apply a compress to the bleeding area and tape it in place.

6. Note the length and extent of unusual behavior or unconsciousness.

7. Seek medical attention promptly, preferably at the nearest hospital emergency department. If someone other than trained medical personnel must take the person to the hospital, transport him or her lying down, face up. Place pads or other suitable material on each side of the person's head to keep it from moving from side to side.

WARNING: DELAYED SYMPTOMS

All head injuries require prompt medical attention, particularly if the person was or is unconscious. However, if the person did not lose consciousness at the time of the injury and did not receive medical care, watch closely for delayed symptoms of brain damage for several days. If you notice any of the symptoms of brain damage—particularly unconsciousness, change in pulse, difficulty breathing, convulsions, severe vomiting, pupils of unequal size, or a generally poor or ill appearance—seek medical attention promptly.

▪ CONCUSSIONS

Concussions are common and caused by a direct blow to the head. The individual does not have to black out to have a concussion. Concussions can occur in contact sports such as football. But every concussion, no matter how mild, injures your brain. This injury needs time and rest to heal properly. Luckily, most concussions are mild and people usually recover fully, though mild difficulty in the ability to concentrate may persist.

> Symptoms

- Confusion
- Amnesia (forgetting the event occurred or the cause of the injury)
- Headache
- Dizziness
- Ringing in the ears

- Nausea or vomiting
- Slurred speech

> What to Do

Seek immediate medical attention if someone blacks out (suffers loss of consciousness).

■ CONCUSSIONS IN INFANTS AND TODDLERS

Concussions can be difficult to recognize in infants and toddlers because they can't readily communicate how they feel. Nonverbal clues of a concussion may include:

- Listlessness, tiring easily
- Irritability, crankiness
- Change in eating or sleeping patterns
- Lack of interest in favorite toys

Any child who has lost consciousness after a blow to the head should be seen by a doctor. Seek immediate medical attention if you notice persistent vomiting, seizures, or a large bruise on the scalp.

> Preventing Concussions

Wear a helmet during recreational activities. When bicycling, motorcycling, skiing, horseback riding, skating, or engaging in any recreational activity that may result in head injury, wear protective headgear.

REMOVING A HELMET

After an accident involving a person who is wearing a helmet, you should not try to remove the helmet because doing so could cause harm. You can sometimes remove the face guard with a screwdriver without risking further injury. Remove the helmet only if the person is having trouble breathing or has stopped breathing and requires CPR, if the person's neck needs to be stabilized, or if the person has severe bleeding from the head. In any of these situations, call 911 (or your local emergency medical dispatch number) first and then carefully remove the helmet following the steps below (note that this procedure requires at least two people):

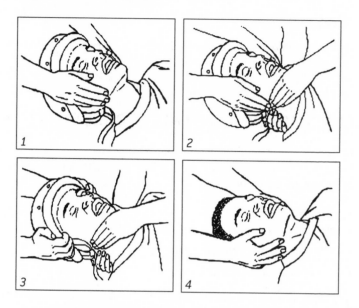

1. Facing the top of the person's head, place your hands on each side of the helmet, with your fingers on the person's lower jaw to immobilize the head.

2. Have another person immobilize the person's head from below by applying pressure to the jaw with the thumb and fingers of one hand and pressure to the base of the skull with the other hand. The hands must hold the head immobile until the helmet is completely removed.

3. Stretch out the sides of the helmet as much as you can and gently and carefully remove it.

4. Keep the person's head immobilized from above by placing your hands on both sides of the head, with your palms over the ears. CPR can now be administered if necessary. (See pp. 33–49.)

LOW BACK PAIN

Lower back pain can occur for a variety of reasons: a strain or tear in a muscle or ligament, injury to a disc or vertebra, pressure on a nerve, or fatigue. Lower back pain can be caused by a repetitive motion or by a sudden force exerted on the back.

> Symptoms

Symptoms can range from a dull ache to a sharp pain in the lower back. If a muscle tears, you may feel a slight pull when the injury occurs, with pain intensifying several hours after the injury. A herniated disc may produce sharp pains that make movement difficult. Sciatic nerve damage may produce sharp pains that radiate down the back of one or both legs. A back that is fatigued may be stiff and ache all over.

> What to Do

1. Call 911 or the local emergency medical dispatch number if you suddenly have problems holding urine or controlling bowel movements, or if you have sudden and noticeable weakness in your legs.

2. See your doctor if your back pain is caused by a blow to the back, if the pain is severe or radiates down the back of both legs, if you have numbness or tingling in your lower back or legs, or if the pain gets worse when you cough or sneeze.

3. For muscle pulls or tears, place an ice pack on the area intermittently (20 minutes every hour while you're awake) for the first 24 hours after the injury. Cold treatments help stop internal bleeding and the accumulation of fluids in and around the injured area, thereby decreasing swelling. Thereafter, use a heating pad on your back at least once a day until the injury heals. Heat increases blood circulation in the area, providing vital nutrients to the injury and helping speed recovery. Do not apply heat before the swelling has subsided, or swelling in the injured area may increase. Take aspirin, ibuprofen, naproxen, or ketoprofen as directed to reduce pain and inflammation.

4. For stiffness or fatigue, place a heating pad on the back to help relax the muscles. Soreness in the lower back can also be relieved by lying down, which takes pressure off the back; by placing one

foot on a foot rest when you're standing, which shifts the angle of the sacrum, lessening the arch of the back; or by getting a good night's rest. The ideal position of rest is lying flat on your back with knees bent; pillows under your knees will help maintain this position.

5. Unless your doctor has prescribed another medication, take aspirin, ibuprofen, naproxen, or ketoprofen with food as directed. (Acetaminophen may not contain as much of the anti-inflammatory agents as aspirin, ibuprofen, naproxen, or ketoprofen; ask your doctor or pharmacist for guidance.)

6. Avoid physical activity until the injury has had time to heal or until the pain is gone. The length of time that it takes the injury to heal depends on the type and severity of the injury and can range from 2 to 6 weeks or longer. Once the injury has healed, gradually and carefully do exercises that stretch the muscles in your back. See your physician if the pain continues or recurs.

> Preventing Low Back Pain

Talk with your doctor about exercises to strengthen the muscles in your back and abdomen. Stretch the muscles in your back before engaging in sports. Avoid sudden movements that could reinjure your back.

NECK INJURIES

A neck injury should be suspected if a head injury has occurred. There are times when a head-injured person will be unconscious, less alert, or distracted by other injuries. You must always assume that these people have a suspected neck injury. Never move a person with a suspected neck injury without trained medical assistance unless the person is in imminent danger of death (such as from fire, an explosion, or a collapsing building).

KEEP THE HEAD IMMOBILE

Any movement of the head of a person with a neck injury—forward, backward, or from side to side—can result in paralysis or death. The head, neck, and shoulders must remain immobile as a unit.

> Symptoms

A neck injury may involve any or all of the following symptoms:

- Headache
- Stiff or painful neck
- Inability to move any part of the body
- Inability to move specific parts of the body (such as arms or legs)
- Tingling sensation in feet and hands

> What to Do

If the person must be moved because of immediate danger to his or her life:

1. Call 911 (or your local emergency medical dispatch number) immediately.

2. Immobilize the neck with a rolled towel, shirt, or newspaper about 4 inches wide, placed as splints on the sides of the head to the shoulders and tied loosely in place. (Do not allow the tie to interfere with the person's breathing.) If you are able to quickly find a wide and short board, then secure the patient's head on both sides to immobilize the head and neck together. You may place a support on either side of the head and neck and secure it with tape or a small piece of cloth. It is very important that you make every attempt not to bend the neck forward or backward. If the person is being rescued from an automobile or from water, place a reasonably short, wide board behind the person's head and back. The board should extend at least to the buttocks. If possible, tie the board to the person's body around the forehead and under the armpits. Move the person very slowly and gently. Keep the person's body as still as possible and do not let the person's body bend or twist.

3. If the person is not breathing or is having great difficulty breathing, push the jaw forward, being very careful not to tilt the head forward or backward. The most common reason for airway obstruction is positioning of the tongue. Performing this jaw movement often moves the tongue out of the way to allow for easier breathing. Restore breathing and circulation if necessary. (See CPR, pp. 33–49.)

4. Lay folded towels, blankets, clothing, sandbags, or other suitable objects around the person's head, neck, and shoulders to keep the head and neck from moving. Place bricks or stones next to

the blankets for additional support. If available, you may also use tape to secure these items to the head and neck.

5. Keep the person comfortably warm while waiting for medical help to arrive.

If the person must be taken to the hospital by someone other than trained medical personnel:

1. The person must be transported lying down on his or her back face up, unless there is danger of vomiting, in which case the person's entire body must be rolled together onto his or her side, keeping the head in the same line with the body in which it was found.

2. Place a well-padded, rigid support such as a door, table leaf, or wide board next to the person. Gather something suitable for tying the person to the board (such as rope, neckties tied together, or strips of strong cloth) and slide them underneath the board in three or four places.

IMMOBILIZING A BROKEN NECK

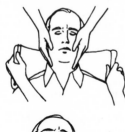

Carefully immobilize the neck by placing rolled towels, sweaters, newspapers, or some other cushioned item, about 4 inches wide, at the side of the person's head and neck, keeping the head as still as possible. It is very important not to bend the person's neck in any direction.

Tie the wrap in place, being careful not to interfere with the person's breathing.

If the person is being rescued from an automobile or from water, place a board behind the head and back. The board should extend at least to the buttocks. If possible, tie the board to the body around the forehead and under the armpits. Move the person slowly and gently as one unit.

MOVING A PERSON WITH A HEAD, NECK, OR BACK INJURY

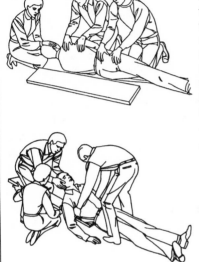

If the person with a suspected head, neck, or back injury must be taken to the hospital by someone other than trained medical personnel, he or she must be transported lying down. Place a well-padded rigid support, such as a door or table leaf, next to the person. The support should extend from beyond the head at least to the buttocks.

The person's head must be held so that it stays in the same line with the body in which it was found. Helpers should grasp the person's clothes and slide him or her onto the support. Move the entire body as a unit.

3. If the person is breathing on his or her own, hold the person's head in the same line with the body in which it was found. Always be sure to support the head and neck to prevent a neck injury or protect one that has already occurred. Other helpers should grasp the person's clothes and slide the person onto the support, moving the entire body together as a unit.

4. Place folded towels, blankets, or cloths around the person's head and neck to keep them from moving and, if possible, tie the person's body to the support.

5. Gently lift the board into the transporting vehicle.

6. Drive carefully to the hospital to prevent further injury.

NOTE: If a pregnant woman who has had a head, neck, or back injury needs to be transported to a hospital by someone other than trained medical personnel, keep her on her back but very gently push the protruding belly to the left side; this improves blood flow to the developing baby.

SEIZURES

A seizure (convulsion) results from a disturbance in the electrical activity of the brain, causing a series of uncontrollable muscle movements. These may occur during a state of total or partial unconsciousness and there may be a temporary loss of breathing. Most seizures last 1 to 2 minutes.

Seizures may occur with a head injury, brain tumor, poisoning, electric shock, withdrawal from drugs, heatstroke, scorpion bites, poisonous snakebites, hyperventilation, or high fever. Seizures also occur in people who have epilepsy, a disorder that results when brain cells temporarily become overactive and release too much electrical energy. A person with epilepsy sometimes has a warning sensation (aura)—a particular taste, smell, or hallucination—that indicates a seizure is about to occur.

You should consider a seizure a medical emergency unless the person having it is known to have epilepsy. However, a person with epilepsy requires emergency medical attention if he or she has a seizure that lasts longer than 5 minutes.

A person having a seizure is not in danger of biting off or swallowing his or her tongue. Do not put any object into the person's mouth. The most important thing to remember when someone is having a seizure is to protect the patient from surrounding objects. Remove any objects in the surrounding environment such as furniture and always protect the head by placing something soft underneath if on a hard floor. Make sure that you keep the person's airway clear of any objects or secretions. Injuries may result from falling during the seizure or from bumping into surrounding objects.

> Symptoms

Seizures may involve any or all of the following symptoms:

- A short cry or scream
- Rigid muscles followed by jerky, twitching movements
- Breathing temporarily stops
- Face and lips turn blue

- Eyes roll upward
- Rapid heart rate
- Loss of bladder and bowel control
- Drooling or foaming at the mouth (foam may be bloody)
- Unresponsiveness
- Sleepiness and confusion after the seizure is over

> ## What to Do

1. Call 911 (or your local emergency medical dispatch number) if the person having the seizure is not known to have epilepsy or if a person with epilepsy has a seizure that lasts longer than 5 minutes.

2. If the person starts to fall, try to catch him or her and lay him or her down gently.

3. Remove any surrounding objects that the person might strike during the seizure, or remove the person from dangerous surroundings (such as stairs, glass doors, or a fireplace).

4. If breathing stops and does not start again immediately, maintain an open airway (see CPR, pp. 33–49). Check to make sure the person's tongue is not blocking his or her throat. Restore breathing if necessary after the seizure.

5. Make sure that the person does not injure himself or herself but do not interfere with his or her movements. Do not try to hold the person down because muscle tears or fractures may result.

6. Do not force any object such as a spoon or pencil between the person's teeth.

7. Do not throw any liquid on the person's face or into his or her mouth.

8. Do not place the patient in the shower.

9. Loosen tight clothing around the person's neck and waist.

10. After the seizure is over, turn the person's head to the side or place the person on his or her side to prevent choking on secretions, blood, or vomit.

11. Keep the person lying down after the seizure is over because he or she may be confused for up to 30 minutes to 1 hour.

12. If necessary, ask bystanders to leave the area.

13. Check for other injuries, such as bleeding and broken bones, and administer appropriate treatment.

14. Stay with the person while he or she recovers.

■ SEIZURES IN INFANTS AND CHILDREN

Seizures in young children are fairly common. The most frequent cause is a rapid rise in temperature due to an acute infection. These seizures (called febrile seizures) usually occur in children between 6 months and 6 years of age and seldom last longer than 2 to 3 minutes. The child should awaken and be alert almost immediately.

Although all seizures in young children must be taken seriously, they are usually more frightening to see than they are dangerous. If these seizures—also called convulsions—last longer, or if the child does not awaken and become alert after the seizure stops, call 911 or your local emergency medical dispatch number. If you do not call 911 for a febrile seizure, you should notify your child's physician to discuss the incident. The symptoms for febrile seizures are the same as for regular seizures (see pp. 150–152).

> What to Do

1. Do not panic.

2. If breathing stops and does not start again immediately, maintain an open airway (see pp. 35–42). Check to make sure the person's tongue is not blocking his or her throat. Restore breathing if necessary after the seizure.

3. After the seizure, turn the child's head to one side or place the child on his or her side so that he or she will not choke on vomit.

4. If the seizure lasts more than 2 to 3 minutes or the child does not regain consciousness after the seizure and become awake and alert or the child is having difficulty breathing and/or is turning blue, call 911 or your emergency medical dispatch number.

5. Have someone else call the child's doctor during the seizure so you do not have to leave the child unattended. If the doctor is not available, take the child to the nearest hospital emergency department.

See also: Drug and Alcohol Problems, p. 198; Fever, p. 208; Head, Neck, and Back Problems, p. 138; Headaches, p. 139; Heat-Related Problems, p. 330; Poisoning, p. 217; Pregnancy Danger Signs, p. 231; and Shock, p. 160.

STROKE

A stroke results from an interruption in blood flow to part or all of the brain. This interruption in circulation may be caused by the formation of a clot inside an artery supplying blood to the brain. This clot can occur by traveling from elsewhere in the body and blocking the blood supply to the brain, by the narrowing of a blood vessel, or by the bursting of an artery within the brain. The brain must receive adequate amounts of blood to function properly. The sooner a stroke victim receives treatment, the more successful treatment is likely to be in preventing or reversing any brain damage.

> Symptoms

A major stroke can cause any or all of the following symptoms:

- Sudden headache
- Sudden paralysis, weakness, or numbness on one side of the body; the corner of the mouth may droop
- Loss or slurring of speech
- Possible unconsciousness or mental confusion
- Sudden fall
- Impaired vision or double vision
- Pupils of different size
- Lack of coordination
- Difficulty breathing, chewing, talking, and/or swallowing
- Loss of bladder and/or bowel control
- Strong, slow pulse

Sudden loss of sensation or motion in an arm or leg may result from a stroke or a brain tumor. The condition should be brought to the attention of a physician without delay. Dial 911 or call your local emergency medical dispatch number immediately. Do not wait until the symptom goes away. Even if the symptom disappears, seek medical attention.

> What to Do

1. Call 911 (or your local emergency medical dispatch number) or take the person to the nearest emergency department immediately. The sooner treatment is begun, the more successful it is likely to be.

2. Maintain an open airway. Restore breathing and circulation if necessary. (See CPR, pp. 33–49.)

3. Place the person on his or her weak side so that secretions can drain from the mouth. Do not give fluids or food to the person. He or she may vomit or choke on them.

4. Keep the person comfortably warm and quiet. Reassure and calm the person.

TRANSIENT ISCHEMIC ATTACK

A transient ischemic attack (TIA) is a temporary clot that traveled to a blood vessel in the brain. Symptoms usually occur in people between the ages of 50 and 70 and clear up within 24 hours. A TIA is a precursor to a stroke, and those who have experienced a TIA have a much higher likelihood of having a stroke in the near future. Only time differentiates a TIA from a stroke.

> Symptoms

A TIA can cause any or all of the following symptoms:

- Slight mental confusion
- Slight dizziness
- Minor speech difficulties
- Muscle weakness
- Visual disturbances

> What to Do

1. Call 911 (or your local emergency medical dispatch number) or take the person to the nearest emergency department immediately. The sooner treatment is begun, the more successful it is likely to be.

2. Maintain an open airway. Restore breathing and circulation if necessary. (See CPR, pp. 33–49.)

3. Place the person on his or her weak side so that secretions can drain from the mouth. Do not give fluids or food to the person. He or she may vomit or choke on them.

4. Keep the person comfortably warm and quiet. Reassure and calm the person.

HEART AND CIRCULATION PROBLEMS

BLEEDING

See External Bleeding, p. 52; Internal Bleeding, p. 112.

FAINTING

Fainting is a brief loss of consciousness due to a reduced blood supply reaching the brain. Recovery usually occurs within a few minutes. Fainting sometimes occurs during the first 5 days of exposure to hot weather, before a person's body becomes adapted to the heat. People who are taking diuretics are at increased risk of fainting in hot weather.

> Symptoms

Fainting may be preceded by any or all of the following symptoms:

- Pale, cool, and wet skin
- Light-headedness or dizziness
- Nausea
- Feeling of restlessness
- Frequent yawning

> What to Do

If the person is about to faint or feels faint:

1. Have the person lie down with legs elevated 8 to 12 inches, or have him or her sit down and slowly bend the body forward so that his or her head is between the knees.

2. Move any harmful objects out of the way and calm and reassure the person.

3. If you suspect the person's condition may be caused by hot weather, assist him or her to a cooler place. Encourage him or her to drink plenty of fluids to prevent dehydration.

If the person has fainted and is not breathing:

1. Call 911 (or your local emergency medical dispatch number).

2. Maintain an open airway. Restore breathing and circulation, if necessary. (See CPR, pp. 33–49.)

If the person has fainted and is breathing:

1. If you suspect that the fainting may have been caused by hot weather, move the person to a cooler place. Encourage him or her to drink plenty of fluids to prevent dehydration.

2. Keep the person lying down. Elevate his or her feet 8 to 12 inches (unless the person has fallen and a head injury is suspected).

3. Maintain an open airway.

4. Loosen tight clothing, particularly around the neck. Do not give the person anything to drink unless he or she seems fully recovered.

5. If the person vomits, place him or her on his or her side. Or, turn the head sideways to prevent choking on vomit.

6. Gently bathe the person's face with cool water. Do not pour water on the face.

7. Check for injuries that may have been caused by falling.

8. Observe the person after he or she regains consciousness. Calm and reassure him or her.

9. If recovery does not seem complete within a few minutes, seek medical attention.

HEART ATTACK

A heart attack is a life-threatening emergency. A heart attack occurs when there is not enough blood and oxygen reaching a portion of the heart. This is due to a narrowing or obstruction of the coronary arteries that supply the heart muscle. A prolonged lack of blood and oxygen can cause part of the heart muscle to die or trigger an abnormal heartbeat that can be fatal. The sooner a heart attack victim receives medical treatment, the less damage the heart is likely to undergo and the better the prognosis.

> Symptoms

A heart attack can cause any or all of the following symptoms:

- Central chest pain or chest tightness that is severe, crushing (not sharp), constant, and lasts for several minutes (pain may feel like indigestion)
- Chest discomfort that moves through the chest radiating to either arm or the shoulder, neck, jaw, mid-back, or stomach
- Profuse sweating
- Nausea and vomiting
- Extreme weakness
- Anxiety and fearfulness
- Pale skin; blue fingernails and lips
- Extreme shortness of breath
- Dizziness or fainting

> What to Do

If the person is unconscious and not breathing or is having difficulty breathing:

1. Call 911 (or your local emergency medical dispatch number).
2. Maintain an open airway.
3. Restore breathing and circulation. (See CPR, pp. 33–49.)

If the person is conscious at the onset of the heart attack:

1. Call 911 (or your local emergency medical dispatch number) and inform the dispatcher of the need for immediate assistance for a possible heart attack. If help is not possible, take the person immediately to the nearest hospital emergency department.
2. Gently help the person to a comfortable position, either sitting up or in a semi-sitting position. A pillow or two may provide greater comfort. The person should not lie down flat because this position makes breathing more difficult.

3. If aspirin is available (preferably in chewable form) and the person is not allergic to it, have him or her chew a 325-milligram tablet or four 81-milligram baby aspirin. Aspirin helps prevent the formation of blood clots.

4. Loosen tight clothing, particularly around the person's neck.

5. Keep the person comfortably warm by covering him or her with a blanket or coat.

6. Calm and reassure the person.

7. If it is readily available, bring the person's current list of medications to the hospital with him or her.

If you are alone and think you're having a heart attack:

1. Call 911 (or your local emergency medical dispatch number) immediately and inform the medics of a possible heart attack and of the need for oxygen.

2. If aspirin is available (preferably in chewable form) and you are not allergic to it, chew a 325-milligram tablet or four 81-milligram baby aspirin. Aspirin helps prevent the formation of blood clots.

3. Get into a comfortable position, either sitting up or in a semi-sitting position. A pillow or two may provide greater comfort.

4. Loosen tight clothing, particularly around your neck.

5. Keep yourself comfortably warm.

6. Do not eat or drink anything.

NOTE: Not all chest pains are symptoms of a heart attack, but it is always a good idea to report any chest pains to a doctor. If you experience persistent or intermittent chest pain and your doctor is unavailable, call 911 (or your local emergency medical dispatch number) or go straight to the nearest emergency department.

See also: Shock, p. 160; Unconsciousness, p. 233.

HEART PALPITATIONS

Heart palpitations are a common medical complaint and are described as the sensation of rapid, fluttering or pounding heartbeats. Palpitations are usually self-limiting and they're often harmless. Common causes of heart palpitations include caffeine, nicotine, stress, anxiety, fever, exercise, hormone changes associated with menstruation, pregnancy, or menopause, and certain medications, such as pseudoephedrine, an ingredient in some cold and allergy medicines. However, occasionally, heart palpitations can be a sign of a serious, underlying problem such as hyperthyroidism or an abnormal heart rhythm (arrhythmia).

> ## Symptoms

- Sudden rapid fluttering of heartbeats
- Pounding sensation in chest

> ## What to Do

Notify your doctor if you develop heart palpitations. He or she may recommend further evaluation such as heart monitoring tests. Seek immediate medical attention if heart palpitations are accompanied by:

- Chest pain
- Shortness of breath
- Dizziness
- Fainting

> ## Preventing Heart Palpitations

Limiting caffeine intake and stress reduction can be considered if the cause is not a serious underlying medical issue.

SHOCK

Shock is a life-threatening situation in which the body's vital functions, such as breathing and heartbeat, are seriously threatened by insufficient oxygenated blood reaching body tissues, such as the lungs, the brain, and the heart. Shock usually results from a serious illness or injury—such as severe bleeding or burns, a heart attack, spinal cord injury, persistent vomiting or diarrhea, perforation of an organ, poisoning, a severe allergic reaction, or a bacterial infection in the blood. **You should seek immediate medical attention.**

> Symptoms

- Pale or bluish and cool skin
- Moist and clammy skin
- Overall weakness
- Rapid (over 100 beats per minute) and weak pulse
- Increased rate of breathing; shallow and irregular breathing or deep sighing
- Restlessness and anxiety
- Unusual thirst
- Vomiting
- Dull, sunken look to the eyes; widely dilated pupils
- Confusion
- Blotchy or streaked skin
- Unconsciousness (in severe cases)

> What to Do

1. Call 911 (or your local emergency medical dispatch number). Maintain an open airway. Restore breathing and circulation, if necessary. (See CPR, pp. 33–49.)

2. Keep the person lying down. In a severely injured patient, you must assume that the patient has a head and neck injury. Do not move the person unless he or she is in danger of further injury. Always protect and support the head and neck to avoid any further injury. Position the jaw forward to open the airway, avoiding any movement of the head or neck.

3. Elevate the person's feet 8 to 12 inches unless he or she is unconscious or has injuries to the neck, spine, head, back, chest, lower face, or jaw. If he or she is having trouble breathing, perform airway and breathing support, being sure to stabilize the head and neck.

4. Keep the person as warm as you can. If possible, place a blanket under and over top any person who is on the ground or on a damp surface.

5. Watch the person very closely for changes in consciousness. Look for other injuries such as internal bleeding (see p. 112) and broken bones (see p. 79) and give first aid for those problems. This may decrease the severity of the shock. Do not give the person fluids to drink if you suspect that the patient is in shock from a severe injury. This could lead to untoward consequences such as aspiration and severe vomiting.

6. Reassure the person. Gentleness, kindness, and understanding play an important role in treating a person in shock.

7. If possible, obtain information about the nature of the accident, estimate blood loss, and gather as much information about the scene as you can.

UNCONSCIOUSNESS

See p. 233.

LUNG AND RESPIRATORY PROBLEMS

Shortness of breath for no apparent reason may mean the onset of an asthma attack or an acute allergic reaction, a heart attack, or congestive heart failure. Seek medical attention immediately to rule out a serious medical condition. Dial 911 or call your local emergency medical dispatch number immediately.

ASTHMA

Asthma is a chronic condition where a patient is susceptible to either gradual or sudden narrowing of the airways in the lungs, causing difficulty in breathing. Breathing may be especially difficult when exhaling. There are many things that can trigger an asthma attack, including infections, exercise, cold weather, inhaled irritants in the air, allergic reactions, and emotional factors. If you have asthma, you can swim, but if you use an inhaler regularly, you should always leave it in an easy-to-reach spot by the water.

> Symptoms

An asthma attack can cause any or all of the following symptoms:

- Difficulty in exhaling (you might hear a wheezing or whistling sound as air is forced out through narrow airways)
- Always sitting upright (because doing so makes it easier for the person to breathe)
- Nervousness, tenseness, fright
- Coughing
- Perspiration on forehead
- Choking sensation
- Vomiting
- Fever

- Bluish tinge to the skin in severe attacks (due to the lack of adequate oxygen intake)

> What to Do

If this is the first episode of suspected (but undiagnosed) asthma:

- Seek medical attention immediately. Report all details of the attack.

- If you can't reach a doctor, take the person to the nearest hospital emergency department.

- Comfort and reassure the person, particularly a child who may be frightened by the experience, because emotional stress may make asthma worse.

- Keep the person in a sitting position—don't force him or her to lie down.

RESPIRATORY FAILURE/SEVERE RESPIRATORY DISTRESS
If the person tries to pull up the shoulders and chin to expand the chest to get air, seek medical attention at once. Call 911 or your local emergency medical dispatcher. The person may be near respiratory failure and could collapse.

If the person has had attacks before:

- Give him or her prescribed medications according to the instructions on the container.

- Do not give anything else without a physician's advice.

- Report the attack to the person's physician.

If the symptoms continue and one or more of the following happens, call 911 or the local emergency medical dispatch number:

- Failure to improve with medication

- Difficulty inhaling or inability to exhale (breathing becomes barely audible)

- Inability to cough or talk

- Increased bluish tinge to skin, especially around the mouth or in nail beds

- Increased pulse rate to more than 120 beats per minute in an adult at rest

- Increased breathing rate of more than 30 breaths per minute in an adult at rest
- Increased anxiety; sweating
- Constant cough
- Flaring of nostrils in children
- Grunting in infants
- Inability to breathe when lying down
- Confusion or sleepiness

BREATHING PROBLEMS IN CHILDREN

Breathing problems in infants and young children are common and usually are not serious. However, in some instances, a serious condition does arise that requires immediate medical attention.

▪ CROUP

Croup is a group of symptoms arising from various respiratory conditions that occur most frequently in children under 3 years of age. Croup is generally caused by a virus, but can also be a spasmodic form. Its symptoms occur most often in fall and winter.

Croup symptoms tend to get worse at night and then improve during the day to then worsen the next day. The illness usually lasts approximately 5 days with the worst symptoms being on days 2 and 3. Often the child has had a mild cold before the attack.

> Symptoms

Croup can cause any or all of the following symptoms:

- High fever
- Croaking sound upon inhaling (stridor)
- Hoarseness
- Hacking, bark-like cough

In more severe cases, there can also be:

- Difficulty breathing, particularly inhaling
- Bluish tinge to the skin and lips when the attack is severe
- Restlessness

> What to Do

1. Reassure the child so that he or she does not become overly frightened.

2. To help the child breathe, place a cool-mist vaporizer in the child's room, or sit with the child in a closed, steam-filled bathroom. (To create steam, let hot water run from the shower or tub for several minutes with the bathroom door closed and a towel under the door.) Do not put the child in the water and only bring him or her into the room after the steam has been produced and the water has been turned off. Remain in the bathroom for 20 to 30 minutes. A small child can be held up high where the steam accumulates.

3. Call your health care provider to discuss what to do.

4. Call 911 (or your local emergency medical dispatch number) or take the child immediately to the nearest hospital emergency department if symptoms continue and one or more of the following happens:

   - Difficulty breathing
   - Croaking sound (stridor) while inhaling, even when the child is calm
   - Blue skin and lips
   - The child becomes agitated or appears exhausted and incapacitated

▪ BLOCKED WINDPIPE

If the child begins to drool, which may indicate a life-threatening condition called epiglottitis, seek medical attention promptly. Call 911 (or your local emergency number) or take the child immediately to the nearest hospital emergency department. *Keep the child in a sitting position.* (See Epiglottitis, p. 121.)

HYPERVENTILATION

Hyperventilation is breathing faster and more deeply than normal, usually due to stress or emotional upset. The person feels as if he or she is not getting enough air into the lungs. Feeling out of breath, he or she increases breathing in an attempt to take in more air. As rapid breathing continues, the level of carbon dioxide in the blood is lowered, causing muscle tightness in the throat and chest, which further aggravates the symptoms.

> Symptoms

Hyperventilation can cause any or all of the following symptoms:

- Light-headedness
- Numbness and tingling in the hands and feet and around the mouth and lips
- Feeling of tightness in the throat
- Muscle twitching
- Difficulty getting a deep, "satisfying" breath
- Convulsions

> What to Do

1. Encourage the person to relax and try to breathe deeply, slowly, and easily.

2. Briefly breathing in and out of a paper bag will increase the carbon dioxide level in the blood, and may help stop the symptoms.

3. If breathing does not return to normal, seek medical attention. Even after breathing returns to normal, it is a good idea to see a doctor to determine the underlying cause of hyperventilation.

See also: Seizures, p. 150.

INFLUENZA (THE "FLU")

Influenza, commonly known as the flu, is a viral infection that attacks the respiratory system, including your nose, throat, bronchial tubes, and lungs. The flu is usually seasonal and typically begins in

November and ends in March. Young children, older adults, people with weakened immune systems and those with chronic illnesses are especially vulnerable.

> Symptoms

- Fever over 101°F in adults (103°F to 105°F in children)
- Chills and sweats
- Muscle aches and pains
- Runny nose
- Cough
- Fatigue
- Loss of appetite

> What to Do

1. Treat the flu with bed rest and plenty of fluids.

2. Acetaminophen every 6 hours can be used to lessen the fever and muscle aches. In some cases, your doctor may prescribe an antiviral medication such as oseltamivir (Tamiflu) or zanamivir (Relenza) if symptoms have begun in the last day or two.

3. Seek immediate care if you or someone exhibits difficulty breathing or confusion or is unable to tolerate liquids.

> Preventing the Flu

It is important to consider getting an annual flu vaccination. While the Centers for Disease Control and Prevention (CDC) recommends that anyone who wants to reduce their risk of getting the flu should be vaccinated, the CDC strongly recommends that specific groups are vaccinated each year. These include persons who are at high risk of having serious flu complications or persons who live with or care for those at high risk for serious complications.

Persons who should be vaccinated each year are:

- Children aged 6 months up to their 19th birthday
- Pregnant women
- People 50 years of age and older

- People of any age with certain chronic medical conditions
- People who live in nursing homes and other long-term care facilities
- People who live with or care for those at high risk for complications from flu, including:
  > Healthcare workers
  > Household contacts of persons at high risk for complications from the flu
  > Household contacts and out-of-home caregivers of children less than 6 months of age (these children are too young to be vaccinated)

Although the vaccine doesn't offer 100 percent protection, it can reduce your chance of infection and help prevent serious complications if you do get sick. Hand washing and proper cough hygiene should also be considered (See Prevent Infections, p. 7).

PNEUMONIA

Pneumonia is an inflammation of the lungs that is typically caused by infection with bacteria, viruses, fungi, or other organisms. Older adults and people with chronic illnesses or impaired immune systems can be vulnerable to pneumonia. Pneumonia often follows a cold or the flu, but it can also be associated with other illnesses or occur on its own.

> Symptoms
- Chest pain
- Fever
- Chills
- Cough
- Shortness of breath

> What to Do

Seek medical attention. Serious pneumonia can be life threatening, particularly for older adults with underlying chronic disease.

> Preventing Pneumonia

Infections can be prevented by hand washing and cough etiquette (see Prevent Infections, p. 7). Talk to your doctor about getting a pneumonia vaccination.

SUDDEN INFANT DEATH SYNDROME (SIDS)

SIDS is the death of an apparently healthy infant under 1 year (usually 6 months or younger) for which no cause can be found. SIDS occurs most frequently during the winter months.

> What to Do

1. Call 911 (or your local emergency medical dispatch number).
2. Attempt to restore breathing and circulation. (See CPR, pp. 40–42.)

> Preventing SIDS

Here are some steps you can take to reduce your baby's risk of SIDS:

- Always put your infant to sleep on his or her back.
- Make sure the crib mattress is firm and flat.
- Never put your baby to sleep on a beanbag chair or waterbed.
- Do not place soft, fluffy toys, pillows, blankets, comforters, or sheepskins in the crib.
- Do not let your child get overheated while sleeping—remove any unnecessary coverings from the crib and don't swaddle or overdress him or her.
- Never use plastic sheets.
- Do not allow smoking in or near your child's sleeping area.

MUSCLE AND JOINT PROBLEMS

BRUISES

A bruise is the most common type of injury. It occurs when a fall or blow to the body causes small blood vessels to break beneath the skin. The discoloration and swelling in the skin are caused by the blood seeping into the tissues, which change colors as the bruise heals.

> Symptoms

Bruises can involve any or all of the following symptoms:

- Pain
- Area initially turns reddish blue
- Area later turns green
- Lump (hematoma) may form
- Area becomes yellow then brown before fading

> What to Do

1. As soon as possible, apply cold compresses or an ice bag to the affected area. Cold or ice decreases local bleeding and swelling.

2. If a bruise is on an arm or leg, elevate the limb above the level of the heart to decrease local blood flow.

3. After 24 hours, apply moist heat (a warm, wet compress) to aid healing. Heat dilates or opens blood vessels, increasing circulation to the affected area.

4. If the bruise is severe, or painful swelling develops, seek medical attention, because there is the possibility of a broken bone or other injury.

See Also: External Bleeding, p. 52; Bone Injuries, p. 79; Shoulder Dislocation, p. 75; Bumps, p. 81; Muscle Aches and Pains, p. 172; Sprains, p. 175.

CHILD ABUSE

If you think a child is the subject of abuse, call a local child protective service agency, welfare department, public health department, or the police. (See p. 190.) You should suspect abuse if a child has any of the following:

- Bruises in fleshy areas such as the face, back, abdomen, thighs, or buttocks
- Bruises in generally protected areas such as the neck, chest, or genitals
- Bruises with distinctive,

recognizable shapes of objects such as cords, clothes hangers, or belt buckles

- Multiple bruises in various stages of healing
- Bruises around the neck (from choking)

MUSCLE ACHES AND PAINS

Pain in the muscles is common and usually not serious. Muscle pain is often caused by tension, infection, fatigue (particularly in children), and over exercising. Gently massaging the area, taking a warm bath, applying warm, wet compresses, and resting are often helpful in relieving the pain. Stretching exercises (begun slowly) also may be helpful treating and preventing muscle pain (see Sports First Aid, p. 235). Any pain that is severe or prolonged needs medical attention.

> Symptoms

If you experience any of the following symptoms, stop exercising immediately and seek treatment:

- Sudden, severe pain
- Swelling
- Extreme tenderness
- Extreme weakness in a limb
- Inability to place weight on a leg or foot
- Inability to move a joint through its full range of motion
- Visible dislocation or broken bone

- Numbness or tingling—this could be a sign of nerve compression and should especially not be ignored

> What to Do

1. For any muscle pain, swelling, or inflammation, the R.I.C.E. method can help reduce damage and speed healing:

   Rest: Stop whatever you are doing that is causing the pain. For sprains and strains, take weight off the affected limb. For delayed soreness, rest the sore muscle group for a day.

   Ice: Cool the affected area to help reduce inflammation and risk of further damage. It is important not to expose skin directly to the ice. Wrap ice, or an ice pack, in a towel to apply it indirectly. Place the ice on the affected area for 10 to 20 minutes, four to eight times a day. Don't apply ice for more than 20 minutes or you risk skin damage. Don't apply heat immediately to an injury, either. This can increase swelling, bruising, or internal bleeding. Heat can be used once healing is progressing, days later, to help relax the muscle.

   Compress: Wrap the injured limb in a snug elastic bandage to help reduce swelling.

   Elevate: Raise the injured limb above the level of the heart to help reduce swelling.

2. After 24 hours, apply warm, moist compresses to the area.

3. You may take nonsteroidal anti-inflammatory medications to relieve pain.

4. Seek medical attention if the pain or swelling is severe.

■ MUSCLE CRAMPS

Muscle cramps can be particularly painful and often occur in the middle of the night, usually in the feet, calves, or thighs. Cramps usually result from fatigue or from keeping a limb in one position for a prolonged period. Massaging the area to relax the muscle is usually effective, because it stimulates local circulation, but do not massage the muscle if the problem could be heat cramps (see Heat-Related Problems, p. 330).

If the cramp is in the foot, turn the toes up toward your body. If the cramp is in the calf, stand up (with most of your weight on the unaffected leg) and massage the cramp. You may also stand up and place the foot of the affected leg flat on the floor and lean your body weight forward, stretching the affected calf. For a cramp in the thigh, lie down while massaging the area. Applying a heating pad or taking a warm bath can also be helpful.

Recurrent muscle cramps can also be an indication of dehydration and electrolyte abnormalities in your body. It is important for you to seek medical attention if your symptoms are recurrent. Your doctor may decide to examine you or review your medication list to determine a possible cause. Cramps in the legs and thighs often occur during pregnancy. The treatment is the same as described above for other muscle cramps. Also, be sure to get plenty of rest.

See also: Bites and Stings, p. 177; Bone Injuries, p. 79; Bruises, p. 171; Cold-Related Problems, p. 318; Shoulder Dislocations, p. 75; Digestive Problems, p. 96; Heat-Related Problems, p. 330; Muscle Strains, below; Sprains, p. 175; and Sports First Aid, pp. 235–290.

MUSCLE STRAINS

A strain results from pulling or overexerting a muscle. Back strains are common injuries. This mainly occurs from improper body mechanics during lifting, running, or exercise.

> Symptoms

Muscle strains can cause one or both of the following symptoms:

- A dull pain in the affected muscle that worsens with movement
- Swelling and tenderness of a particular muscle group

> What to Do

1. Rest the affected area immediately.

2. Apply ice or a cold compress to the area intermittently (20 minutes every hour while you are awake) for the first 24 hours after the injury to decrease swelling. Do not use heat or hot water soaks during the first 24 hours following the injury.

3. Wrap the injured limb in a snug elastic bandage to help reduce swelling.

4. After 24 hours, apply warm, moist compresses to the area.

5. If possible, elevate the strained area above the level of the heart.

6. You may take nonsteroidal anti-inflammatory medications to relieve pain.

7. Seek medical attention if the pain or swelling is severe.

See also: Muscle Aches and Pains, p. 172; Sports First Aid, pp. 235–290.

SPRAINS

A sprain is an injury to the ligaments—strong, flexible bands of fibrous tissue that bind bones together and support the joints. A ligament may be stretched or completely torn. A sprain usually results from overextending or twisting a limb beyond its normal range of movement.

> Symptoms

A sprain can cause any or all of the following symptoms:

- A popping sound or tearing sensation at the time of the injury
- Pain on moving the injured part and/or pain in the joint
- Swelling of the joint
- Tenderness on touching the affected area
- Black and blue discoloration of skin around the area of the injury

> What to Do

If you are uncertain about whether an injury is a sprain or a broken bone, treat it as a broken bone. (See Broken Bones, p. 79.)

If the ankle or knee is sprained:

1. Place cold packs or a small ice bag wrapped in a cloth over the affected area intermittently (20 minutes every hour while you are awake) for the first 24 hours after the injury to decrease swelling.

Do not use heat or hot water soaks during the first 24 hours following the injury.

2. Apply a supporting bandage, pillow, or blanket splint to the injury. (See Splinting and Other Procedures, p. 80.) Loosen the support if the swelling increases.

3. Keep the injured part elevated above the level of the heart and keep the person from walking, if possible.

4. After the first 24 hours, apply heat to the area or soak it in warm water periodically for several minutes at a time.

5. Seek medical attention for an evaluation of the injury and to rule out a broken bone.

If the wrist, elbow, or shoulder is sprained:

1. Place the injured arm in a sling. For a wrist injury, apply a supporting bandage. Loosen the bandage if swelling increases. (See Bandages, p. 26.)

2. Place cold packs or a small ice bag wrapped in a cloth over the affected area. Do not use heat or hot water soaks during the first 24 hours following the injury.

3. Seek medical attention for an evaluation of the injury and to rule out a broken bone.

See also: Bone Injuries, p. 79; Shoulder Dislocations, p. 82; Muscle Aches and Pains, p. 172; Sports First Aid, pp. 235–290.

SKIN PROBLEMS

BITES AND STINGS

Rashes may appear after insect stings, tick bites, brown recluse spider bites, and rat bites. Rashes that result from bites and stings should be seen by a doctor. Some may rapidly lead to breathing difficulties.

■ HUMAN BITES

Any human bite that breaks the skin needs immediate medical treatment. Human bites can lead to serious infections from bacteria or viruses that may contaminate the wound. A bite on the hand can cause loss of the use of the fingers and hand.

> What to Do

1. Immediately clean the wound thoroughly with soap and running water for 5 minutes or more to wash out contaminating organisms. Do not put medication, antiseptics, or home remedies on the wound.

2. Put a sterile bandage or clean, dry cloth over the wound. If it is bleeding, apply continuous pressure to the wound for 5 minutes or until the bleeding stops.

3. Seek medical attention promptly, particularly for a bite on the face, neck, or hands, which can develop into a serious infection. If some skin tissue, such as a part of an ear or a nose, is bitten off, bring it to the hospital emergency department or doctor's office with the person. (See Amputations, p. 60.)

See also: Animal and Insect Bites, p. 295; Insect and Marine Life Stings, p. 334.

BLISTERS

Blisters are usually caused by clothing (such as shoes) or equipment repeatedly rubbing against the skin. In general, the best way to handle blisters is to leave them alone. They usually heal on their own.

> What to Do

If the blister is small and unopened and will receive no further irritation:

Cover it with a sterile gauze pad and bandage in place. The fluid in the blister will eventually be absorbed by the skin and it will heal itself.

If the blister accidentally breaks, exposing raw skin:

Wash the area gently with soap and water and cover with a sterile bandage. The skin will regrow its outer layers.

If the blister is large and likely to be broken by routine activity:

Seek medical attention for treatment.

If medical attention is not readily available:

1. Gently clean the area with soap and water. Sterilize a needle by holding it over an open flame. Puncture the lower edge of the blister with the needle. Press the blister gently to force out fluid. Cover the area with a sterile bandage.

2. Always look for signs of infection such as redness, pus, or red streaks leading from the wound. Seek medical attention promptly if these symptoms appear.

See Also: External Bleeding, p. 52.

FINGERTIP INJURIES

Injuries to the fingertip resulting from a hammer hit or slammed door are extremely painful. Small blood vessels under the fingernail may break, causing a collection of blood to form. Within 1 to 2 days, the nail turns black. The area becomes very painful from the pressure of the blood clot.

It is recommended that a doctor drain the blood if the area of discoloration covers more than half of the fingernail. However, if medical assistance is not available for a few days and the pain is severe, drain the blood clot yourself by following these instructions.

> What to Do

1. Sterilize a paper clip (straightened out) by holding it over an open flame until it is red hot.

2. Gently puncture the collection of blood to allow it to drain by pushing the paper clip through the fingernail into the middle of the area of discoloration.

3. Cover the area with a sterile bandage. The fingernail should not be pulled off if it becomes loose. Keep the nail in place with a bandage to allow the new fingernail to push off the old one.

4. If the pain is not relieved immediately or it gets worse, see a physician right away.

FROSTBITE

See Cold-Related Injuries, p. 318.

HIVES

See Hives, p. 56.

RASHES

Skin rashes occur for many reasons, including allergic reactions, fever, heat, or infectious diseases. Some rashes may indicate a serious problem. Medical attention should always be sought if blue, purple, or blood-red spots appear (these may mean bleeding in and under the skin); the rash becomes worse; signs of infection such as pus or red streaks occur; itching is severe; or if other symptoms are present.

> Infections

Rashes are present with many infectious diseases. Infections that can cause rashes include chickenpox, measles, rubella, Lyme disease (p. 314), Rocky Mountain spotted fever (p. 316), scarlet fever, certain forms of meningitis, roseola infantum, and infectious mononucleosis.

> Plant Reactions

Contact with plants often produces a rash in sensitive persons. The most common offenders are poison ivy, poison oak, and poison sumac. (See Plant Irritations, p. 346.)

> Reaction to Medications

A skin reaction may appear with any medication, although these rashes are more likely to appear with the use of powerful drugs such as barbiturates, tranquilizers, and antibiotics. If a rash appears while the person is on a medication, call the doctor immediately to see if a rash is to be expected from the illness for which the medication was prescribed or if it is a reaction to the drug. Once it has been determined that you are allergic to a certain drug or substance, it is very important to write it down or remember it. Be sure to always inform health care providers that you are allergic to this substance to avoid accidental exposure in the future.

▪ RASHES IN INFANTS

Infants often have rashes. The most common is diaper rash, which is not dangerous but can cause a lot of discomfort. Diaper rash usually is a burn that occurs when bacteria react with urine on the skin and break down the urine into ammonia. Diaper rash may also be caused by fungi from an infant's stool. Thorough skin cleansing followed by complete drying will help. It is often helpful to be sure that the skin has completely dried before replacing the diaper. Very absorbent, dry diapers should be used and changed frequently. Various ointments are available, but it is best to ask a doctor for specific instructions.

A common rash in newborns appears during the early weeks of life. It may appear anywhere on the body and often moves from one place to another. The affected area should be kept clean and dry. It is always a good idea to report all infant rashes to a doctor.

Rashes on infants can also be caused by food allergies and by contact with substances such as clothes washed in strong detergents, rubber in pants, skin-care products, and soap left behind the ears. These rashes should also be reported to a doctor.

▪ HEAT RASH

Heat rash, or prickly heat, is a common rash caused by high body temperature due to fever or hot, humid weather. The sweat ducts are blocked and the area affected is covered with tiny red pinpoints. Both prevention and treatment consist of avoiding extreme heat.

Dusting powders and soothing lotions are also helpful. Light, dry, loose clothing should be worn in hot weather. Heat rash usually disappears in a cool environment. If heat rash persists, a doctor should be consulted.

SPLINTERS

A splinter, or sliver, is a small piece of wood, glass, or other material that becomes lodged under the surface of the skin.

> What to Do

1. Wash your hands and the person's skin around the splinter with soap and water.

2. Place a sewing needle and tweezers in boiling water for about 5 minutes or hold over an open flame to sterilize.

3. If the splinter is sticking out of the skin, gently pull the splinter out with the tweezers at the same angle at which it entered.

4. If the splinter is not deeply lodged beneath the skin and is clearly visible, gently loosen the skin around the splinter with the needle and carefully remove the splinter with the tweezers at the same angle at which it entered. Make sure you remove the entire splinter.

5. Squeeze the wound gently to allow slight bleeding to wash out any germs. Or rinse out the wound under running water for at least 5 minutes.

6. If the splinter breaks off in the skin, is easily broken, or is deeply lodged, seek medical attention for removal and a possible tetanus shot. You should also seek medical attention for any damage due to a fingernail.

7. After the splinter is removed, wash the area with soap and water and apply a bandage.

8. Watch for any signs of infection such as redness, pus, or red streaks leading up the body from the wound; see a doctor immediately if you notice any of these symptoms.

See Also: External Bleeding, p. 52.

STAPHYLOCOCCAL SKIN INFECTIONS

Recent attention has shifted to bacteria that are resistant to antibiotics. MRSA is methicillin-resistant strain of *Staphylococcus aureus*, a type of bacteria that is normally found on our skin. "Staph" skin infections, including MRSA, typically begin as small red bumps that resemble pimples, boils, or spider bites. These can quickly become painful abscesses that may require surgical draining. Sometimes the bacteria remain confined to the skin. But they can also penetrate into the body, causing potentially life-threatening infections in bones, joints, surgical wounds, the bloodstream, heart valves, and lungs.

Keep an eye on minor skin problems—pimples, insect bites, cuts, and scrapes—especially in children. If wounds become infected, see your doctor.

> Symptoms

Signs and symptoms of a wound infection:

- Redness, warmth, and tenderness of the wound
- Pus (a yellowish-white fluid that may have a foul smell)
- Fever

> What to Do

1. Wash your hands with soap and water before treating the wound.

2. Wash the injured area well with soap and water to remove any dirt. Gentle scrubbing may be necessary. It is important to remove all dirt to prevent infection. Bits of dirt left in the wound may also cause permanent discoloration of the skin. Rinse the wound under running water. Do not put medication on the wound unless a doctor recommends it.

3. Leave minor scrapes and scratches exposed to the air. Cover larger wounds, or those likely to be reinjured, with a sterile pad or clean cloth and tape it in place. Change the dressing and inspect the wound for signs of infection at least once a day.

4. You should also seek medical attention if the wound is large or deep or there is a question about the person having had a tetanus immunization within 5 years.

> Preventing Staph Skin Infections

Protecting yourself from staph infections can seem daunting, given how widespread and virulent the bacteria have become. But these commonsense precautions can help lower your risk:

1. Hand washing is your best defense against germs. If your hands aren't visibly dirty, you can use a hand sanitizer. These sanitizers are convenient and may actually kill more germs than soap and water do. (See Prevent Infections, p. 7.)

2. Keep cuts and abrasions clean and covered with sterile, dry bandages until they heal. The pus from infected sores often contains staph bacteria, and keeping wounds covered will help keep the bacteria from spreading.

3. Athletes in contact sports can be vulnerable to staph infections. Athletes should check with their physician about screening and school prevention protocols.

WOUNDS

Always seek medical attention if:

- The wound is deep or associated with loss of tissue.

- Bleeding does not stop.

- The injury was caused by an obviously dirty object.

- The wound was caused by an animal or human bite.

- A foreign material or object is embedded in the wound.

- You notice signs of infection such as fever, redness, swelling, increased tenderness at the site of the wound, pus, or red streaks leading from the wound toward the body.

- There is any doubt about the person having had a tetanus immunization within 5 years.

If medical assistance is not readily available and the wound shows signs of infection, keep the person lying down with the injured area immobilized and elevated. Apply warm wet cloths over the wound until medical assistance can be obtained.

▪ ABDOMINAL WOUNDS

Deep abdominal wounds are a medical emergency. Surgery is usually necessary to repair the wound.

> What to Do

1. Call 911 (or your local emergency medical dispatch number) or take the person to the nearest emergency department.

2. Maintain an open airway. Restore breathing and circulation, if necessary. (See CPR, pp. 33–49.)

3. Keep the person lying down on his or her back.

4. Bend the person's legs at the knees and place a pillow, rolled towel, blanket, or clothing under his or her knees to relax the abdominal muscles.

5. Apply direct pressure to the abdomen if necessary to control bleeding. (See Internal Bleeding, p. 112.) The abdomen is soft and applying pressure can decrease or stop internal bleeding.

6. Do not try to push the intestines back in place if they are sticking out of the wound. If medical assistance is not readily available and the intestine is sticking out of the wound, dampen a pad with sterile or boiled water that has cooled to body temperature (drinking water or clean seawater may be used in an emergency) and place the pad over the intestine.

7. Cover the entire wound with a sterile pad such as gauze (preferably) or a clean cloth, clothing, towel, plastic wrap, aluminum foil, or other suitable material.

8. Apply an adhesive bandage to hold the pad in place. Do not bandage too tightly.

9. Keep the person comfortably warm. Do not give the person anything to eat or drink, including water, because surgery will probably be necessary and the stomach should be empty.

▪ CHEST WOUNDS

A deep, open chest wound is a serious emergency. Damage to the lungs may occur, resulting in air flowing in and out of the wound with breathing and not in and out of the lungs where it is needed.

> What to Do

1. Call 911 (or your local emergency medical dispatch number).

2. Do not remove any object remaining in the wound, because very serious bleeding or other internal life-threatening problems may result.

3. Immediately cover the entire wound and about 2 inches all around it with a pad, such as dry sterile gauze (preferably), a clean cloth, clothing, plastic wrap, aluminum foil, or other suitable material. The pad must be at least 2 inches larger all around the wound and must be airtight.

4. If no pad is available, place a hand on each side of the wound and firmly push the skin together to close the wound. Apply an airtight bandage with tape or other suitable material, if available.

5. If air is bubbling from the chest wound, then place an occlusive dressing over the wound and tape on three sides only. This allows for venting of air from the chest cavity and prevents life-threatening pressure changes within the chest.

6. Maintain an open airway. Restore breathing and circulation if necessary. (See CPR, pp. 33–49.) It may be necessary to slightly raise the person's shoulders to aid breathing.

7. Do not give the person anything to eat or drink because this may cause choking. Also, the stomach should be empty in case surgery is necessary.

8. Reassure the person. Gentleness, kindness, and understanding play an important role in treating a person who may be in shock.

▪ CUTS

> What to Do

If bleeding is severe:

Use direct pressure to control bleeding. (See Bleeding, p. 52.)

If bleeding is not severe:

1. Wash your hands thoroughly with soap and water before handling the wound to prevent further contamination of the injury.

2. If the cut is still bleeding, apply direct pressure over the wound with a sterile or clean cloth.

3. When the bleeding has stopped, wash the wound thoroughly with soap and water to remove any dirt or other foreign material near the skin's surface. Gentle scrubbing may be necessary. It is very important to remove all dirt to prevent infection. Foreign particles close to the skin's surface may be carefully removed with tweezers that have been sterilized over an open flame or boiled in water. Do not attempt to remove any foreign material that is deeply embedded in a muscle or other tissue, because serious bleeding may result.

4. Rinse the wound thoroughly under running water for 5 to 10 minutes.

5. Pat the wound dry with a sterile or clean cloth. Do not apply ointments, medication, antiseptic spray, or home remedies unless told to do so by a doctor.

6. Cover the wound with a sterile dressing and tape it in place. If the cut is slightly gaping, apply a butterfly bandage (see p. 27) or tape the edges of the wound together as close as possible.

■ CUTS IN THE SCALP

Cuts in the scalp may bleed heavily even if the wound is minor. With any cut or puncture, you should consult a physician about the necessity for a tetanus shot.

> What to Do

If the cut is severe or there is the possibility of a skull fracture:

1. Do not clean the wound or remove any foreign bodies from the scalp.

2. Gently apply a sterile compress and bandage it in place. If bleeding persists, apply pressure firmly to the wound until the bleeding stops.

3. Seek medical attention promptly.

If the cut is minor:

1. Control the bleeding by applying a sterile compress to the wound and pressing firmly.

2. When bleeding stops, clean the wound with soap and water or hydrogen peroxide.

3. Apply a bandage.

■ OPEN WOUNDS

An open wound is an injury in which the skin is broken through its entire thickness. The objectives in treating an open wound consist of:

- Stopping the bleeding

- Preventing contamination and infection

- Preventing shock

- Seek medical attention if the wound is severe or if the person has not had a tetanus shot within 5 years.

■ PUNCTURE WOUNDS

A puncture wound results when a sharp object—such as a nail, a large splinter, a knife, a needle, a bullet, a firecracker, or an ice pick—pierces the skin and underlying tissue. The wound is usually deep and narrow, with little bleeding, which increases the chance for infection because the germs are imbedded deeply and not washed out by the flow of blood.

Tetanus is a danger with any wound, but is greater with puncture wounds because the tetanus bacteria grow well in a deep wound where there is little oxygen. All puncture injuries should be seen by a doctor.

> What to Do

1. Wash your hands with soap and water before examining the wound.

2. Do not poke or put medication into the wound. Look to see if any part of the object that caused the injury has broken off and

become lodged in the wound. Do not attempt to remove any foreign object that is deeply embedded in the wound because the foreign object may break off in the wound and serious bleeding may result.

3. In obviously minor puncture wounds, objects sticking in no deeper than the skin's surface may be carefully removed with tweezers that have been sterilized over an open flame or boiled in water.

4. Encourage bleeding to wash out germs from inside the wound by gently pressing on the edge of the wound. Do not press so hard that you cause additional injury.

5. If the puncture wound is obviously minor, wash the wound with soap and water and rinse it under running water.

6. Cover the wound with a sterile or clean dressing and bandage it in place.

7. Seek medical attention promptly.

8. If medical attention is not readily available and the wound shows signs of infection—such as fever, redness, swelling, increased tenderness at the site of the wound, pus, or red streaks leading from the wound toward the body—keep the person lying down with the injured area immobilized and elevated. Apply warm wet cloths to the wound until medical assistance can be obtained.

SCRAPES AND SCRATCHES

Scrapes can easily become infected because the outer, protective skin layer is damaged.

> What to Do

1. Wash your hands with soap and water before treating the wound.

2. Wash the injured area well with soap and water to remove any dirt. Gentle scrubbing may be necessary. It is important to remove all dirt to prevent infection. Bits of dirt left in the wound may also cause permanent discoloration of the skin. Rinse the wound under running water. Do not put medication on the wound unless a doctor recommends it.

3. Leave minor scrapes and scratches exposed to the air. Cover larger wounds, or those likely to be reinjured, with a sterile pad or clean cloth and tape it in place.

4. If you notice any signs of infection—such as redness, swelling, increased tenderness at the site of the wound, pus, or red streaks leading from the wound toward the body—keep the person lying down with the injured area immobilized and elevated. Apply warm wet cloths to the wound and seek medical assistance immediately.

5. You should also seek medical attention if the wound is large or deep or there is a question about the person having had a tetanus immunization within 5 years.

OTHER POTENTIAL MEDICAL EMERGENCIES

ABUSE, ASSAULT, AND NEGLECT

Reported cases of child abuse, and abuse of other individuals, such as spouses and the elderly, have risen dramatically. Abuse can take many forms—emotional, physical, or sexual—or can involve neglect. In most instances, the abuser is a parent or other family member, a neighbor, or some other adult. People who abuse often were abused themselves as children.

Making an assessment that abuse has occurred or is occurring can be difficult. Always call the police if you suspect with good reason that a child or other person is being abused or is in danger of losing his or her life. If you are abusing a child or other person, help is available to you. Call a child abuse hotline or other community agency that offers counseling.

> Symptoms

Some symptoms and signs of abuse are more obvious than others. If a person has been **physically abused**, he or she may exhibit any or all of the following:

- Frequent complaints of pain
- Frequent broken bones
- Unexplained cuts, bruises, or burn marks
- Bleeding
- Multiple injuries on different parts of the body that are healing in different stages
- Withdrawal, depression, or inattentiveness
- Excessive aggression

If a child has been **sexually abused**, he or she may exhibit any or all of the following:

- Complaints of pain when urinating
- Unusual fear of adults
- Injury to genital or rectal area
- Difficulty walking or sitting
- Withdrawal, depression, or inattentiveness
- Excessive masturbation
- Promiscuous or sexually precocious behavior

If a person (usually a child or elderly person) has been **neglected**, he or she may exhibit any or all of the following:

- An unkempt appearance; poor hygiene
- Lack of appropriate medical care for a chronic illness or injury; lack of required immunizations
- Malnourishment
- Lack of appropriate supervision

> What to Do

For a victim of physical or sexual abuse:

1. Treat noticeable injuries, such as cuts, bruises, or burns.
2. Do not allow the person to take a shower, bathe, brush his or her teeth, or eat or drink anything until he or she has been examined professionally; this preserves any evidence of abuse.
3. Comfort the person as much as possible.
4. Do not leave the person alone.
5. Call 911 (or your local emergency medical dispatch number) or take the person to a hospital emergency department or doctor's office immediately.

For a victim of negligence:

1. Do not directly confront the person you suspect of negligence.
2. Contact a local service agency such as a child protective services agency, a senior agency or aging department, welfare department, public health authorities, or the police. Professionals in these organizations are trained to help people who are the victims of negligence and their families; they will keep your information confidential and anonymous. If your claim later

turns out to be unwarranted, you cannot legally be held responsible for providing the information in good faith.

When you seek medical treatment for a victim of sexual or physical abuse, he or she will probably be given a private room or a secluded area at the physician's office or hospital emergency department. A social worker, police officer, and medical personnel may all be present to help. You or the person may be asked to describe several times what happened and to give a description of the abuser.

A physician will recommend that the person have a complete physical examination. The exam is performed to protect the person from disease and to support possible criminal charges of rape or other physical abuse. The exam will include taking samples from the mouth, vagina, and rectum and testing for sexually transmitted infections (such as HIV, chlamydia, gonorrhea, or syphilis) and for a pre-existing pregnancy. The tests will determine the person's health status at the time the incident occurred.

The person will be advised to seek follow-up medical treatment, depending upon the injuries and test results. Medical personnel may advise the person to seek counseling for assistance in handling the emotional aspects of physical abuse or rape. Doctors also recommend that the siblings of an abused child be examined within 24 hours.

▪ RAPE/SEXUAL ASSAULT

Sexual assault is forced or manipulated sexual contact without consent or agreement. Sexual assault includes forced vaginal or anal intercourse, oral sex, or penetration with an object. These activities are usually referred to as rape. Sexual assault also includes involuntary sexual contact such as forced touching or fondling.

Rape is a crime in every state. Some state laws have been expanded to include rape in marriage and between individuals of the same sex. The motives of the rapist are dominance and control.

If you are alone and you have been raped, or if another person has been raped, call the police immediately to report the crime. Next, call a relative, friend, or rape hotline (or other community agency with rape counseling available). Then call your doctor or the hospital emer-

> **IF A RAPE HAS OCCURRED, DO NOT ALLOW THE PERSON TO:**

- Change clothes
- Take a shower
- Brush his or her teeth
- Eat or drink
- Urinate

> **YOU SHOULD:**

- Call the police.
- Call a relative or friend to assist you.
- Call a doctor, a hospital emergency department, or an abuse hotline for instructions on how to proceed.

gency department to let them know that a rape has occurred and that you or another individual will be seeking medical treatment.

> Symptoms

Injuries from a sexual assault vary according to the manner of attack and may involve any or all of the following symptoms:

- Blood on underwear
- Bleeding from the vagina or anus
- Cuts, burns, bruises (especially on inner thighs or in genital area)
- Fearfulness, anxiety, depression, shame, embarrassment

> What to Do

- Treat noticeable injuries, such as cuts, bruises, or burns.
- Do not allow the person to take a shower, bathe, brush his or her teeth, or eat or drink anything.
- Comfort the person and provide emotional support; be nonjudgmental.

- Believe the person.
- Do not leave the person alone.
- Take the person to a hospital emergency department or doctor's office immediately for further treatment.

The rape victim will probably be given a private room or taken to a private area at the physician's office or hospital emergency department. A social worker, police officer, and medical personnel may all be present to help. The person may be asked several times to describe what happened and to give a description of the assailant. It is very important for the person to attempt to describe the circumstances involved and medical symptoms experienced before and after the sexual assault occurred.

A physician will recommend that the person have a complete physical examination. The exam is performed with the person's consent to protect him or her from disease and to collect physical evidence of the assault. The exam will include taking samples from the mouth, vagina, and rectum, and testing for sexually transmitted infections such as chlamydia, gonorrhea, syphilis, and HIV. A test may also be done for a pre-existing pregnancy. Pictures may be taken as evidence of sexual assault. The tests will determine the person's health status at the time the crime occurred. The person may be given antibiotics or offered the "morning after pill" to prevent any sexually transmitted disease or unplanned pregnancy. All evidence collected during the exam should be sealed and given directly to the police by the examiner.

The person will be asked to seek follow-up medical treatment, depending on the injuries and test results. He or she should also seek counseling for assistance in handling the emotional aspects of the assault.

> How to Prevent Rape From Occurring

- Teach your children about areas to stay away from and not to interact with strangers.
- Avoid carrying large purses or bags. High heels also make it very difficult to be balanced and maintain agility when in dangerous situations.
- Stay away from dark and deserted areas when alone.
- Always stay with a group of people when possible.
- Be alert to any strangers around you.

- Carry self-defense spray.
- Take self-defense classes.
- Be careful with whom you leave a social establishment. Do not leave your group of people.

▪ DATE RAPE DRUGS

Date rape drugs are powerful tranquilizers that alter consciousness and can induce the sleepiness of a deep coma within 30 minutes. They get their name from the most common situation in which they are used: A prospective sexual assailant, usually a man, targets a potential rape victim, usually a woman, and secretly places a pill or a small amount of a colorless, odorless, tasteless liquid into the woman's alcoholic beverage at a party or bar. The drugs that are used most frequently for this purpose include flunitrazepam (known on the street as the forget-me pill, roofies, R-2, or roach) and gamma hydroxyl butyrate (known on the street as GHB, scoop, liquid G, or grievous bodily harm). Alcohol intensifies the action of these drugs.

> Symptoms

A person who has been given a date rape drug will have any or all of the following symptoms, which can last up to 8 hours:

- Drowsiness within half an hour of drinking a beverage or ingesting a pill containing the tranquilizer
- Complete or partial amnesia; the person may later recall only snapshot-like images of the sexual assault.
- Lack of coordination
- Slow breathing
- Unexplained bruises
- Confused behavior and impaired judgment

> What to Do

1. Call 911 (or your local emergency medical dispatch number) or take the person to the nearest hospital emergency department. Doctors can perform examinations and tests that can help determine what happened; these procedures are most reliable when they are performed soon after an assault.

2. Treat any injuries.

3. Tell the person not to bathe or shower, eat or drink, change clothes, or brush his or her teeth.

4. Give the person emotional support.

> Avoiding Date Rape Drugs

Here are some steps you can take to avoid being the victim of a drug-induced date rape:

• Closely watch the preparation of your drinks.

• Do not set your glass down or look away from it; keep your hand over the top of your drink if you have to look away or are distracted for a moment.

• Do not drink any liquid that has a white film on the surface or on the glass (this can indicate a partially dissolved drug).

• Be careful when getting drinks from punch bowls or large containers of alcoholic beverages when you are at a party at which you don't know or trust the host or other guests (large containers of beverages are easy to contaminate intentionally).

CHILLS

Chills may be a symptom of many medical problems, including flu, kidney and bladder infections, bacterial pneumonia, food poisoning, and spider bites. Chills are also associated with exposure to cold.

Chills are nature's way of raising the body temperature. Chills occur when there is decreased blood circulation to the body surface due to narrowing of the blood vessels in the skin. Muscles in the body contract. Shivering and shaking associated with chills produce heat in the body, thus allowing the body temperature to rise. Often, chills are followed by fever and indicate the onset of an infection.

■ CHILLS BROUGHT ON BY MEDICATION

Call 911 (or your local emergency medical dispatch number) or take the person to the nearest emergency department if the chills and tremors are associated with taking tranquilizers or antidepressants. This situation can indicate a life-threatening imbalance of chemicals in the brain and nervous system.

> What to Do

1. Make the person comfortably warm, but do not use hot water bottles or heating pads.

2. Offer warm drinks and liquids such as tea or soup if the person is not nauseated or vomiting.

3. Seek medical attention; a serious infection may be present.

See also: Insect Bites (Spider and Tick Bites), pp. 177, 308–317, 334–337; Cold-Related Problems, p. 318; Fever, p. 208; Digestive Problems, p. 96; Heat-Related Problems, p. 330.

DIZZINESS AND VERTIGO

Dizziness can be caused by a number of medical problems including low blood sugar, inner ear infection, pregnancy, medications, and dehydration, as well as serious life threatening emergencies such as a cardiac arrhythmia (fast heart rate, slow heart rate) and brain attack (stroke). The good news is that dizziness rarely signals a serious, life-threatening condition.

Vertigo is a feeling of dizziness commonly described as "the walls are spinning." The cause of vertigo is usually viral but can be from a disturbance of the inner ear. Symptoms typically last for 24 to 48 hours and usually go away without treatment. However, vertigo can also be a symptom of a brain attack (stroke) or cardiovascular problem. It is important to notify your physician if you experience these symptoms.

> Symptoms

Dizziness is a term used to describe a number of symptoms. Common symptoms include feeling lightheaded, faint, weak, unsteady, or vertigo (the walls are spinning). Dizziness may also include nausea, unsteadiness, wooziness, fatigue, difficulty concentrating, and blurred vision during quick head movements.

> What to Do

1. Sit or lie down immediately when you feel dizzy. The symptoms should resolve or improve quickly.

2. If a person complains of vertigo, reassure the person that he or she is not turning or spinning around. Assist the person so that he or she does not fall.

3. Call a physician if the symptoms persist or whenever you experience any unexplained, prolonged, or recurrent dizziness.

4. Seek medical attention immediately if you have any cardiovascular history or experience any of the following:

    > Chest pain or rapid or slow heart rate

    > Leg or arm weakness or numbness

    > Speech impairment

    > Loss of consciousness

    > Falling or difficulty walking

    > Head injury

    > A new, different or severe headache

    > A fever higher than 101° F (38.3° C)

    > A very stiff neck

    > Blurred vision or loss of vision

    > Hearing loss

    > Numbness or tingling

(See Stroke, Transient Ischemic Attack (TIA), pp. 153–154).

DRUG AND ALCOHOL PROBLEMS

Drug abuse is the regular or excessive use of a drug outside the usual standards of medical practice or medical need. Drug abuse often results in physical and psychological dependence on the drug. If you are using drugs, this section will provide you with information about drug overdose and withdrawal and first aid measures for yourself or for another person. See a physician for a confidential discussion about your drug use and information about treatment.

Questions to ask yourself if you suspect that someone you know is using drugs: How is the individual acting differently than normal? Is he or she moody, overly quiet, or easily agitated? Are there physical manifestations that might suggest drug use, such as a sudden loss of weight or an inattention to personal hygiene? Has the individual's group of friends changed within the past 6 months? Do you know who they are? Has the person stopped seeing his or her old friends? Does he or she spend more time alone?

Mild changes in behavior, especially in teenagers, do not necessarily mean that an individual is taking drugs. If you suspect drug use, however, other clues may be helpful in identifying the problem. For example, use of any drug either depresses the central nervous system or stimulates it. Depending on the type of drug and the amount taken, a person's behavior under the influence of that drug may range from extreme sluggishness to hyperactivity. With drugs that are injected into the body, you may notice needle marks on the person's arms or legs (or elsewhere). In cases of drug withdrawal, you may notice frequent blinking or jerky eye movements, along with the symptoms listed on the following pages.

Paraphernalia that may signal drug use include needles and syringes, eyedroppers, teaspoons, pills, capsules, vials, pipes, or glass bulbs ("bongs").

Information to help you recognize the symptoms of drug or alcohol abuse, or withdrawal from dependence on some drugs, is given in the following pages, under categories of drugs. Here are some general guidelines for dealing with drug-related emergencies:

- Professional medical treatment for a person who is suffering withdrawal from drugs or who has overdosed on drugs will vary according to the type of drug and the amount taken.

- For the first-aid provider faced with an emergency situation in which drug use is suspected, first assess whether it is safe for you to handle the situation on your own. If it is not, call out for help.

- If the person is unconscious, ensure that he or she is breathing. Restore breathing and circulation if necessary. (See CPR, pp. 33–49.)

- If the person is conscious and you are the first person providing first aid, ask the person what drug he or she took, the amount, and when it was taken. (Report all information, including first-aid treatment, to the doctor later.)

For help in dealing with health effects from drug and other chemical exposures, contact a Regional Poison Control Center at 800-222-1222.

▪ ALCOHOL

Ethanol is the active or "toxic" ingredient in alcoholic beverages that causes intoxication. Alcohol can appear to act as a stimulant but, in fact, is a depressant. It slows down or depresses the activities of the central nervous system (the brain and spinal cord), which controls psychomotor skills such as reaction time and coordination, and areas of the brain that control speech, hearing, and eye movement. Alcohol also impairs reasoning by relaxing an individual's social inhibitions and self-control. Ingesting alcoholic beverages can give a false sense of euphoria.

▪ ALCOHOL OVERDOSE

> Symptoms

Excessive consumption of alcohol can cause any or all of the following symptoms:

- Lack of coordination
- Slurred speech
- Abnormal breathing
- Unconsciousness
- Vomiting
- Coma
- Red streaks in the whites of the eyes
- Odor of alcohol on the breath
- Fast heart rate

> What to Do

1. If the person appears to be sleeping, with normal breathing and pulse, and he or she can be roused with a shout or a shake, no immediate treatment is required. Place the person so that he or she will not hurt himself or herself. Check on the person at regular intervals.

2. If the person has abnormal breathing, is unconscious (cannot be roused), or is in a coma, maintain an open airway. Restore breathing and circulation, if necessary. (See CPR, pp. 33–49.) Seek medical attention promptly.

■ ALCOHOL WITHDRAWAL

> Symptoms

Withdrawal from alcohol dependence can cause any or all of the following symptoms:

- Trembling of hands and head
- Nausea
- Vomiting
- Fear of sounds, ordinary objects, or lights
- Hallucinations (seeing objects that are not present)
- Unusual behavior
- Fast heart rate
- Seizures

> What to Do

1. Seek medical attention promptly.
2. If the person is vomiting, see that he or she does not choke on vomit.
3. Calm and reassure the person.

■ DEPRESSANTS

Depressants are drugs that slow down or depress the activities of the central nervous system (the brain and spinal cord), which controls psychomotor skills such as reaction time and coordination, and areas of the brain that control speech, hearing, eye movement, and perception.

Depressants include all alcoholic beverages, narcotics, sedatives, cannabis drugs, and all depressant tranquilizers. Examples are opium, morphine, heroin, fentanyl (synthetic heroin), codeine, phenobarbital, sleeping pills, marijuana, and hashish. Some of these substances are referred to on the street as weed, downers, goofballs, yellow jackets, red devils, and rainbows.

▪ DEPRESSANT OVERDOSE

> Symptoms

An overdose of a depressant drug can cause any or all of the following symptoms:

- Intoxicated behavior
- Slurred speech
- Deep sleep, possibly leading to coma
- Shallow breathing
- Slow pulse
- Low body temperature
- Heavy sweating
- Very relaxed muscles
- Very small pupils

> What to Do

1. Call 911 (or your local emergency medical dispatch number). Maintain an open airway. Restore breathing and circulation if necessary. (See CPR, pp. 33–49.)

2. Keep the person awake. Use a cold, wet towel or cloth to slap the person's face gently.

3. Keep the person talking, if possible.

4. Calm and reassure the person.

▪ DEPRESSANT WITHDRAWAL

> Symptoms

Withdrawal from dependence on depressant drugs can cause any or all of the following symptoms, which may not occur at the same time:

- Nervousness or restlessness
- Trembling
- Muscle twitching
- Abdominal cramping
- Hot and cold flashes
- Sweating
- Weight loss
- Enlarged pupils
- Tears
- Runny nose
- Yawning
- Muscle aches
- Vomiting
- Loss of appetite
- Rise in body temperature
- Craving for the drug

> What to Do

1. Seek medical attention.
2. Calm and reassure the person.

■ HALLUCINOGENS

Hallucinogenic drugs, sometimes called psychedelic drugs, change the chemical makeup of the brain and distort perception. The most well-known hallucinogens include lysergic acid diethylamide (LSD or acid), phencyclidine (PCP or angel dust), mescaline and peyote, and psilocybin (magic mushrooms). The effects of hallucinogens can last up to 12 hours. Some stimulants and tetrahydrocannabinol (THC, the active ingredient in marijuana and hashish) can also be hallucinogenic.

▪ HALLUCINOGEN USE

> Symptoms

Even one dose of a hallucinogen can cause any or all of the following symptoms:

- Delusions (misinterpretation of sounds, movements, or objects)
- Hallucinations (seeing things that are not present)
- Fast heartbeat
- Increased blood pressure
- Enlarged pupils
- Reddish face
- Lack of emotional control (periods of laughing and crying or behavior not appropriate for the situation)
- Depression (appearing sad or slow to move or talk)
- Panic, fear, or tension
- Varying levels of consciousness
- Disorientation or poor recent memory

> What to Do

1. Ensure that the person does not harm himself or herself or others.

2. Seek medical attention promptly.

3. Reassure the person and try to talk him or her through the experience in a quiet place.

4. Do not move suddenly in front of the person. Keep your voice calm and do not turn away from the person. The person could try to harm you.

▪ INHALANTS

Increasing numbers of children are inhaling common household products to get high. When used in this way, these substances are called inhalants. Inhalants include glues and adhesives, nail polish remover, marking pens, paint thinner, spray paint, butane lighter fluid, gasoline, propane gas, correction fluid, household cleaners, cooking sprays, deodorants, fabric protectors, whipping cream aerosols, and air-conditioning coolants. These products are usually snorted from a plastic bag or breathed in ("huffed") from a chemical-soaked rag. Using an inhalant even once can damage the brain and nervous system or cause sudden death. While a person is using an inhalant or immediately after, his or her heart may begin to overwork, beating rapidly but unevenly and causing cardiac arrest.

▪ INHALANT USE

> Symptoms

Use of inhalants can cause any or all of the following symptoms:

- Intoxicated behavior, loss of coordination, or slurred or disoriented speech
- State of excitement quickly followed by extreme drowsiness
- Hallucinations
- Severe mood swings
- Numbness and tingling of the hands and feet
- Heart palpitations
- Difficulty breathing
- Dizziness
- Red or runny eyes or nose
- Headache
- Death

> What to Do

1. Seek medical attention and intervention immediately.

2. If the person is not breathing, call 911 (or your local emergency medical dispatch number). Maintain an open airway. Restore breathing and circulation if necessary. (See CPR, pp. 33–49.)

▪ STIMULANTS

Stimulants increase the activities of the central nervous system (brain and spinal cord), which controls psychomotor skills such as reaction time and coordination, and areas of the brain that control speech, hearing, eye movement, and perception.

Stimulants include amphetamines, cocaine, and inhalants. Some of these substances are referred to on the street as crack, ice (crystal meth), speed, crank, uppers, pep pills, bennies, whites, and dexies.

▪ STIMULANT OVERDOSE

> Symptoms

An overdose of a stimulant can cause any or all of the following symptoms:

- Overly active behavior
- Aggressive behavior
- Mental confusion
- Disorganization
- Suspiciousness
- Unconsciousness
- Repetition of a particular act
- Irritability
- Fear
- Exaggerated perceptions of personal abilities
- Sweating
- Fast heart rate
- Seizures

> What to Do

1. Approach the person carefully.
2. Maintain an open airway. Restore breathing and circulation if necessary. (See CPR, pp. 33–49.)

3. Seek immediate medical attention.

4. Keep the person from harming himself or herself or others.

▪ STIMULANT WITHDRAWAL

> Symptoms

Withdrawal from dependence on stimulants can cause any or all of the following symptoms:

- Extreme lack of energy
- Depression
- Extreme hunger
- Hallucinations
- Deep sleep
- Dehydration

> What to Do

1. Seek medical attention.

2. Calm and reassure the person.

FALLS IN THE ELDERLY

Falls are a leading cause of injury and injury-related death among those older than 65. The risk of falling is greater due to age-related physical changes and medical conditions, as well as from medications prescribed to treat these conditions.

In older adults, a hip fracture is most often a result of a traumatic event, such as falling. Hip fractures are a common fracture in people older than 65. As you age, bones become less dense and lose minerals, which increases the risk of fracture. Women are more likely than men to experience a hip fracture because women lose bone density at a greater rate as they age. A hip fracture is a serious injury, and complications can be life threatening.

Seek immediate care for any elderly person who has fallen. It is important to determine the underlying cause of the fall and rule out any acute medical cause and/or traumatic injuries. Because this is a traumatic event, it is important to adhere to trauma principles and protect the head, neck, back, and pelvis (hip).

> What to Do

1. Call 911 (or your local emergency medical dispatch number) or transport the person immediately to the nearest hospital emergency department. An injury to the pelvis can cause severe internal bleeding and always requires evaluation by a doctor.

2. Keep the person lying down on his or her back.

3. Legs may be straight or bent at the knees, whichever is more comfortable for the person.

4. Tie the person's legs together at the ankles and knees whether the legs are straight or bent.

5. If the person must be taken to the hospital by someone other than trained medical personnel, place the person on a well-padded rigid support such as a board, door, or table leaf. (See Head, Neck, and Back Problems, p. 138.)

> Preventing Falls

Many falls and fall-related injuries are preventable. Individuals older than 65 should be screened by their doctor to determine the need for ambulatory assistance devices (canes, walkers) and for home-assist devices such as railings in the shower. Safeguarding your home by ensuring adequate lighting in hallways and avoiding common household dangers (for example, keeping toys and other clutter from hallways and stairs) is also important (see Safeguarding Your Home, p. 8). Exercise also is recommended to increase muscle tone and flexibility.

See Also: Head, Neck, and Back Problems, p. 138; Bone Injuries, p. 79; Ankle, Leg, and Hip Problems, p. 62; Arm, Hand, and Shoulder Problems, p. 70.

FEVER

Fever is a common sign of possible health problems. Knowing how to take a temperature can help you evaluate a potential problem and provide important information to doctors. A fever is the body's way of indicating that something is wrong—most commonly that an infection is present. A fever is the body's defensive mechanism to combat infection. You should always call a doctor if a fever suddenly changes from slight (99°F to 100°F) to high (104°F) and persists. If the person with a fever is an infant and a doctor cannot be reached, take the child to the nearest hospital emergency department. The same steps should be taken if a fever is present for no obvious reason and it persists. In this case, it is best not to take any medication to reduce the fever, because this may give the person a false sense of well-being and discourage him or her from consulting a doctor.

▪ FEVER IN ADULTS

The average normal temperature taken by mouth is 98.6° Fahrenheit, plus or minus 1°. A Celsius thermometer, common in Canada and Europe, may be used instead of a Fahrenheit thermometer. An average normal temperature on a Celsius thermometer is 37°, plus or minus 1°.

A rectal temperature is 1° higher than a normal oral temperature. Individual normal temperatures may run slightly above or below the average. Individual temperatures may also vary throughout the day, running lower in the morning and higher in the evening. Slight changes in temperature (other than normal variations during the day) are usually not significant. Fever in adults is a temperature greater than 100.9°F (38.3°C) and often indicates that an infection is present. A major increase in temperature (to approximately 104°F or greater) may indicate a serious condition. Temperatures well below normal also may be significant.

> What to Do

Take acetaminophen, aspirin, or a nonsteroidal anti-inflammatory medication (such as ibuprofen or naproxen) to help reduce the fever. Follow the package recommendations or a doctor's instructions to determine the dose to take. Remove excess clothing and move the person to a cooler environment.

■ FEVER IN INFANTS AND CHILDREN

A normal temperature taken rectally in infants and small children is usually below 100.3°F rectal. Rectal temperature readings run about 1° degree higher than oral temperature readings. Although temperature is the same throughout the body, taking an oral temperature lets air into the mouth, lowering the temperature reading somewhat. Children can run high fevers without being seriously ill. It is always best, however, to report any fever over 101°F to the doctor, particularly if the child does not feel, look, or act well. Report to the doctor any other symptoms the child might have. Infants less than 3 months with a rectal fever of 100.3°F or higher should be taken immediately to the nearest pediatric-capable emergency department.

> ### WARNING: DON'T GIVE ASPIRIN TO CHILDREN
>
> Never give aspirin to a child or teen under 19 during episodes of fever-causing illnesses. The use of aspirin in children has been linked to a life-threatening disorder called Reye's syndrome.

> What to Do

1. Always check with the doctor before giving medication to an infant or small child, particularly one under 1 year of age.
2. Give the child plenty of fluids.

■ TAKING A TEMPERATURE

Several different types of thermometers are available. Digital thermometers are easy to use and record a temperature quickly (in less than 30 seconds) and accurately. Glass thermometers are the least expensive, but they take 3 to 4 minutes to record a temperature and can be difficult to read. Do not use mercury-containing thermometers because if they break, this chemical can be toxic. Tympanic (ear) thermometers, which measure the amount of infrared radiation in the eardrum, are not as accurate in infants under age 1, so doctors don't recommend them for children this age. Ear thermometers are, however, accurate and convenient for older children and adults.

Most temperatures are taken by mouth with an oral (Fahrenheit or Celsius) thermometer. People with mouth injuries should have their temperature taken with an ear thermometer, and children under 3 years should have their temperature taken rectally with a rectal thermometer.

An infant's temperature, taken rectally (with a rectal Fahrenheit or Celsius thermometer), usually registers 1 degree higher than a normal oral temperature. A temperature taken by mouth registers lower than a temperature taken rectally because air entering the mouth cools the mouth slightly, lowering the temperature reading.

> How to Read a Thermometer

Digital thermometers and ear thermometers are easy to read because they display the temperature reading on a small screen. To read a glass thermometer, hold the end without the bulb between the thumb and the first finger. Use good light. Look through the pointed edge toward the flat side until you see a thin silver or red line coming out of the bulb. Rotate the thermometer slightly if the silver line is not visible. The temperature reading is at the end of the silver line. The long lines mark the degrees of temperature and the short lines indicate two-tenths of a degree. An arrow points to the normal reading of 98.6°F (37°C). Readings higher than this indicate a fever, except in a rectal temperature, which is normally 1 degree higher.

Before taking a temperature with a glass thermometer, you need to shake the thermometer until the silver or red line reads below the 98.6°F (37°C) mark to approximately 95°F (35°C). Hold the thermometer as described above and shake it sharply downward with a snapping wrist movement. Read the thermometer to make sure the mercury is shaken down.

> How to Take an Oral Temperature

If you are using an oral thermometer, insert the bulb under the tongue. Keep the thermometer in place for 2 to 3 minutes if you are using a glass thermometer or 30 seconds or until you hear the beep for a digital thermometer. Warn the person not to talk or bite on the thermometer. Do not take a temperature for at least 10 minutes after a person has taken a bath, smoked, eaten hot or cold foods, or drunk water; this can affect the temperature reading.

If you have trouble reading the glass thermometer, set it aside until someone else can read it. The temperature reading on a glass thermometer will stay the same until the thermometer is shaken down. The temperature display on a digital thermometer lasts about 3 minutes.

> How to Take a Rectal Temperature

To take a rectal temperature, place the infant or young child on his or her stomach on a firm surface or on your lap. Lubricate the bulb end of the thermometer with petroleum jelly, separate the cheeks of the child's buttocks so that the rectum is visible, and gently insert the thermometer into the rectum about ½ to 1 inch. Never use force. If you meet resistance, change the direction of the thermometer slightly. Hold the thermometer firmly between your fingers and squeeze the child's buttocks together with your other hand. Leave the thermometer in place for about 30 seconds or until you hear the beep for a digital thermometer. Do not use glass thermometers for rectal temperatures. If the child struggles, hold him or her steady by placing your hand on the small of his or her back.

TAKING A RECTAL TEMPERATURE

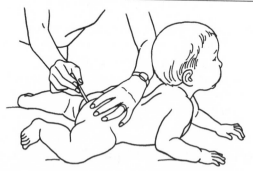

To take an infant's or young child's temperature rectally, place the child on his or her stomach on a firm surface (or on your lap). Separate the cheeks of the child's buttocks and gently insert the thermometer into the rectum about ¹/₂ to 1 inch. Hold the thermometer firmly between your fingers and squeeze the child's buttocks together with your other hand.

MENTAL HEALTH PROBLEMS

▪ ANXIETY/PANIC ATTACKS

A panic attack is a common disorder described as a sudden episode of intense anxiety or fear that develops for no apparent reason and that triggers severe physical reactions. Panic attacks can be very frightening and may resemble a heart attack or even dying.

> Symptoms

Because panic attack symptoms can resemble life-threatening conditions, it's important to seek an accurate diagnosis and treatment. Panic attack symptoms include:

- Rapid heart rate
- Chest pain
- Shortness of breath
- Sweating
- Trembling
- Hyperventilation
- Chills
- Hot flashes
- Nausea
- Abdominal cramping
- Sense of impending death

> What to Do

1. Because panic attack symptoms can resemble life-threatening conditions such as a heart attack, it is important to seek medical help as soon as possible. Panic attacks are hard to manage on your own, and they may get worse without treatment.

2. The main treatment options for panic attacks are medications and psychotherapy. Both are equally effective.

▪ DEPRESSION

Depression is one of the most common health conditions in the world. Feeling sad or upset is a normal human emotion, but with depression, these feelings persist for weeks, months, or even years. And these feelings are much more intense and can significantly interfere with work and daily activities, relationships, and even daily tasks. Feelings of depression can also lead to suicide. Depression usually doesn't get better if ignored and may even get worse unless treated.

Certain risk factors associated with depression include:

- Having other biological relatives with depression
- Having family members who have taken their own life
- Stressful life events, such as the death of a loved one
- Having a depressed mood as a youngster
- Illness, such as cancer, heart disease, Alzheimer's, or HIV/AIDS
- Long-term use of certain medications, such as some drugs used to control high blood pressure, sleeping pills, or, occasionally, birth control pills
- Certain personality traits, such as having low self-esteem and being overly dependent, self-critical, or pessimistic
- Alcohol, nicotine, and drug abuse
- Having recently given birth

> What to Do

If you have symptoms of depression, contact your doctor to discuss your condition. Seek immediate medical care if you have thoughts of hurting yourself or someone else.

Taking steps to control stress, to increase your resilience, and to boost low self-esteem may help. Friendship and social support, especially in times of crisis, can help you through tough and stressful situations.

DRUG AND ALCOHOL ABUSE

See p. 198.

PSYCHOSIS (HEARING VOICES, HALLUCINATION, DELUSIONS)

A person exhibiting sudden bizarre behavior such as hearing voices in his or her head, seeing things that do not exist, or believing that he or she is some other person is a sign of acute medical illness (delirium) and requires immediate medical attention. Such individuals can be harmful to themselves as well as to others. Causes of such behavior can range from drugs and acute poisoning, to infection, to acute mental illness. It is important to seek medical attention to determine the underlying cause of the behavior.

> What to Do

Seek immediate medical attention.

SUICIDE, THREATENED

Take all threats of suicide seriously—even if you cannot imagine that a person could be feeling so unhappy that he or she would want to die. A person who threatens to take his or her life sees the situation as hopeless and death as the only answer. Your response could make the difference between life and death—a person who is contemplating suicide very often changes his or her mind when given the chance. You can provide that chance by diverting the person's attention from immediate thoughts of self-destruction.

If the threat of suicide is unmistakable and immediate:

1. Immediately phone for help; call 911 (or your local emergency medical dispatch number), a suicide hotline, the police, or other trained professionals.

2. De-escalate the situation. Even though you may feel very nervous, speak calmly and move slowly. Sometimes a suicidal person is feeling very angry and may lash out at those who are closest.

Do not argue with the person or show anger; these actions could intensify the situation.

3. Give the person your full attention. Try to get him or her to talk to you, but don't insist. Simply being there and showing a willingness to respond when the person is ready to talk can be very reassuring. You may find it difficult to sit without talking, but even your silent presence can be very soothing to a person who is suicidal. When he or she chooses to open up and talk to you, listen attentively. It is okay to sympathize with the person's feelings; showing that you understand can make him or her feel less alone. Do not leave the person alone. If you are unable, have someone else come to be with the person until help arrives.

4. Once the immediate, critical situation is under control, seek professional help for the person. If possible, you or someone else the person trusts should go along to the therapy sessions.

If the person is talking about suicide but does not have the means at hand:

1. Remain calm, listen attentively, or simply sit silently with the person. Although the immediate situation is not critical, it is still extremely serious.

2. Get the person to agree to get help from a medical professional as soon as possible; call your doctor and ask him or her to recommend a qualified professional. If you would feel better getting immediate help, take the person to an emergency department or counseling center right away.

3. Remove or lock away any firearms or medications (including over-the-counter drugs).

4. If possible, prevent the person from driving.

5. If the person refuses to seek help, call 911 (or your local emergency medical dispatch number) or a suicide hotline immediately for help. Don't be concerned about overreacting—that is better than if you find out later that you could have helped and didn't.

> Signs to Watch For In an Adult

There are no clear-cut ways to tell in advance who will succeed at suicide and who won't. Always err on the side of safety and seek professional help if you suspect a person may be suicidal. The following signs may indicate that an adult is at risk of committing suicide:

- Severe depression that lasts longer than a few weeks and is characterized by symptoms that can include loss of appetite, a change in sleep patterns (sleeping less than usual or more than usual), and lack of interest in formerly enjoyable activities

- Not eating or taking care of themselves like usual
- Excessive alcohol ingestion or abuse of other drugs
- A previous suicide attempt
- A history of suicide in the family
- Giving away or selling valuable possessions
- Recent filing of a will
- Failure to renew a rental lease or other indications that the person is not thinking about the future

> Signs to Watch For In a Child

The signs of depression and suicide risk are different in children than in adults. A suicide threat by a child is extremely serious because children do not have the same judgment as adults and don't always understand the consequences of their actions. A child who talks about suicide should not be left alone until he or she has had a thorough evaluation by a mental health professional, preferably a child psychiatrist. Call your doctor or a suicide hotline immediately if you notice any of the following signs in a child. Even if the child is not suicidal, these are indications that he or she has a physical or emotional problem that requires the attention of a physician:

- An obvious change in behavior such as worsening performance in school, withdrawal from friends and family, change in sleep patterns or appetite, or lack of interest in formerly enjoyable activities
- Anger that may be displayed in disruptive, unmanageable behavior or physical violence against other children or adults
- Irritability
- Moodiness
- Use of alcohol or other drugs

POISONING

It is extremely important to call the poison control center, hospital emergency department, a doctor, or 911 (or your local emergency medical dispatch number) for instructions before doing anything for a person who has swallowed a poison. When calling, be sure to give the following information:

- Person's age
- Name of the poison
- How much poison was swallowed
- When the poison was swallowed
- Whether the person has vomited
- How much time it will take to get the person to a medical facility

For help in dealing with health effects from chemical exposures, contact a Regional Poison Control Center at 800-222-1222.

Emergency treatment for victims of swallowed poisons consists of:

- Seeking prompt medical attention by calling 911, your local emergency medical dispatch number, or the local poison control center
- Following the instructions of the emergency dispatch operator or poison control center
- Getting the poison out of the person or neutralizing the poison with water or milk. Inducing vomiting is rarely done and should be undertaken on medical advice only (preferably from the staff at the poison control center).

Do not induce vomiting if the person is unconscious or is having seizures. Do not induce vomiting if you do not know what the person has swallowed.

Do not induce vomiting if the person has swallowed:

- A strong acid or alkali such as toilet bowl cleaner, rust remover, chlorine bleach, dishwasher detergent, or glucose-test tablets
- A petroleum product such as kerosene, gasoline, furniture polish, charcoal lighter fluid, or paint thinner

Vomiting after ingesting strong acids and alkalis may cause further damage to the throat and esophagus. Petroleum products, if vomited, can be drawn into the lungs and cause chemical pneumonia. It is important to note, however, that the poison control center may recommend inducing vomiting for some of the products mentioned above (particularly the petroleum products) because of other chemicals in the swallowed product that may be even more harmful to the body.

Always follow the instructions of the poison control center. If the person vomits, whether induced or spontaneously, keep the person on his or her side with the head tilted to either side and lower than the rest of the body so that he or she will not choke on the vomit. Place a small child facedown across your knees. Be sure to take the poison container and any vomited material to the hospital for inspection.

NOTE: The information or instructions on labels of poisonous substances are not always correct, particularly if the container is old. It is always best to consult the poison control center, if possible.

> ## What to Do

If the person is not breathing:

1. Call 911 (or your local emergency medical dispatch number), the poison control center, an ambulance, the fire department, or other rescue personnel for transportation to the hospital.

2. Maintain an open airway. Restore breathing and circulation, if necessary. (See pp. 33–49.)

3. Take the poison container and any vomited material to the hospital with the person.

If the person is unconscious or having seizures:

1. Seek medical attention immediately. Call 911 (or your local emergency medical dispatch number), the poison control center, an ambulance, the fire department, or other rescue personnel for transportation to the hospital. The person should be transported lying on his or her side or stomach.

2. Maintain an open airway if possible. Restore breathing and circulation if necessary. (See CPR, pp. 33–49.)

3. Loosen tight clothing around the person's neck and waist. Do not give any fluids to the person. Do not try to induce vomiting. If the person vomits on his or her own, turn his or her head to the side so that he or she will not choke on the vomit.

4. Take the poison container and any vomited material to the hospital with the person.

If the person is conscious:

1. Have someone else (if possible) call 911 (or your local emergency number), the poison control center, hospital emergency department, or a doctor for instructions while you continue to care for the person.

2. Follow the instructions from the poison control center.

If vomiting occurs:

1. Keep the person in a position with their head lower than the rest of the body or lying on his or her left side to prevent choking on vomit.

2. Seek medical attention immediately.

3. Take the poison container and any vomited material to the hospital with the person.

See also: Burns (Chemical Burns), p. 89; Carbon Monoxide Poisoning, below; Diarrhea, p. 102; Drug Abuse, pp. 198–207; Food-Related Illness, p. 104; Lead Poisoning, p. 222; Mercury Poisoning, p. 224; Rashes, p. 179; Seizures, p. 150; Unconsciousness, p. 233.

▪ CARBON MONOXIDE POISONING

Carbon monoxide—a colorless, odorless, tasteless gas—is a common cause of poisoning death. Most accidental cases of carbon monoxide poisoning occur in the home during the winter months, usually at night when people are sleeping. The gas can be produced by any source of heat or fire that is enclosed without proper ventilation and is present in the exhaust of motor vehicles and generators. Sources of carbon monoxide in the home include faulty forced-air gas furnaces or other gas appliances, unventilated space heaters, poorly ventilated fireplaces, and indoor cooking with grills that use charcoal or chemical fuels.

Be extremely cautious when rescuing a person from an area filled with smoke or chemical or gas fumes. Do not attempt a rescue alone. Before entering the area, rapidly inhale and exhale two or three times; take a deep breath and hold it. Remain close to the ground (crawl) while entering and rescuing the person so that you will not inhale hot air or fumes. If the area is extremely hot or heavy with fumes, it is best to leave the rescue to someone who has an independent air supply. Do nothing at the site but remove the person.

> Symptoms

Poisoning from carbon monoxide or other dangerous fumes can cause any or all of the following symptoms (in an infant, the only noticeable symptoms are often irritability and lethargy):

- Headache
- Dizziness
- Nausea
- Weakness and light-headedness
- Inability to move or concentrate
- Chest pain
- Shortness of breath
- Seizures
- Coma

> What to Do

1. Seek medical attention immediately even if the person seems to partially or completely recover. Call 911 (or the local emergency medical dispatch number) and inform the dispatch operator of your concern of exposure to carbon monoxide.

2. Get the person into fresh air immediately (upwind of the poisonous fumes).

3. Maintain an open airway. Restore breathing and circulation if necessary. (See CPR, pp. 33–49.)

4. Loosen tight clothing around the person's neck and waist.

> Preventing Carbon Monoxide Poisoning

Here are some steps you can take to help keep your family safe from carbon monoxide poisoning:

- Install carbon monoxide detectors (available at hardware and houseware stores) on each floor of your home, including every bedroom. (Most cases of carbon monoxide poisoning occur at night while sleeping.)

- Make sure that all furnaces and gas appliances are properly installed and adequately ventilated.

- Have all furnaces and gas appliances inspected and maintained every year by a trained professional.

- Do not burn fuels such as gas or kerosene in confined spaces or rooms. Never use a barbecue grill indoors.

- Make sure that space heaters are adequately ventilated.

■ FOOD POISONING

(See Food-Related Illness, p. 104.)

■ LEAD POISONING

Lead poisoning is a disease that results from an excessive level of lead in the body. Lead poisoning most often occurs in young children who nibble on paint chips, plaster, putty, and other substances containing lead. Brain, kidney, and bone marrow damage may result from prolonged exposure to lead. It is extremely important to seek medical attention as soon as lead poisoning is suspected.

> Symptoms

Lead poisoning can cause any or all of the following symptoms:

- Vomiting
- Weakness
- Fatigue
- Irritability
- Trouble sleeping
- Fever
- Paleness
- Convulsions

- Abdominal pain
- Poor appetite
- Headache
- Hair loss
- Decreased intelligence quotient (IQ)

> What to Do

For any symptoms of lead poisoning, or to examine the possibility of lead poisoning in the absence of symptoms, see a doctor for a complete examination and evaluation, which will include testing the level of lead in the blood.

> Preventing Lead Poisoning

Here are some steps you can take to help keep your children safe from lead poisoning:

- Have your children wash their hands and face after playing outside and before eating.
- Wash toys often; discard any toys that might have lead-based paint (such as those made in other countries).
- Give your child foods high in iron and calcium (both of which help prevent lead absorption by the body) and low in fat (fat promotes lead absorption); don't store food in opened cans or in pottery.
- Use cold tap water for cooking (hot water draws lead from pipes). Before using cold water from the tap, let it run for a few minutes.
- Remove chipping and peeling paint and paint dust. Leave the house during remodeling.

WARNING: LEAD IN OLDER HOMES

If you live in a house or an apartment built before 1978, ask your doctor about blood lead testing for your child and keep your child away from peeling paint. Peeling paint needs to be removed from all surfaces up to 5 feet above the floor. It is also a good idea to repaint the rooms to seal in the lead paint.

■ MERCURY POISONING

Mercury, the silver-colored liquid metal in fever thermometers, is a poisonous substance that can be absorbed by the body. Other sources of metallic mercury include thermostats and blood pressure monitors. The most dangerous way to be exposed to this form of mercury is by inhaling it over a long period of time, usually in an industrial workplace. Swallowing small amounts of metallic mercury, such as that in a fever thermometer, is usually not harmful. Without treatment, severe mercury poisoning can cause birth defects, damage organs, or even be fatal. Students sometimes steal mercury from school chemistry labs to play with at home or conduct their own experiments. If you notice a substance resembling mercury in a glass jar, immediately call your local environmental health department, board of health, poison control center, or doctor to find out how to dispose of the metal properly.

> Symptoms

Contact with mercury or mercury poisoning can cause any or all of the following symptoms:

- An allergic-type rash on the skin (on skin contact)
- Nausea, vomiting, diarrhea, and abdominal pain (on inhalation)
- Shortness of breath or coughing (on inhalation)

> What to Do

If the amount of mercury is greater than that from a small fever thermometer or if mercury from a thermometer spills on a porous surface (such as upholstered furniture or unfinished wood):

1. Do not touch the mercury or try to clean it up, even with a vacuum cleaner.

2. Call your local environmental health department, board of health, poison control center, or doctor (even if no one has any noticeable symptoms).

3. Open the windows to ventilate the area.

4. Leave the area until a health professional has evaluated the situation and the mercury has been cleaned up.

If the amount of mercury is small (such as that in a fever thermometer) and it spills on a nonporous surface (such as ceramic tile or finished wood):

1. Remove any gold jewelry you are wearing (mercury adheres to gold) and be careful to avoid any skin contact with the mercury (only special gloves designed to handle hazardous materials are protective against mercury poisoning).

2. Use an index card or stiff paper to scoop up the mercury droplets and place them in a glass jar with a tight lid or in a reclosable plastic bag. Alternatively, you can use masking tape, duct tape, or cellophane tape to remove the mercury; put the wad of tape and mercury in a glass jar or reclosable plastic bag.

3. Call your local environmental health department, board of health, poison control center, or doctor and ask how to dispose of the mercury.

4. Ventilate the area of the spill for at least 2 days.

■ MUSHROOM POISONING

See Food-Related Illness, p. 108.

PREGNANCY AND EMERGENCY CHILDBIRTH

Occasionally, childbirth occurs at an unexpected time or labor proceeds more quickly than expected. In such cases, the mother sometimes cannot get to the hospital in time for the delivery. If the mother's contractions are 2 to 3 minutes apart, if she feels the urge to push down, or if the baby's head is visible in the vaginal opening (about the size of a half-dollar or larger), birth will usually occur very soon.

If at all possible, summon a doctor to deliver the infant. Sometimes a doctor can give instructions over the telephone during the delivery. Try to remain calm. Most births occur naturally and normally. Do not try to delay or prevent the birth of the baby by crossing the mother's legs or pushing on the baby's head or by any other means. This could be very harmful to the infant.

▪ EMERGENCY CHILDBIRTH

Before the Baby Arrives

> What to Do

1. Place clean sheets on the bed. If time allows, a shower curtain or rubber sheet placed underneath the clean linen will help protect the mattress. If a bed is not available, place clean cloths, clothes, or newspapers underneath the mother's hips and thighs on the floor or ground. A fresh newspaper is generally very clean and almost sterile.

2. Have the mother lie on her back with her knees bent, her feet flat, and her knees and thighs wide apart.

3. Sterilize scissors or a knife in boiling water for at least 5 minutes if possible or hold over a flame for 30 seconds. Leave the scissors or knife in the water until you are ready to use it. Either may be used to cut the umbilical cord.

4. Gather together:

   > Clean, soft, cotton blanket, sheet, or towel to wrap the baby

   > Clean, strong string or clean shoelaces, cord, or strips of cloth to tie off the umbilical cord

   > Pail or bucket in case the mother vomits

   > Large plastic bag, container, or towel in which to place the afterbirth (placenta) for later inspection by medical personnel

---

PREPARING FOR DELIVERY

Place clean sheets on the bed. If no bed is available, place clean cloths, clothes, or newspapers underneath the mother's hips and thighs on the floor, leaving room for the birth of the baby. Have the mother lie on her back with her knees bent, her feet flat, and her knees and thighs wide apart.

> Sanitary napkins or clean, folded cloths or handkerchiefs to be placed over the vagina after the birth of the baby and after the delivery of the afterbirth

> Diapers and safety pins

Delivering the Baby

> What to Do

1. Wash your hands with soap and water. Do not place your hands or other objects in the vagina. Do not interfere with the delivery or touch the baby until the head is completely out of the vagina. Usually the baby will be born facedown.

2. Once the baby's head is out, guide and support it to keep it free of blood and other secretions.

3. If the baby's head is still inside a liquid-filled bag, carefully puncture the bag with the sterile scissors or your finger and open it to allow the fluid to escape. Remove the membranes from the baby's face so the baby can breathe.

4. Check to make sure the umbilical cord is not wrapped around the baby's neck. If the umbilical cord is not wrapped around the baby's neck, do not worry about cutting the cord until after the baby's birth. If the umbilical cord is wrapped around the baby's neck, gently and quickly slip the cord over the baby's head. If the cord is wrapped too tightly to slip over the baby's head, the cord must be cut now to prevent the baby from strangling. If you have cut the cord and if someone is available to help you, have that individual tie off the umbilical cord ends. (See Immediate Care of the Baby, p. 228.)

5. Continue to support the head as the baby is being born. The baby will be very slippery, so be gentle and very careful.

6. Once the baby's head and neck are out of the vagina, the baby will turn on his or her side to allow passage of the shoulders. The upper shoulder usually emerges first. Carefully and gently guide the baby's head slightly downward. Once the upper shoulder is out, gently lift the baby's head upward to allow the lower shoulder to emerge. Do not pull the child out by the armpits.

7. Carefully hold the slippery baby as the rest of his or her body slides out.

Immediate Care of the Baby

> What to Do

1. To help the baby start breathing, hold the baby with his or her head lower than the feet so that secretions can drain from the lungs, mouth, and nose. Support the head and body with one hand while grasping the baby's legs at the ankles with the other hand.

2. Wipe out the mouth and nose gently with sterile gauze or a clean cloth to make sure that nothing interferes with breathing.

3. If the baby has not yet cried, slap your fingers against the bottom of the baby's feet or gently rub the baby's back.

4. If the baby is still not breathing, give artificial respiration through both the baby's mouth and nose, keeping the head extended. (See CPR, pp. 40–42.) Give very gentle puffs every 3 seconds.

5. Note the time of delivery.

6. Once the baby starts breathing, wrap him or her, including the top and back of his or her head, in a blanket or sheet to prevent heat loss. Place the baby on his or her side on the mother's stomach with the baby's head slightly lower than the rest of the body and facing the mother's feet. The umbilical cord should be kept loose. It is very important to keep the baby warm and breathing well.

7. Do not clean the white cheesy coating covering the baby's skin. This is a protective covering. Do not clean the baby's eyes or ears.

8. It is not necessary or desirable to cut the umbilical cord immediately. It is best to wait about a minute, until the cord stops pulsating. If the mother can be taken to the hospital immediately after the delivery of the afterbirth (which occurs 5 to 20 minutes after

---

AFTER THE DELIVERY

After the baby is born, hold the baby with his or her head lower than the feet so that secretions can drain from the lungs, mouth, and nose. Support the head and body with one hand while grasping the baby's legs and ankles with the other hand.

TYING THE UMBILICAL CORD

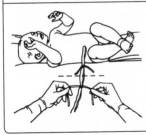

If the umbilical cord is to be cut, tie a clean string around the cord at least 4 inches from the baby's body. Tie in a tight square knot so that circulation is cut off in the cord. Use a second piece of string to tie another tight square knot 6 to 8 inches from the baby (2 to 4 inches from the first knot). Cut the cord between the two ties.

delivery of the baby), the baby can be left attached to the umbilical cord and afterbirth, particularly if there are no clean scissors to cut the cord. Also, the cord must be cut properly.

9. If you must cut the cord, tie a clean string or strip of cloth around the cord at least 4 inches from the baby's body. Tie the string in a tight square knot so that circulation is cut off in the cord. Using a second piece of string or strip of cloth, tie another tight square knot 6 to 8 inches from the baby (2 to 4 inches from the first knot).

10. Cut the cord between the two ties with sterilized or clean scissors or a knife.

11. Keep the baby warm with his or her head covered and close to the mother. The baby's head should still be slightly lower than the rest of his or her body to allow drainage of secretions.

Delivery of the Afterbirth

Delivery of the afterbirth (placenta) usually occurs 5 to 20 minutes after the birth of the baby. It is usually preceded by a gush of dark red blood from the vagina.

> What to Do

1. Be patient in waiting for the delivery of the afterbirth. Do not pull on the umbilical cord to quicken delivery of the afterbirth. The mother's uterine contractions will eventually push out the afterbirth.

2. Place the afterbirth in a container and take it with the mother and baby to the hospital so that it may be examined.

Care of the Mother

After the infant has been born and the afterbirth has been expelled:

1. Place sanitary napkins or clean, folded cloths against the mother's vaginal opening to absorb blood.

2. To help control the flow of blood from the mother, place your hands on the mother's abdomen and gently massage the uterus, which can be felt just below the mother's navel and feels like a large smooth ball. Continue to massage gently until the uterus feels firm. Continue to do this every 5 minutes or so for an hour, unless medical assistance is obtained. If the bleeding is very heavy and/or prolonged, seek medical attention immediately.

3. If she wishes, sponge the mother's face with cool water.

4. Give the mother water, tea, coffee, or broth. Do not give her alcoholic beverages.

5. Keep the mother warm and comfortable. And remember, congratulations are in order!

Medical Attention

Regardless of how smoothly the delivery goes, it is very important that both the mother and baby be examined by a physician to make certain all is well. Most serious problems occur in the first 24 hours after birth.

See also: Miscarriage, below; Pregnancy Danger Signs, p. 231.

▪ MISCARRIAGE

A miscarriage is the loss of a fetus usually occurring before the 12th week of pregnancy. Miscarriages are common and occur in approximately 15 percent of pregnancies, usually in the first 3 months. Miscarriages are unpredictable and often unavoidable.

The first signs of a possible miscarriage are usually bleeding followed by lower abdominal cramping.

> What to Do

1. Although vaginal bleeding and/or cramping do not always indicate a miscarriage, if either of these symptoms appears, notify a doctor immediately

2. If heavy or continuous bleeding occurs, seek medical attention immediately, preferably at the nearest hospital emergency department.

See also: Abdominal Pain, p. 96; Emergency Childbirth, p. 225; Pregnancy Danger Signs, below.

■ PREGNANCY DANGER SIGNS

Certain symptoms during pregnancy should be reported immediately to a doctor. They may or may not indicate a serious condition, but only a doctor can evaluate the situation. The symptoms to report immediately include:

- Any vaginal bleeding
- Stomach pain or cramps
- Persistent vomiting
- Severe, persistent headaches
- Swelling of the face or fingers
- Blurring or dimness of vision
- Chills and fever
- Sudden leaking of fluid from the vagina
- Convulsions
- Difficulty breathing
- Chest pain

Headaches During Pregnancy

Severe or persistent headaches in the last 3 months of pregnancy can be a sign of danger to both the mother and the baby. Headaches may indicate a serious condition known as preeclampsia in which the mother's body reacts negatively to the presence of the fetus. Other symptoms of preeclampsia include swelling of the face and fingers, blurred vision, and rapid weight gain. Any severe or persistent headache at any time during pregnancy or up to 2 months after pregnancy requires prompt medical attention.

See also: Cold-Related Problems, p. 318; Drug and Alcohol Problems, p. 198; Head, Neck, and Back Problems, p. 138; Heat-Related Problems, p. 330; Poisoning, p. 217; Stroke, p. 153.

SLEEP-RELATED PROBLEMS

■ INSOMNIA

Insomnia is a common problem and is typically caused by stress, anxiety, depression, excess caffeine, and eating too much, among other causes. Insomnia can affect not only your energy level and mood but also your health because sleep helps bolster your immune system. Fatigue, at any age, leads to diminished mental alertness and concentration. Lack of sleep caused by insomnia is linked to accidents both on the road and on the job.

> Symptoms

Symptoms of insomnia include:

- Difficulty falling asleep at night
- Waking up during the night or too early
- Daytime fatigue, sleepiness, and irritability

> What to Do

If you are having frequent nights of insomnia or if insomnia has been interfering with your daytime functioning for a month or longer, see your doctor to determine what might be the cause of your sleep problem and how it might be treated. Your doctor may prescribe a sleeping pill; however, this will be only temporary because there is a risk of dependency associated with these medications. Your doctor also may provide guidance for some behavioral therapy.

> Preventing Insomnia

Exercise, stress relief therapy, avoiding excess caffeine or alcohol, and avoiding meals before going to bed are some ways to prevent insomnia.

▪ SNORING

Snoring is a common problem and is caused when air flows past relaxed tissues in your throat, causing the tissues to vibrate as you breathe, creating hoarse or harsh sounds. However, loud and frequent snoring may indicate a serious health condition called obstructive sleep apnea.

> What to Do

1. Seeking medical advice about your snoring can help both you and your partner. For you, snoring may indicate another health concern, such as obstructive sleep apnea, nasal obstruction, or obesity. Your willingness to see a doctor may also result in more restful sleep for your partner.

2. If your partner notices a pattern of loud snoring followed by a period of silence (lasting 10 seconds or longer), you may be at risk for sleep apnea. Your doctor may refer you to an ear, nose, and throat (ENT) specialist (otolaryngologist) or sleep specialist for additional testing and evaluation. This may require that you stay overnight at a sleep center to undergo in-depth analysis of your sleep habits by a team of specialists.

3. Lifestyle changes, such as losing weight, avoiding alcohol or heavy meals close to bedtime, or sleeping on your side can help stop snoring.

UNCONSCIOUSNESS

There are many causes of unconsciousness including heart attack, stroke, head injury, bleeding, diabetic coma, or insulin shock. Poisoning, heatstroke, choking, gas inhalation, severe allergic reaction to insect stings, and electrical burns can also cause unconsciousness. You should always seek medical attention for anyone who is unconscious, regardless of the cause.

> Symptoms

A person who is unconscious is:

- Unresponsive
- Unaware of his or her surroundings
- Unable to speak or respond to you

> What to Do

1. Call 911 (or your local emergency medical dispatch number) immediately.

2. Loss of consciousness that occurs suddenly and without warning may indicate a stroke or a heart attack, or that a person has stopped breathing. The person may require CPR to restore breathing and circulation if necessary. (See CPR, pp. 33–49.)

If the unconscious person is breathing:

1. Call 911 (or your local emergency medical dispatch number) or take the person to the nearest emergency department.

2. Maintain an open airway.

3. Loosen tight clothing, particularly around the person's neck. Keep the person comfortably warm but not hot. Do not give an unconscious person anything to eat or drink and do not leave him or her alone.

4. Keep the person lying down. If the cause of unconsciousness is unknown, always suspect a head, neck, or back injury and do not move the person except to maintain an open airway. If the cause of unconsciousness is known and it is not a head, neck, or back injury, place the person on his or her side to allow secretions to drain and to prevent choking on fluids and vomit. When placed on his or her side, the person should have the head slightly lower than the rest of the body.

Check for bleeding (p. 52), broken bones (p. 79), or a head injury (p. 140), and give first aid.

Part IV

SPORTS
FIRST AID

WARM-UP, STRETCH, AND COOL DOWN

Whenever exercising, include some type of warm-up and cool-down period. Warming-up prior to any physical activity has numerous benefits. A proper warm-up increases the blood flow and delivery of oxygen and nutrients to the working muscles, which can decrease muscle stiffness and lower the risk of injury. A proper warm-up also will help increase the body's core temperature, including muscle temperature. By increasing muscle temperature, you are helping to make the muscles loose, supple, and pliable. Warm muscles and tendons are less prone to injury and may improve physical performance. An effective warm-up also has the effect of increasing both your heart rate and your respiratory rate. Ultimately, a proper warm-up helps prepare your body and mind for more strenuous activity.

The warm-up period can be divided into three simple steps: (1) general warm-up, (2) stretching, and (3) activity-specific warm-up. This is followed by a cool-down period.

> General Warm-up

The general warm-up routine should begin with light exercise that slightly increases your heart rate. If you plan to go running, begin your warm-up with a steady walk. If you will be playing basketball, begin with some free throws and simple shots. Remember to start slow and do not wear yourself out during your warm-up.

> Stretching

Once your muscles are warm, take time to stretch. Muscles are much more flexible when they are warm compared to when they are cold. Focus on stretching large muscle groups such as in the legs (hamstrings and quadriceps) but stretch all the muscles that you will be using in your activity.

Key Points About Stretching

- Always complete a warm-up session prior to stretching.
- To help improve flexibility, stretch and hold the muscle for

20 to 60 seconds. Stretches should be performed slowly and under control. Repeat each stretch 2 to 3 times.

- Stretch until you feel slight pulling but no pain. As you hold the stretch the muscle will relax. As you feel less tension you can increase the stretch again until you feel the same slight pull. Hold this position until you feel no further increase.

- Be sure not to stretch so far that you cause pain, and maintain proper breathing during each stretch. Correct stretching should feel comfortable with no discomfort.

- Hold the stretch steady and do not bounce.

- Avoid stretching to injured muscles, bones, or joints.

- Take your time and do not rush through your stretching routine.

- Make sure you stretch all of the major muscle groups, which include your legs, arms, shoulders, and back.

> Activity-specific Warm-up

After stretching, the final step is to do some exercises that are specific to the activity you will be undertaking. If you plan to lift weights, begin with light weights and perform a few repetitions before increasing the amount of weight and number of repetitions. If you will be playing basketball, run up and down the sidelines for a few minutes and perform some game-related drills. The warm-up session should last about 5 to 10 minutes, although more time may be necessary if preparing for more intense exercise. If you are exercising in cold weather, take more time to be sure your body is ready. Once you are sufficiently warm and flexible, your body is ready for exercise.

> Cool Down

Any game or workout should be followed by a cool-down period. This is just as important as the warm-up period. A proper cool-down allows you to lower your heart and breathing rate and prevent the pooling of blood within your muscles. This can help minimize dizziness and fainting. The cool-down period also allows waste products to be removed from your muscles, which can help reduce soreness after strenuous activity.

Begin the cool down period by decreasing the intensity of your activity (such as by walking or jogging after a hard run) for about

5 to 10 minutes. This should be followed by light stretching to help relax the muscles and prevent soreness. It is important that you remain active during the cool-down period. Upon completion of your exercise routine, be sure to drink plenty of water and replenish lost nutrients. (See also Cold-Related Problems, p. 318, and Heat-Related Problems, p. 330.)

ANKLE INJURY

The ankle consists of the bones of the lower leg (the fibula and tibia) and the top of the foot (the talus). These bones form the ankle joint and are connected by a group of ligaments. Two important ligaments that help add stability to the joint are the anterior talofibular ligament, which runs from the outer ankle "knob" to the top of the foot, and the calcaneofibular ligament, which connects the outer ankle knob to the heel bone. The ankle is a hinge joint that allows up-and-down bending and limited side-to-side movement of the foot.

SPRAINED ANKLE

A sprained ankle occurs when a person steps down on the outside of the foot, causing the ligaments on the outside of the ankle to stretch or

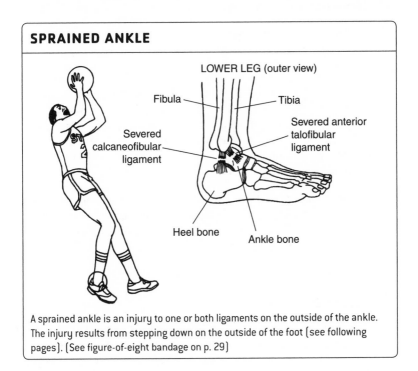

SPRAINED ANKLE

LOWER LEG (outer view)

Fibula — Tibia

Severed anterior talofibular ligament

Severed calcaneofibular ligament

Heel bone

Ankle bone

A sprained ankle is an injury to one or both ligaments on the outside of the ankle. The injury results from stepping down on the outside of the foot (see following pages). (See figure-of-eight bandage on p. 29)

tear. The injury, which may involve one or both ligaments, can range from a tiny tear to complete severing of the ligaments. A sprained ankle can be more painful than a break in a bone and may take as long to heal. Sprained ankles are the most common injuries in all sports, including baseball, basketball, football, soccer, rugby, jogging, track and field, and tennis, and can also occur during everyday activities, including walking.

> Symptoms

At the time of the injury, you may feel a flash of heat or a tearing sensation on the outside of the ankle or hear a popping sound. Pain, swelling, and bruising may develop on the outside of the ankle or the top of the foot, and you may not be able to walk on it. Your ankle may feel warm for several hours. Depending on the severity of the sprain, symptoms may appear immediately or 6 to 12 hours after the injury.

> Immediate Treatment

If the pain is severe or persistent or if your ankle is swollen, see your doctor to determine proper treatment. He or she can rule out a broken bone in the foot, ankle, or lower leg.

Stop the activity that caused the sprain. As soon as possible, elevate your ankle, preferably above the level of your heart, and place an ice pack on the ankle intermittently (20 minutes every hour while you're awake) for the first 24 hours after the injury. Cold treatments help stop internal bleeding and the accumulation of fluids in and around the injured area, thereby decreasing swelling.

Unless your doctor has prescribed another medication, take aspirin, ibuprofen, naproxen, or ketoprofen with food as directed to relieve pain and inflammation. (Acetaminophen relieves pain but has no effect against inflammation; ask your doctor or pharmacist for guidance.)

> Continued Care

Do not engage in the activity that caused the injury until the pain has subsided. Your physician may put a brace on the ankle to immobilize or restrict movement. Alternately, use of an elastic bandage on the ankle may aid stability. (If you have peripheral vascular disease or diabetes, consult your physician before using an elastic bandage.) Take aspirin, ibuprofen, naproxen, or ketoprofen as directed to relieve pain and inflammation. See your physician if the pain and swelling continue.

Once an ankle has been sprained, it may be susceptible to recurring sprains because of instability in the joint. Swelling and the development of bone spurs (small, spoke-like calcium growths) can make the ankle susceptible to arthritis.

> How to Prevent Recurring Injury

Wear properly fitting shoes appropriate for the activity and replace them when they wear out. You may have to tape your ankle to make it more stable. With your physician's okay, work with a trainer or physical therapist to strengthen the muscles around the ankle and lower calf.

See also: Ankle Sprain, p. 63; Sprains, p. 175.

BACK INJURY

The lower back consists of the vertebrae and discs of the lower spine, the sacrum and coccyx (tailbone), and many muscles and ligaments that connect the ribcage to the pelvis. The spine and muscles that run alongside it provide support for the trunk and protect the spinal cord.

LOWER BACK PAIN

Lower back pain can occur for a variety of reasons: a strain or tear in a muscle or ligament, injury to a disc or vertebra, pressure on a nerve, or fatigue. Lower back pain can be caused by a repetitive motion, such as a golf swing over time, or by a sudden force exerted on the back, such as from a football block. It can also result from an insufficient warm-up period before athletic activity.

LOW BACK PAIN

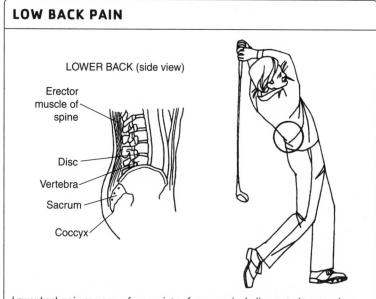

LOWER BACK (side view)

Erector muscle of spine

Disc

Vertebra

Sacrum

Coccyx

Lower back pain can occur for a variety of reasons, including a strain or tear in a muscle or ligament, injury to a disc or vertebra, pressure on a nerve, or fatigue. Over time, a repetitive motion such as a golf swing can also bring on lower back pain.

> Symptoms

Symptoms can range from a dull ache to a sharp pain in the lower back. If a muscle tears, you may feel a slight pull when the injury occurs, with pain intensifying several hours after the injury. A herniated disc may produce sharp pains that make movement difficult. Sciatic nerve damage may produce sharp pains that radiate down the back of one or both legs. A back that is fatigued, such as from a long-distance athletic activity, may be stiff and ache all over. (See Back Injuries, pp. 138–140, and Lower Back Pain, pp. 145–146.)

> Immediate Treatment

See your doctor if your back pain is caused by a blow to the back, if the pain is severe or radiates down the back of both legs, if you have numbness or tingling in your lower back or legs, or if the pain gets worse when you cough or sneeze. Go to the nearest hospital emergency department if you suddenly have problems holding urine or controlling bowel movements or if you have sudden and noticeable weakness in your legs.

For muscle pulls or tears, place an ice pack on the area intermittently (20 minutes every hour while you're awake) for the first 24 hours after the injury. Cold treatments help stop internal bleeding and the accumulation of fluids in and around the injured area, thereby decreasing swelling.

For stiffness or fatigue, place a heating pad on the back to help relax the muscles. Soreness in the lower back can also be relieved by lying down, which takes pressure off the back; by placing one foot on a foot rest when you're standing, which shifts the angle of the sacrum, lessening the arch of the back; or by getting a good night's rest. The ideal position of rest is lying flat on your back with knees bent; pillows under your knees will help maintain this position.

Unless your doctor has prescribed another medication, take aspirin, ibuprofen, naproxen, or ketoprofen with food as directed. (Acetaminophen may not contain as much of the anti-inflammatory agents as aspirin, ibuprofen, naproxen, or ketoprofen; ask your doctor or pharmacist for guidance.)

> Continued Care

For a muscle pull or tear, place an ice pack on the injury intermittently (20 minutes every hour while you are awake) for the first 24 hours after the injury. Thereafter, use a heating pad on your back at least once a day until the injury heals. Heat increases blood circulation in the area, providing vital nutrients to the injury and helping speed recovery. Do not apply heat before the swelling has subsided or swelling in the injured area may increase. Take aspirin, ibuprofen, naproxen, or ketoprofen as directed to reduce pain and inflammation.

Avoid athletic activity until the injury has had time to heal or until the pain is gone. The length of time that it takes the injury to heal depends on the type and severity of the injury and can range from 2 to 6 weeks or longer. Once the injury has healed, gradually and carefully do exercises that stretch the muscles in your back. Use an ice pack to reduce any swelling that may occur, and after the swelling has subsided, apply heat to help relax the injured muscle. See your physician if the pain continues or recurs. For stiffness or fatigue, apply heat as directed under Immediate Treatment (p. ii).

> How to Prevent Recurring Injury

Work with a trainer or physical therapist on exercises that strengthen the muscles in your back and abdomen. Stretch the muscles in your back before engaging in sports. Avoid sudden movements that could reinjure your back.

ELBOW INJURY

The elbow is a hinge joint that allows the wrist and hand to rotate and the forearm to extend and flex. The elbow consists of three main bones—the humerus of the upper arm and the ulna and radius of the forearm—that converge to form the elbow joint. The forearm bone in line with the thumb is the radius, and the forearm bone in line with the little finger is the ulna. The bony protrusions on the inside and outside of the elbow are called epicondyles. Ligaments connect and support the three bones in the elbow. Tendons are strong, flexible cords that connect the surrounding muscles to the bones. Bursas—fluid-filled sacs or saclike cavities—surround and cushion the bones at the joint.

ELBOW BURSITIS

Elbow bursitis (sometimes referred to as student's elbow or miner's elbow) is inflammation and swelling of the olecranon bursa, a fluid-filled sac at the base of the elbow, beneath the ulna bone in the forearm. The bursa (which lies just under the skin) cushions the bones at the joint and allows the skin to glide smoothly over the muscles and tendons of the outer elbow. Bursitis results from repetitive stress (such as from leaning on the point of the elbow for long, frequent intervals) or from a direct blow (such as from a fall).

> Symptoms

Elbow bursitis may cause a painless swelling about the size of a golf ball on the outer elbow. Unless the swelling is severe, the condition usually does not affect the elbow's range of motion.

> Immediate Treatment

If the swelling is painful, if your skin at the site of the swelling is warm or red, or if you have a fever, see your doctor to determine proper treatment.

Rest the elbow in a sling or an elastic wrap bandage until the swelling subsides. Unless your doctor has prescribed another medication, take aspirin, ibuprofen, naproxen, or ketoprofen with food as directed to relieve pain and inflammation. (Acetaminophen relieves pain but has no effect against inflammation; ask your doctor or pharmacist for guidance.) For a recurring case, your doctor may recommend an injection of a corticosteroid drug such as cortisone. Once the elbow has healed, no other treatment is necessary. The condition seldom has any long-term effects.

> How to Prevent Recurring Injury

Use elbow pads when you participate in contact sports, or in sports in which you may fall. If the injury frequently recurs or if it becomes chronic, your physician may recommend surgically removing the bursa.

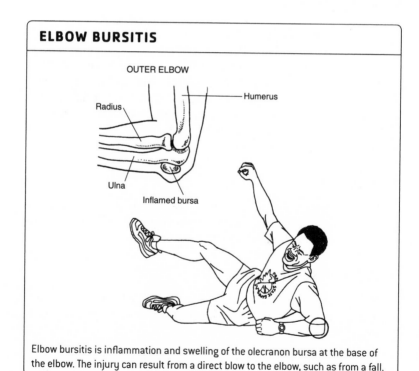

ELBOW BURSITIS

OUTER ELBOW

Humerus

Radius

Ulna

Inflamed bursa

Elbow bursitis is inflammation and swelling of the olecranon bursa at the base of the elbow. The injury can result from a direct blow to the elbow, such as from a fall.

GOLFER'S ELBOW

Golfer's elbow is inflammation or a tiny tear in the tendon that attaches the flexor muscle group to the medial epicondyle (inner "knob"). The flexor muscles run down the inside of the forearm and help flex the wrist and bend the fingers.

Golfer's elbow, which occurs in both tennis players and golfers, is usually associated with a repetitive motion over time. It can develop from an improper downward stroke in golf, hitting the ground during the golf swing, or improperly executing the forehand stroke in tennis. The condition can also result from underdeveloped flexor muscles. Other sports that can cause golfer's elbow include racquetball, table tennis, rowing, bowling, archery, waterskiing, and weight lifting. Construction work and other kinds of physical activities, such as housework, moving furniture, painting, and gardening, can also cause golfer's elbow.

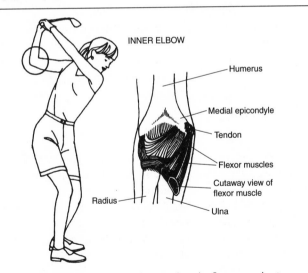

GOLFER'S ELBOW

INNER ELBOW

Humerus

Medial epicondyle

Tendon

Flexor muscles

Cutaway view of flexor muscle

Ulna

Radius

Golfer's elbow is inflammation of the tendon that attaches the flexor muscles to the inner "knob" of the elbow (the medial epicondyle). The condition, also called tendonitis of the elbow, can result from a repetitive motion such as an incorrect downward swing in golf.

> Symptoms

Symptoms of golfer's elbow include pain on the inside of the elbow, which can be intense and limit movement. For example, you might feel pain when picking up a child, carrying a heavy tray, or lifting a heavy box.

> Immediate Treatment

In serious cases of golfer's elbow (such as if you can't bend or straighten the elbow without pain or you feel numbness or weakness in your arm or hand), see your doctor to determine proper treatment.

Stop the activity that is causing the pain. Place an ice pack on the elbow intermittently (20 minutes every hour while you're awake) for the first 24 hours after the pain began. Cold treatments help stop internal bleeding and the accumulation of fluids in and around the injured area, thereby decreasing swelling.

Unless your doctor has prescribed another medication, take aspirin, ibuprofen, naproxen, or ketoprofen with food as directed to relieve pain and inflammation. (Acetaminophen relieves pain but has no effect against inflammation; ask your doctor or pharmacist for guidance.) For severe inflammation or for a recurring case, your doctor may recommend an injection of a corticosteroid drug such as cortisone.

> Continued Care

Rest the arm for 4 to 8 weeks. Use an ice pack for the first 24 hours (20 minutes every hour while you're awake) after stopping the activity to reduce swelling and inflammation. Use a heating pad thereafter. Heat increases blood circulation in the area, providing vital nutrients to the injury and helping speed recovery. Do not apply heat before the swelling has subsided, or swelling in the injured area may increase. Take aspirin, ibuprofen, naproxen, or ketoprofen with food as directed to reduce pain and inflammation.

Do not engage in the activity that caused the injury until the pain has subsided. Ease into limited muscle workouts—swing a golf club or tennis racket, lift light weights, and work with a trainer or a physical therapist on hand, wrist, and forearm exercises that strengthen the flexor muscles. Muscle strengthening exercises also help strengthen the supporting ligaments and tendons. If these measures do not relieve the symptoms, see your physician.

With proper treatment and rest, golfer's elbow seldom has any long-term effects. However, some people experience recurring tendonitis even with preventive measures. In rare cases, surgery to release tension on the tendon, which involves severing the tendon from the bone, may be recommended.

> How to Prevent Recurring Injury

Allow plenty of time for healing. After the pain goes away, use weights and do exercises recommended by a trainer or physical therapist. You may need to continue these measures throughout your life to avoid or reduce pain. Get recommendations from a golf or tennis pro about proper equipment and technique. Your doctor may recommend wearing an elbow brace, which helps constrict the extensor and flexor muscles and helps reduce tension in the areas at which the muscles attach to the elbow. This measure alone can often greatly reduce the pain.

TENNIS ELBOW

Tennis elbow is a catchall phrase for inflammation or a tiny tear in the tendon that connects the extensor muscle group to the lateral epicondyle (the outer "knob"). The extensor muscles—the long muscles on the outside of the forearm—help to extend the wrist.

Tennis elbow, also called elbow tendonitis, is usually associated with a repetitive motion over time. In tennis, it usually develops from an improperly executed backhand stroke. It may also be caused by improper equipment such as a racket that is too stiff or too heavy, a grip that is too small or too large, or strings that are too loose. Other causes include snapping the wrist on a tennis serve or having underdeveloped extensor muscles. Other sports that can cause tennis elbow include racquetball, table tennis, bowling, fly-fishing, archery, skiing, and golf. Construction work and other kinds of physical activity such as housework, painting, writing, and gardening can also cause tennis elbow.

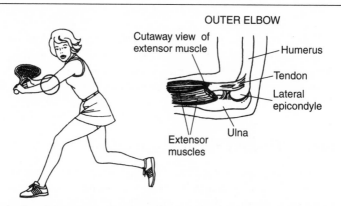

TENNIS ELBOW

OUTER ELBOW

Cutaway view of extensor muscle

Humerus

Tendon

Lateral epicondyle

Ulna

Extensor muscles

Tennis elbow is inflammation of the tendon that attaches the extensor muscles to the outer "knob" of the elbow (the lateral epicondyle). The condition can result from an improperly executed backhand tennis stroke.

> Symptoms

The major symptom of tennis elbow is pain on the outside of the elbow, which can be severe and limit movement. Even everyday activities such as shaking hands, holding a coffee cup, turning a doorknob, or picking up a piece of paper may be extremely painful.

> Immediate Treatment

Stop the activity that is causing the pain. Place an ice pack on the elbow intermittently (20 minutes every hour while you're awake) for the first 24 hours after the pain began. Cold treatments help stop internal bleeding and the accumulation of fluids in and around the injured area, decreasing swelling.

Unless your doctor has prescribed another medication, take aspirin, ibuprofen, naproxen, or ketoprofen with food as directed to relieve pain and inflammation. (Acetaminophen relieves pain but has no effect against inflammation; ask your doctor or pharmacist for guidance.) If these measures do not relieve the symptoms, see your physician. He or she may prescribe a different medication to help reduce the pain and swelling. For severe inflammation or for a recurring case, he or she may recommend an injection of a corticosteroid drug such as cortisone.

> Continued Care

Rest the arm for 4 to 8 weeks. Use an ice pack for the first 24 hours (20 minutes every hour while you're awake) after stopping the activity to reduce swelling and inflammation. Use a heating pad thereafter. Heat increases blood circulation in the area, providing vital nutrients to the injury and helping speed recovery. Do not apply heat before the swelling has subsided, or swelling in the injured area may increase. Take aspirin, ibuprofen, naproxen, or ketoprofen with food as directed to reduce the pain and inflammation.

Do not engage in the activity that caused the injury until the pain has subsided. Ease into limited muscle workouts—swing a racket gently, exercise with light weights, and work with a trainer or a physical therapist on hand, wrist, and forearm exercises that strengthen the extensor muscles. Muscle-strengthening exercises also help strengthen the supporting ligaments and tendons. See your physician if the pain is severe and limits forward motion of the arm.

With proper treatment and rest, tennis elbow seldom has any long-term effects. However, some people experience recurring tendonitis even with precautionary measures. In rare cases, surgery to release tension on the tendon, which involves severing the tendon from the bone, may be recommended.

> How to Prevent Recurring Injury

Allow plenty of time for healing. Use weights and do exercises recommended by a trainer or physical therapist after the pain goes away. You may need to continue these measures throughout your life to avoid or reduce pain. Get recommendations from a tennis pro about proper equipment and technique. Your doctor may recommend wearing an elbow brace, which helps constrict both the extensor and flexor muscles and helps reduce tension in the areas at which these muscles attach to the elbow. This measure alone can often greatly reduce the pain.

FOOT INJURY

The forefoot, or front third of the foot, is composed of five singular long bones (metatarsals) that look like the fingers of your hand. The tips of these bones form the toes (phalanges). These bones provide balance for the body.

MORTON'S NEUROMA

Morton's neuroma is pain in the front third of the foot caused by swelling of a nerve between two metatarsal bones, usually those between the third and fourth toes. Poorly fitting shoes and stress on the feet caused by repetitive athletic activity, such as running, are common factors contributing to Morton's neuroma. Genetic susceptibility can also play a part; if the joints of the metatarsal bones are larger than usual, they may compress the nerve between these bones, especially during athletic activity, and cause swelling of the nerve. The condition is common in many sports. Wearing high heels—especially shoes that crowd the toes—may make women more susceptible.

> Symptoms

The major symptoms of Morton's neuroma are pain on the top of the foot, in the ball of the foot, and/or on the bottom of the toes. The pain may be severe enough to limit athletic participation. Wearing shoes can worsen the pain. In severe cases, the toes may become numb.

> Immediate Treatment

If the pain is severe or persistent, if your toes are numb, or if walking causes severe pain, see your physician to determine proper treatment.

Stop the activity that is causing the pain. Remove your shoes and walk barefoot or in stocking feet. Place an ice pack on the site of the pain intermittently (20 minutes every hour while you're awake) for the first 24 hours after the injury. Unless your doctor has prescribed another medication, take aspirin, ibuprofen, naproxen, or ketoprofen with food as directed to relieve pain and inflammation. (Acetamino-

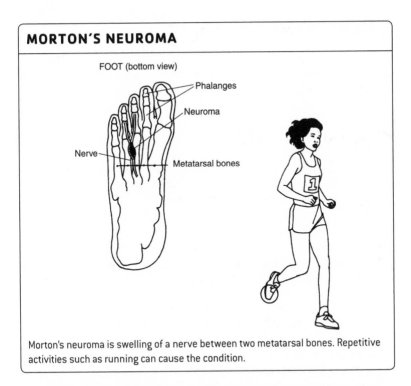

FOOT (bottom view)

Phalanges

Neuroma

Nerve

Metatarsal bones

Morton's neuroma is swelling of a nerve between two metatarsal bones. Repetitive activities such as running can cause the condition.

phen relieves pain but has no effect against inflammation; ask your doctor or pharmacist for guidance.) For severe inflammation or for a recurring case, your doctor may recommend an injection of a corticosteroid drug such as cortisone.

> Continued Care

Rest the foot for 3 to 6 weeks. Do not engage in the activity that caused the neuroma until the pain has subsided. Take aspirin, ibuprofen, naproxen, or ketoprofen with food to relieve pain and inflammation. See your physician if the pain in your foot or the numbness in your toes continues. With proper treatment and rest, Morton's neuroma seldom has any long-term effects.

> How to Prevent Recurring Injury

The most important preventive measure is to wear shoes that give your foot room to move. If the pain returns, immediately stop the activity that prompted it.

PLANTAR FASCIITIS

Plantar fasciitis, or heel spur, is a common injury to the plantar fascia, a band of protective tissue that runs from the heel along the bottom of the foot to the base of the toes. In plantar fasciitis, the plantar fascia detaches slightly from the heel, causing pain and inflammation in the bottom of the heel that hurts more when standing on the toes. The injury can range from a tiny tear to a more serious, but rare, severing of the plantar fascia. Regardless of the extent of the tear, a spoke-like calcium deposit, or "spur," can form at the heel bone, aggravating the condition.

Plantar fasciitis is usually caused by overuse, as in frequent running. It also can result from poor arches, from wearing shoes with a stiff heel, or from running or competing in sports on hard terrain, such as concrete. The condition can also result from an increase in body weight. Other sports in which the injury can occur include aerobics, baseball, basketball, football, hiking, rugby, soccer, tennis, and track and field. Women who regularly wear high heels and do not stretch their calf muscles and the plantar fascia before engaging in sports may be susceptible to this injury.

> Symptoms

The major symptom of plantar fasciitis is pain in the heel, especially when waking. Ironically, walking may hurt, but running, once the feet and legs have been warmed up, does not. The pain usually subsides when you are lying down but may return when you get up. Your heel may be swollen and bruised. You may feel as though you are walking on a pea or pebble.

> Immediate Treatment

If you are unable to place any pressure on your foot, or if walking or climbing stairs causes intense pain, see your doctor to determine proper treatment.

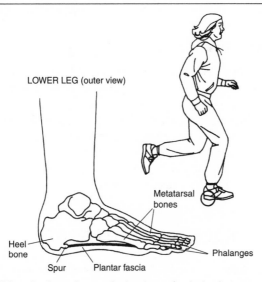

PLANTAR FASCIITIS

LOWER LEG (outer view)

Metatarsal bones

Heel bone

Spur   Plantar fascia

Phalanges

Plantar fasciitis, or heel spur, is a tear in the plantar fascia that is aggravated by a spur that develops at the heel bone. The injury often results from repetitive motion such as running.

Stop the activity that is causing the pain. Place an ice pack on the heel intermittently (20 minutes every hour while you're awake) for the first 24 hours after the injury. Cold treatments help stop internal bleeding and the accumulation of fluids in and around the injured area, thereby decreasing swelling. Elevate your foot above the level of your heart. Unless your doctor has prescribed another medication, take aspirin, ibuprofen, naproxen, or ketoprofen with food as directed to relieve pain and inflammation. (Acetaminophen relieves pain but has no effect against inflammation; ask your doctor or pharmacist for guidance.)

> Continued Care

Do not engage in the activity that caused the injury until the pain has subsided. With your physician's okay, work with a trainer or physical therapist on exercises that stretch the plantar fascia. Take aspirin, ibuprofen, naproxen, or ketoprofen with food as directed to relieve pain and inflammation. If the pain and swelling continue, see your physician. In rare cases, surgery to release tension on the fascia, which involves severing the fascia from the heel bone, may be recommended.

> How to Prevent Recurring Injury

Allow plenty of time for the injury to heal before resuming your activity. Your physician, trainer, or physical therapist may recommend using shoe inserts when you engage in sports to help relieve pressure on the heel. Carefully perform exercises that stretch the calf muscles and the plantar fascia; always do these exercises to warm up before engaging in sports. Wear proper shoes. A stiff heel in running shoes or tennis shoes can cause or aggravate the condition. Run or train on a dirt or wood track and avoid concrete.

STRESS FRACTURE IN THE FOOT

A stress fracture usually occurs in the foot or in the tibia (the larger of the two lower leg bones). A stress fracture in the foot is a hairline crack in one of the metatarsal bones. The injury can result from a repetitive motion, such as running, from sudden stress placed on the foot, such as a change in running routine or running surface, or from participating in sports after a period of inactivity. It also can result from an increase in body weight. Stress fractures are common in many sports other than running, including gymnastics, aerobics, baseball, basketball, tennis, rugby, soccer, and walking. Any activity that puts stress on the feet or legs over time may cause a stress fracture.

> Symptoms

A stress fracture causes intense pain at the site of the fracture. During exercise, the foot or leg may feel like it is on fire. The pain subsides when you stop the activity. In more serious cases, the pain may continue even after stopping the activity.

> Immediate Treatment

If the pain is severe and persistent, see your physician to determine proper treatment.

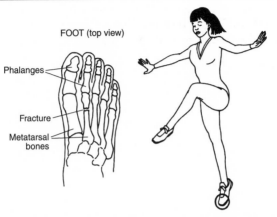

FOOT (top view)

Phalanges

Fracture

Metatarsal bones

A stress fracture usually occurs in the foot or in the tibia, the larger of the two lower leg bones. A stress fracture in the foot is a hairline crack in one of the metatarsal bones, which can occur when all the weight of the body is put on these bones.

Stop the activity that is causing the pain. Place an ice pack on the area intermittently (20 minutes every hour while you're awake) for the first 24 hours after the injury. Cold treatments help stop internal bleeding and the accumulation of fluids in and around the injured area, thereby decreasing swelling. Elevate your foot above the level of your heart. Unless your doctor has prescribed another medication, take aspirin, ibuprofen, naproxen, or ketoprofen with food as directed to relieve pain and inflammation. (Acetaminophen relieves pain but has no effect against inflammation; ask your doctor or pharmacist for guidance.)

> Continued Care

Rest the foot for 4 to 6 weeks. Do not engage in the activity that caused the injury until the pain has subsided. Take aspirin, ibuprofen, naproxen, or ketoprofen with food as directed to reduce pain and inflammation. See your physician if the pain continues after you resume activity. With proper treatment and rest, stress fractures seldom have any long-term effects.

> How to Prevent Recurring Injury

Resume activity gradually, especially sports that involve running. Wear proper shoes. Run or train on a soft surface, such as a dirt or wood track, and avoid concrete. Increase your speed or distance gradually.

See Broken Bones, pp. 79–81.

HAND INJURY

The hand consists of the bones and joints of the fingers and thumb (called phalanges), the five metacarpal bones of the palm, and eight small, oblong bones that together form the wrist. Beneath the skin is a complex network of ligaments, tendons, and muscles. Muscles in the forearm allow the hand to perform a wide range of motion and tasks. (For more information, see Hand Fracture, pp. 72–73, and Fingertip Bandages, p. 29.)

BASEBALL FINGER

Baseball finger is a tear in a tendon at the joint at the end of the finger. Depending on the severity of the injury, you may not be able to straighten the finger. The injury is caused by sudden force exerted on the end of the finger, such as from a thrown or hit baseball.

BASEBALL FINGER

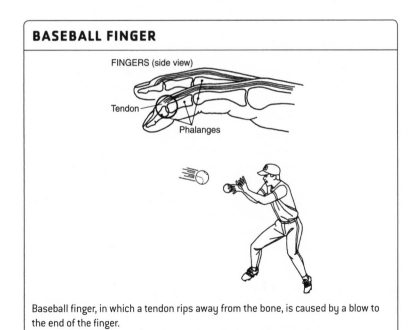

FINGERS (side view)

Tendon

Phalanges

Baseball finger, in which a tendon rips away from the bone, is caused by a blow to the end of the finger.

> Symptoms

Baseball finger causes immediate pain and may cause swelling and bruising at the site of the injury.

> Immediate Treatment

Place an ice pack on the finger intermittently (20 minutes every hour while you're awake) for the first 24 hours after the injury. Cold treatments help stop internal bleeding and the accumulation of fluids in and around the injured area, thereby decreasing swelling. Elevate your finger above the level of your heart. See your physician to determine the extent of the injury. Your physician may recommend using a splint on the finger to aid healing.

Unless your doctor has prescribed another medication, take aspirin, ibuprofen, naproxen, or ketoprofen with food as directed to relieve pain and inflammation. (Acetaminophen relieves pain but has no effect against inflammation; ask your doctor or pharmacist for guidance.)

> Continued Care

Do not engage in the activity that caused the injury until the pain has subsided. Work with a trainer or physical therapist on exercises that strengthen the tendons in the fingers. Take aspirin, ibuprofen, naproxen, or ketoprofen with food as directed to relieve pain and inflammation. See your physician if the pain continues or injury recurs. See your physician if you are unable to straighten your finger all the way; you may need a splint to aid in healing. With proper treatment and rest, this injury seldom has any long-term effects, although it sometimes results in the permanent inability to completely straighten the end joint of the finger. This lack of movement seldom interferes in any way with the functioning of the finger, but you should still see your physician if you cannot straighten the end joint of the injured finger.

> How to Prevent Recurring Injury

Continue doing exercises that strengthen the tendons in the finger. Use good judgment when engaging in your sport.

SKIER'S THUMB

Skier's thumb is a tear or complete severing of the ligament that attaches the thumb to one of the metacarpal bones in the palm. The injury often occurs during a fall in skiing when the ski pole forces the thumb away from the fingers. It can also occur when catching a swiftly thrown baseball, football, or basketball.

> Symptoms

Skier's thumb causes immediate pain and swelling at the base of the thumb. The pain may intensify and bruising may occur several hours after the injury. Pinching may be difficult.

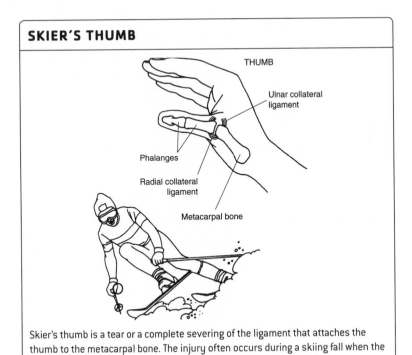

SKIER'S THUMB

THUMB

Ulnar collateral ligament

Phalanges

Radial collateral ligament

Metacarpal bone

Skier's thumb is a tear or a complete severing of the ligament that attaches the thumb to the metacarpal bone. The injury often occurs during a skiing fall when the ski pole forces the thumb away from the fingers.

> Immediate Treatment

Place an ice pack on the base of the thumb intermittently (20 minutes every hour while you're awake) for the first 24 hours after the injury. Cold treatments help stop internal bleeding and the accumulation of fluids in and around the injured area, thereby decreasing swelling. Elevate your hand above the level of your heart. See your physician to determine the extent of the injury. Your physician may recommend using a splint on the thumb to aid healing.

Unless your doctor has prescribed another medication, take aspirin, ibuprofen, naproxen, or ketoprofen with food as directed to relieve pain and inflammation. (Acetaminophen relieves pain but has no effect against inflammation; ask your doctor or pharmacist for guidance.)

> Continued Care

Do not engage in the activity that caused the injury and avoid use of the thumb until the pain has subsided. Work with a trainer or physical therapist on exercises that strengthen the tendons and ligaments in the hand. Use an ice pack when necessary to reduce swelling. Take aspirin, ibuprofen, naproxen, or ketoprofen with food as directed to relieve pain and inflammation. If the pain continues or if the injury recurs, see your doctor.

With proper treatment and rest, the injury seldom has long-term effects. In serious cases, surgery will be necessary to repair the ligament.

> How to Prevent Recurring Injury

Continue doing exercises that strengthen the tendons and ligaments in the hand. Use good judgment when engaging in your sport.

HIP INJURY

The hip consists of the ilium bone (the top of the pelvis), the sacrum and coccyx (tailbone) of the lower spine, the pubic bone, and the ischium bone (the bottom of the pelvis). Several muscle-tendon groups are connected to the hip. The bones of the hip protect the internal organs and allow standing and movement.

HIP POINTER

A hip pointer is a bruise or tear in a muscle that attaches to the top of the ilium bone at the waist. The injury, which is very common in contact sports, is caused by a blow to or fall on the hip.

See also: Hip Pointer, p. 65.

> Symptoms

A hip pointer causes pain and bruising in the hip. The pain may intensify several hours after the injury.

> Immediate Treatment

If the pain is severe or persistent, see your doctor to determine proper treatment.

Place an ice pack on the hip intermittently (20 minutes every hour while you're awake) for the first 24 hours after the injury. Cold treatments help stop internal bleeding and the accumulation of fluids in and around the injured area, thereby decreasing swelling.

Unless your doctor has prescribed another medication, take aspirin, ibuprofen, naproxen, or ketoprofen with food as directed to relieve pain and inflammation. (Acetaminophen relieves pain but has no effect against inflammation; ask your doctor or pharmacist for guidance.)

HIP POINTER

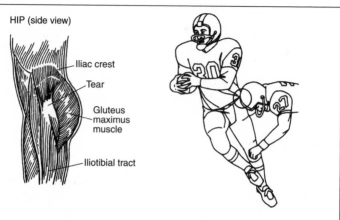

HIP (side view)

- Iliac crest
- Tear
- Gluteus maximus muscle
- Iliotibial tract

A hip pointer is a bruise or tear in a muscle that attaches to the top of the ilium bone at the waist. The injury results from a blow to or fall on the hip.

> Continued Care

Use an ice pack (20 minutes every hour while you're awake) at least once a day for the first 24 hours after the injury. Take aspirin, ibuprofen, naproxen, or ketoprofen with food as directed to relieve the pain and inflammation. After the swelling has stopped, place a heating pad on the hip at least once a day until the injury heals. Heat increases blood circulation in the area, providing vital nutrients to the injury and helping speed recovery. Do not apply heat before the swelling has subsided, or swelling in the injured area may increase. Avoid athletic activity until the injury has had time to heal, or until the pain in the hip has gone. The length of time for the injury to heal depends on the severity of the tear and can range from 3 to 6 weeks or longer.

After the injury has healed, gradually and carefully perform exercises that involve stretching the muscles in your upper legs and waist. Use an ice pack to reduce swelling when necessary. See your physician if the pain continues or if the injury recurs. With proper rest, hip pointers seldom have any long-term effects.

> How to Prevent Recurring Injury

Wear hip padding when you engage in contact sports.

KNEE INJURY

The knee consists of ends of three main bones—the femur of the upper leg and the tibia and fibula of the lower leg. These bones are connected by a series of ligaments to form the knee joint. Resting on top of the knee joint is a fourth bone, the patella (kneecap). Bursas (fluid-filled sacs or saclike cavities) surround and cushion the bones. Muscles, such as the quadriceps in the front upper leg and the hamstrings in the back upper leg, are connected to these bones by tendons. Muscles, tendons, and ligaments add stability to the joint. The knee allows the leg to extend and bend and is a hinge joint like the elbow. (For more information, see Kneecap Dislocation, p. 66.)

RUNNER'S KNEE

Runner's knee, or patellofemoral joint pain, is a common problem that affects runners and other athletes of all abilities. The term refers to damage to and roughness of the cartilage that covers the undersurface of the kneecap. Cartilage covers all bone and joint surfaces and acts as a shock absorber to keep bone from rubbing against bone. When the condition occurs, rough spots on the kneecap can rub directly against the femur, causing pain.

Runner's knee can result from a repetitive motion (such as running) or sudden stress on the knee (which can result from a change in running routine or running surface, using heavier weights in weight lifting, or using a high gear in bicycling). It also may be influenced by genetic factors (a "loose" kneecap or an abnormality in the structure of the kneecap), by a direct or forceful blow to the kneecap, or by unknown factors. Any sport in which pressure is put on the knees—such as weight lifting, football, tennis, rowing, aerobics, or bicycling—can cause runner's knee. Other activities that can cause runner's knee include heavy lifting or stair climbing.

The term runner's knee has also been used to describe a pain on the outside of one or both knees. This condition, although not as common as patellofemoral joint pain, is usually caused by overuse—for example, by increasing running mileage without acclimating first to the new distance. The pain in the knee occurs when the foot strikes

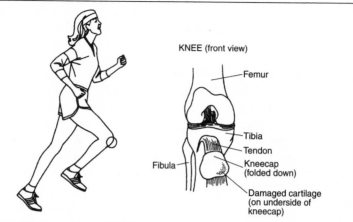

KNEE (front view)

Femur

Tibia

Tendon

Fibula

Kneecap
(folded down)

Damaged cartilage
(on underside of
kneecap)

Runner's knee—pain on or behind the knee—is caused by damage to the cartilage that covers the undersurface of the kneecap. The injury often results from running, which puts repetitive stress on the knee.

the ground at a pronounced angle while running, which causes extra stress and may cause a tiny tear in a strip of connective tissue that extends from the ilium (hipbone) to the top of the tibia. Usually, the outside of the person's shoe and the heel are worn down. If you have any of these signs and symptoms, see your physician for proper diagnosis and treatment. The condition can be corrected with shoe inserts, moldings that fit inside the shoes to give the feet support and help the feet strike the ground properly during running.

> Symptoms

Symptoms of runner's knee include anything from a dull ache to a sharp pain on and behind the kneecap, pain while sitting with the knees bent, pain when kneeling or squatting, or pain when walking up or down stairs. The condition can also cause swelling of the knee, muscle weakness in the quadriceps, or grinding and popping of the knee.

> Immediate Treatment

If the pain is persistent or severe or if your knee is swollen, see your doctor to determine proper treatment.

Stop the activity that is causing the pain. Place an ice pack on the knee intermittently (20 minutes every hour while you're awake) for the first 24 hours after the injury. Cold treatments help stop internal bleeding and the accumulation of fluids in and around the injured area, thereby decreasing swelling. Keep your leg elevated above the level of your heart.

Unless your doctor has prescribed another medication, take aspirin, ibuprofen, naproxen, or ketoprofen with food as directed to relieve pain and inflammation. (Acetaminophen relieves pain but has no effect against inflammation; ask your doctor or pharmacist for guidance.)

> Continued Care

Rest your leg for approximately 3 to 6 weeks. Occasional use of an elastic bandage on the knee may help promote stability and prevent further injury. If you have peripheral vascular disease or diabetes, however, you should consult your physician first before using an elastic bandage. Keep your leg slightly elevated.

Do not engage in the activity that caused the injury until the pain has subsided. With your physician's okay, work with a trainer or physical therapist on exercises that strengthen the quadriceps muscles. Use an ice pack to reduce any swelling that may occur. Take aspirin, ibuprofen, naproxen, or ketoprofen with food as directed to relieve pain and inflammation. If the pain and swelling continue, see your physician.

> Long-term Effects

Some pain may continue when the knee is bent. You may have difficulty kneeling or squatting. In some cases, surgery may be recommended to smooth the roughness on the back of the kneecap.

> How to Prevent Recurring Injury

Keep your quadriceps muscles strong with muscle strengthening exercises that also help strengthen the joint-supporting ligaments and tendons. Use good judgment in increasing your running mileage and intensity or when running on a different surface. Avoid the use of high gears when bicycling. Gradually acclimate yourself to lifting heavy objects. Ensure that your shoes fit properly.

TORN CARTILAGE IN THE KNEE

The meniscus, or knee cartilage, is a crescent-shaped band of elastic tissue inside joints. The knee joint has two menisci that sit on top of the tibia, the large lower leg bone. The medial meniscus is on the inner side of the joint and the lateral meniscus is on the outer side. This cartilage helps the knee joint fit snugly together and helps distribute body weight evenly over the surface of the tibia. Injury to the meniscus can range from a tiny tear, which may not require surgery, to a complete rupture, which in most cases must be repaired surgically. With repeated twists or blows to the knee, a small tear may develop into a complete severing.

The injury is usually caused by a severe twist or forceful blow to the knee when the leg is straightened. It also can result from force placed on the knee when the foot is planted while the leg is straightened, causing the knee to twist. Torn cartilage sometimes occurs in conjunction with a torn ligament in the knee. The injury is very common in contact sports such as football. Other sports in which the injury can occur include hockey, lacrosse, soccer, downhill skiing, basketball, and golf. Torn cartilage in the knee can also result from tripping over objects or falling with force on the knee.

> Symptoms

The major symptom of torn cartilage in the knee is pain at the joint line (the area at which the bones of the leg join to form the knee). The knee may lock or buckle, make a popping sound, or swell.

> Immediate Treatment

See a doctor for proper diagnosis of the extent of the tear. Surgery may be recommended to repair or remove the damaged cartilage.

Stop the activity that is causing the pain. (The pain and swelling are likely to keep you from continuing.) Apply an ice pack to the knee

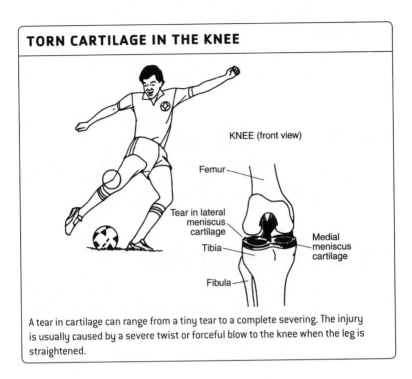

TORN CARTILAGE IN THE KNEE

KNEE (front view)

Femur

Tear in lateral meniscus cartilage

Tibia

Medial meniscus cartilage

Fibula

A tear in cartilage can range from a tiny tear to a complete severing. The injury is usually caused by a severe twist or forceful blow to the knee when the leg is straightened.

intermittently (20 minutes every hour while you're awake) for the first 24 hours after the injury. Cold treatments help stop internal bleeding and the accumulation of fluids in and around the injured area, thereby decreasing swelling. Keep your leg slightly elevated.

Unless your doctor has prescribed another medication, take aspirin, ibuprofen, naproxen, or ketoprofen with food as directed to relieve pain and inflammation. (Acetaminophen relieves pain but has no effect against inflammation; ask your doctor or pharmacist for guidance.)

> Continued Care

Follow your physician's instructions regarding follow-up care. See your doctor if the pain and swelling continue or if your knee locks or buckles.

> Long-term Effects

You may have some stiffness and swelling in your knee. The injury may make you susceptible to developing arthritis or ligament tears in your knee.

> How to Prevent Recurring Injury

With your physician's okay, work with a trainer or physical therapist to strengthen the hamstring muscles in your back upper leg and the quadriceps muscles in the front upper leg.

TORN LIGAMENT IN THE KNEE

There are four ligaments that provide stability to the knee joint: the anterior cruciate ligament (ACL), the posterior cruciate ligament (PCL), the medial collateral ligament (MCL), and the lateral collateral ligament (LCL). The two cruciate ligaments crisscross inside the knee joint and add stability to the joint. The collateral ligaments provide side-to-side stability to the joint, the medial on the inner side (the side closest to the other knee), and the lateral on the outer side of the knee.

The anterior cruciate ligament is the most important ligament for ensuring stability of the knee. A tear of the anterior cruciate ligament is the most common knee ligament injury. An injury can range from a tiny tear to a complete rupture of the ligament, but is usually the latter. With complete rupture, there is rapid and substantial swelling to the knee, and the injured person is usually unable to bear weight on the leg. A tear in this ligament may be accompanied by a tear in another knee ligament or meniscus in the knee. The injury is caused by a traumatic or sudden blow to the knee when the leg is straight or slightly bent. It also can occur from force placed on the knee when the foot is planted while the leg is straight or slightly bent. The injury is very common in contact sports such as football. Other sports in which the injury can occur include lacrosse, soccer, downhill skiing, and basketball. The injury can also result from tripping over an object on the floor.

Partial and sometimes complete tears of either of the collateral ligaments are also common knee injuries. As compared to a tear of the anterior cruciate ligament, there is less swelling, and the injured person is able to bear weight on the leg. When these ligaments are partially torn, surgery can sometimes be avoided; complete tears require surgery. These tears may also be associated with tears in the meniscus. Tears of the posterior collateral ligament are the least common of the four, and many times do not require surgery.

> Symptoms

A torn ligament in the knee can cause swelling and pain from the accumulation of fluid and blood inside the joint. The injury can also cause stiffness, limitation of movement, or displacement of the knee. You may hear a popping sound when the ligament is torn, especially with an anterior cruciate tear, which is also accompanied by immediate substantial swelling and inability to bear weight on the leg. Tears of the collateral ligaments result in less swelling, with a slower onset, and the injured person can bear weight on the leg. In less severe tears, the symptoms may not appear for 6 to 12 hours.

TORN LIGAMENT

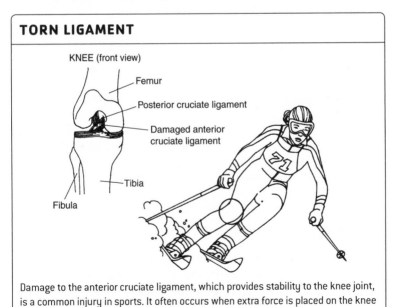

KNEE (front view)

Femur

Posterior cruciate ligament

Damaged anterior cruciate ligament

Tibia

Fibula

Damage to the anterior cruciate ligament, which provides stability to the knee joint, is a common injury in sports. It often occurs when extra force is placed on the knee when the foot is planted while the leg is straight or slightly bent.

> Immediate Treatment

If the pain is severe or persistent, if you are unable to bear weight on your leg, if your knee is swollen, or if the movement in your knee is limited, see your doctor to determine proper treatment. Depending on the severity of the injury, he or she may recommend surgery to reconstruct the ligament.

Stop your activity. Apply an ice pack to the knee intermittently (20 minutes every hour while you're awake) for the first 24 hours after the injury. Cold treatments help stop internal bleeding and the accumulation of fluids in and around the injured area, thereby decreasing swelling. Keep your leg elevated, especially if there is any swelling.

Unless your doctor has prescribed another medication, take aspirin, ibuprofen, naproxen, or ketoprofen with food as directed to relieve pain and inflammation. (Acetaminophen relieves pain but has no effect against inflammation; ask your doctor or pharmacist for guidance.)

> Continued Care

Follow your doctor's instructions regarding follow-up care. See your doctor if the pain or swelling in your knee continues or if your knee buckles.

> Long-term Effects

The knee may be unstable and give out, especially when you turn sharply to the left or right, such as when cutting in football. Your knee may be susceptible to meniscus tears because the ligament is looser than normal. Your knee may also be susceptible to arthritic changes over time.

> How to Prevent Recurring Injury

With your doctor's okay, work with a trainer or physical therapist to strengthen the leg muscles, especially the quadriceps muscle in the front and the hamstring muscle in the back of the upper leg. Muscle-strengthening exercises also help strengthen the joint-supporting ligaments and tendons.

LEG INJURY

ACHILLES TENDONITIS

Achilles tendonitis is a tear in the tendon that attaches the calf muscles to the heel bone. Injury to the Achilles tendon can range from a tiny tear to a complete rupture of the tendon. The Achilles tendon, one of the longest and strongest tendons in the body, allows you to run, climb, and stand on the tips of your toes.

Achilles tendonitis can result from repetitive motion such as running over time, or from sudden stress placed on the tendon, such as in sprinting. A tear can also occur if the tendon is fatigued from overuse or if pressure is placed on it before a sufficient warm-up period, from wearing improper shoes during sports activities or athletic shoes with a stiff heel, or from running or training on a hard surface. The injury can occur in any sport, but is most common in aerobics, baseball, basketball, football, hiking, rugby, soccer, tennis, and track and field.

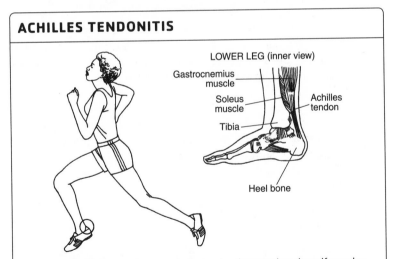

ACHILLES TENDONITIS

LOWER LEG (inner view)

Gastrocnemius muscle

Soleus muscle

Achilles tendon

Tibia

Heel bone

Achilles tendonitis is a strain or tear in the tendon that attaches the calf muscles to the heel bone. The injury frequently results from a repetitive movement such as running.

The injury can also result from everyday activities such as running for a bus or taking long walks without acclimating first to the distance.

> Symptoms

Depending on the extent of the tear, symptoms can range from mild discomfort to severe pain that may be centered at the lower back of the leg (about 2 inches above the ankle). With a mild strain or tear, the pain may be noticeable on waking up in the morning, but as the tendon warms up during walking or exercise, the pain may disappear. However, the discomfort may return the next morning. With a more serious tear or severing of the tendon, you may feel as if someone kicked you in the back of the leg as the tendon ruptures. With both minor and major injuries to the tendon, pain and swelling (from the accumulation of fluids) will worsen several hours after the onset of the injury.

> Immediate Treatment

If the pain is severe or persistent, see your doctor to determine proper treatment. A complete rupture usually has to be repaired surgically.

Stop the activity that caused the injury. Apply an ice pack to the area intermittently (20 minutes every hour while you're awake) for the first 24 hours after the injury. Cold treatments help stop internal bleeding and the accumulation of fluids in and around the injured area, thereby decreasing swelling. Keep your leg elevated as much as possible.

Unless your doctor has prescribed another medication, take aspirin, ibuprofen, naproxen, or ketoprofen with food as directed to relieve pain and inflammation. (Acetaminophen relieves pain but has no effect against inflammation; ask your doctor or pharmacist for guidance.)

> Continued Care

Do not engage in the activity that caused the injury or any other activities that cause pain until the pain has subsided. Gradually and carefully extend or stretch your lower leg and foot. Work with a trainer or physical therapist on light exercises that stretch the calf muscles and the Achilles tendon. He or she may recommend that you wear half-inch lifts in your shoes to take pressure off the heel. Use an ice pack to reduce any swelling that may occur. Take aspirin, ibuprofen, naproxen, or ketoprofen with food as directed to relieve pain and inflammation. See your physician if the pain and swelling persist.

With proper treatment and rest, Achilles tendonitis seldom has any long-term effects. However, some people experience recurring tendonitis regardless of preventive measures. In rare cases, surgery may be recommended to remove scar tissue and part of the tendon.

> How to Prevent Recurring Injury

Allow plenty of time for the injury to heal. Your physician, trainer, or physical therapist may recommend that you wear shoe inserts when you engage in sports to help relieve pressure on your heel. Carefully perform exercises that stretch the calf muscles and the Achilles tendon. Wear proper shoes—a stiff heel in running shoes or tennis shoes can cause or aggravate the condition. Run or train on a dirt or wood track (not on concrete).

CALF MUSCLE TEAR

Injury to the calf muscle can range from a tiny tear to a complete rupture. A tear in the calf muscle usually occurs in people who participate in sports after a period of inactivity. The injury usually occurs when they jump and land on their toes. The calf muscles, the gastrocnemius and the soleus, extend from the back of the knee to the heel. The gastrocnemius muscle starts behind the knee and forms the bulky part of the calf. The soleus muscle starts lower down at the back of the shin. The two muscles join to form the Achilles tendon, which connects them to the heel. The calf muscles pull the heel up to allow a springing movement through the toes, which is important for walking, running, jumping, and hopping.

> Symptoms

Symptoms of a torn calf muscle include an immediate sharp pain in the middle of the calf, sometimes accompanied by a snapping or tear-

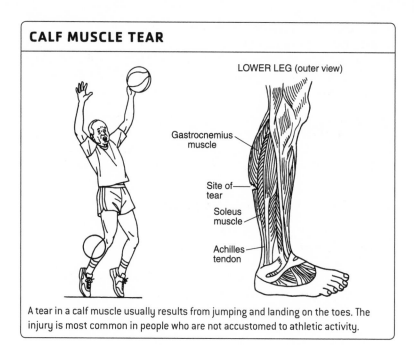

CALF MUSCLE TEAR

LOWER LEG (outer view)

Gastrocnemius muscle

Site of tear

Soleus muscle

Achilles tendon

A tear in a calf muscle usually results from jumping and landing on the toes. The injury is most common in people who are not accustomed to athletic activity.

ing sensation. The middle of the calf muscle may swell and feel tender to the touch.

> ## Immediate Treatment

If your calf swells, if the pain is not relieved by lifting your heel, or if you cannot walk, see your doctor to determine treatment.

Elevate your heel by wearing a heel lift in your shoe to take pressure off the calf muscle. Unless your doctor has prescribed another medication, take aspirin, ibuprofen, naproxen, or ketoprofen with food as directed to relieve pain and inflammation. (Acetaminophen relieves pain but has no effect against inflammation; ask your doctor or pharmacist for guidance.)

> ## Continued Care

Once the injury heals, no treatment is necessary. A tear in the calf muscle seldom has any long-term effects.

> How to Prevent Recurring Injury

Always warm up your calf muscles with a few minutes of stretching exercises before engaging in sports activities.

HAMSTRING MUSCLE PULL

Injury to the hamstring can range from a tiny tear to a more serious tear in the muscle or in the tendons that attach the muscle to bone. Most injuries occur in the muscle. The hamstring is a large muscle on the back of the thigh that runs from the bottom of the pelvis to the top of the knee. About mid-thigh, the hamstring separates into two major muscle-tendon groups. The medial (inner) hamstring tendons attach to the inner knee and the front of the tibia (the larger of the lower leg bones). The lateral (outer) hamstring tendons attach to the outside of the knee at the top of the fibula (the other lower leg bone). The hamstring muscle bends the leg at the knee. (The quadriceps muscle on the front of the thigh extends or straightens the leg.)

HAMSTRING MUSCLE PULL

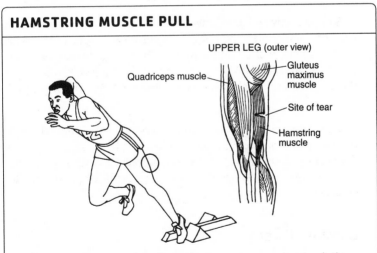

UPPER LEG (outer view)

Quadriceps muscle

Gluteus maximus muscle

Site of tear

Hamstring muscle

Injury to the hamstring can range from a tiny tear to a more serious tear in the muscle or in the tendons that attach the muscle to bone. The injury usually occurs during a quick running start, such as a sprint, when the leg is straightened rather than bent at the knee.

Injury to the hamstring is common among athletes of all abilities. It usually results from a quick start, such as sprinting, when the leg is straightened. The injury can also occur when the quadriceps muscle is overdeveloped in relation to the hamstring muscle or when engaging in sports before a sufficient warm-up period. Some people have naturally tight hamstrings that may or may not make them susceptible to injury. Sports in which hamstring injury is common include baseball, football, basketball, rugby, soccer, and tennis.

> Symptoms

The major symptom of a hamstring muscle pull is pain in the back of the leg. The degree of pain depends on the severity of the tear. With some tears or strains in the muscle, pain may worsen over several hours, making it difficult to walk, sit, or bend over.

> Immediate Treatment

If the pain in the back of the leg is severe or persistent or if you cannot straighten your leg, see your doctor to determine proper treatment.

Stop the activity that is causing the pain. Place an ice pack on the back of the leg intermittently (20 minutes every hour while you're awake) for the first 24 hours after the injury. Cold treatments help stop internal bleeding and the accumulation of fluids in and around the injured area, thereby decreasing swelling. Keep your leg slightly elevated.

Unless your doctor has prescribed another medication, take aspirin, ibuprofen, naproxen, or ketoprofen with food as directed to relieve pain and inflammation. (Acetaminophen relieves pain but has no effect against inflammation; ask your doctor or pharmacist for guidance.)

> Continued Care

Rest your leg for approximately 1 to 3 weeks, depending on the extent of the injury. Use an ice pack on the injury (20 minutes every hour while you're awake) for the first 24 hours after stopping the activity to reduce swelling and inflammation. Use a heating pad thereafter. Heat increases blood circulation in the area, providing vital nutrients to the injury and helping speed recovery. Do not apply heat before the swelling has subsided, or swelling in the injured area may increase. Take aspirin, ibuprofen, naproxen, or ketoprofen with food as directed to reduce the pain and inflammation.

Use of an elastic bandage on the upper leg may help relieve pressure by compressing the quadriceps and hamstring muscles. However, if you have peripheral vascular disease or diabetes, consult your physician first before using an elastic bandage because it can constrict blood circulation. Keep your legs slightly elevated and extended straight out in front of you whenever you can.

Do not engage in the activity that caused the injury until the pain has subsided. Gradually and carefully bend and stretch your leg. Work with a trainer or physical therapist on light exercises that strengthen the hamstring and quadriceps muscles. Use an ice pack to reduce any swelling that may occur. Take aspirin, ibuprofen, naproxen, or ketoprofen with food as directed to relieve pain and inflammation. If the pain continues or if the injury recurs, see your doctor. With proper rest and rehabilitation, a hamstring muscle pull seldom has any long-term effects.

> How to Prevent Recurring Injury

Warm up properly. Perform exercises that strengthen the hamstring and quadriceps muscles.

SHIN SPLINT

While not a medical term, "shin splint" denotes the anatomical location of pain that occurs in the front of the lower leg. A shin splint can be one of several injuries: a tiny tear in a muscle (the posterior tibial muscle) at the point at which it attaches to the tibia in the front of the leg, a stress fracture in the bone, or a tiny tear or inflammation in the thin membrane that covers all the body's bone surfaces. Exercise may increase the size of the muscle in the lower leg, causing the muscle to strain against the surrounding membrane and bone; rarely, in serious cases, blood flow to and from the muscles can be restricted, which is termed anterior compartment syndrome.

A tear in the muscle, a stress fracture in the bone, or a tear or in-flammation in the membrane covering the bone can all result from overuse, such as during intensive athletic training; from a change in running routine or running surface or shoes; or from participating in sports or vigorous exercise after a period of inactivity. A shin splint can also result from an increase in body weight. Compartment syndrome may result when the leg muscles are overdeveloped. Shin splints are common among athletes of all abilities and occur in many sports other than running, including aerobics, baseball, basketball, tennis, rugby, soccer, and walking. (For more information, see Ankle, Leg, and Hip Problems, pp. 62–69.)

> Symptoms

A shin splint causes pain in the lower front portion of the leg. Moving the muscles in the leg worsens the pain.

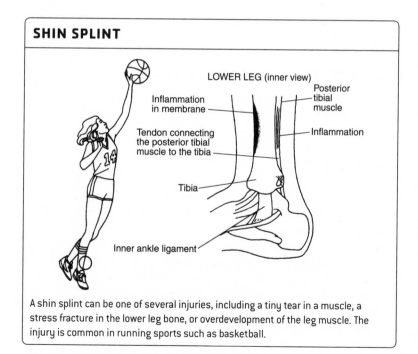

SHIN SPLINT

LOWER LEG (inner view)

Inflammation in membrane

Tendon connecting the posterior tibial muscle to the tibia

Posterior tibial muscle

Inflammation

Tibia

Inner ankle ligament

A shin splint can be one of several injuries, including a tiny tear in a muscle, a stress fracture in the lower leg bone, or overdevelopment of the leg muscle. The injury is common in running sports such as basketball.

> Immediate Treatment

If the pain in your leg is severe or persistent or if you are unable to walk, see your doctor to rule out a stress fracture or anterior compartment syndrome.

Stop the activity that is causing the pain. Place an ice pack on the site of the injury intermittently (20 minutes every hour while you're awake) for the first 24 hours after the injury. Cold treatments help stop internal bleeding and the accumulation of fluids in and around the injured area, thereby decreasing swelling.

Unless your doctor has prescribed another medication, take aspirin, ibuprofen, naproxen, or ketoprofen with food as directed to relieve pain and inflammation. (Acetaminophen relieves pain but has no effect against inflammation; ask your doctor or pharmacist for guidance.)

> Continued Care

Rest your legs for 3 to 6 weeks. Do not engage in the activity that caused the injury until the pain has subsided. Apply a heating pad to the injury. Heat increases blood circulation in the area, providing vital nutrients to the injury and helping speed recovery. Do not apply heat before the swelling has subsided, or swelling in the injured area may increase. Take aspirin, ibuprofen, naproxen, or ketoprofen with food as directed to reduce the pain and inflammation. Use an ice pack on the area to reduce any swelling that may occur. If the pain continues after you resume activity, see your physician.

With proper treatment and rest, a shin splint seldom has any long-term effects. In serious cases of anterior compartment syndrome, surgery may be required to cut the membrane (fascia) covering the muscle.

> How to Prevent Recurring Injury

Work with a trainer or physical therapist to strengthen the surrounding ankle muscles. You may be advised to use shoe inserts that help support the arch and take stress off the lower leg. Resume activity, especially running sports, gradually.

MUSCLE CRAMPS

Muscle cramps occur when the muscles tighten up during or after athletic activity, usually when the activity is prolonged, such as during a marathon, an extended tennis match, or a long bicycle ride. Cramps can occur almost anywhere in the body. During athletic activity, cramps can occur in the stomach, legs, feet, arms, neck, or back. Cramps in the legs are very common, especially in the hamstring muscles in the back upper leg, the quadriceps muscles in the front upper leg, and the calf muscles in the back lower leg. Cramps develop when the muscles deplete their supply of oxygen and glycogen, a carbohydrate energy source that is stored in muscles and in the liver. Cramps can also result from a chemical imbalance in the body, or when the body has insufficient water to help remove waste products. (See Muscle Aches and Pain, p. 172, and Heat-Related Problems, p. 330.)

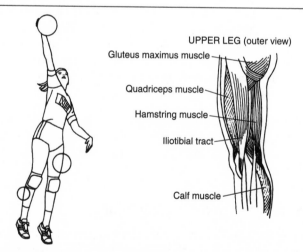

MUSCLE CRAMPS

UPPER LEG (outer view)

Gluteus maximus muscle

Quadriceps muscle

Hamstring muscle

Iliotibial tract

Calf muscle

Muscle cramps occur when the muscles tighten up during or because of continuous athletic activity or when dehydrated.

> Symptoms

Muscle cramps can be very painful. Stopping the activity that is causing the cramp can make it worse. However, continuing the activity is often impossible.

> Immediate Treatment

Some cramps can be severe. If the cramp is not relieved by the steps below, see your doctor to determine proper treatment.

Gently stretch out the muscle if possible. Massage it to help work out the cramp. If a heating pad is available, place it on the muscle to help relieve tightness. Continue massaging the muscle until the cramp goes away. Drink plenty of fluids.

Unless your doctor has prescribed another medication, take aspirin, ibuprofen, naproxen, or ketoprofen with food as directed to relieve pain and inflammation. (Acetaminophen relieves pain but has no effect against inflammation; ask your doctor or pharmacist for guidance.)

> Continued Care

You can usually resume athletic activity after an attack of cramps. If soreness persists, stop the activity and massage the muscle or use a heating pad to relax it. Take aspirin, ibuprofen, naproxen, or ketoprofen with food as directed to help relieve the pain and inflammation. See your physician if the cramps occur regularly during exercise. With proper treatment, muscle cramps rarely have long-term effects.

> How to Prevent Recurring Injury

Include foods in your diet that are high in potassium and calcium, including bananas, high-fiber cereals or bread, fresh vegetables, milk, yogurt, and cheese. Drink plenty of water before and during extended exercise or athletic activity; water helps the muscles eliminate waste products and helps you avoid dehydration. In some situations, such as engaging in sports during hot weather when the body may be working twice as hard, you might get cramps even when you've taken preventive measures.

SHOULDER INJURY

The shoulder is a complex ball-and-socket joint consisting of three main bones—the humerus (the upper part of the upper arm bone), the clavicle (the collarbone), and the scapula (or shoulder blade, the largest bone in the chest-shoulder region). The top of the humerus forms the ball in the joint and is attached by ligaments to the shoulder blade. Muscles travel over, under, and around the shoulder joint and provide stability. Tendons connect the muscles to bone. The shoulder allows the hand and arm to move. (For more information, see Shoulder Dislocation, p. 75, and Shoulder Separation, p. 76.)

SHOULDER DISLOCATION

In most cases of shoulder dislocation, the upper arm bone (humerus) pops out of the joint, usually toward the front. Ligaments, tendons, and other connective tissues are stretched or torn and may injure nerves and blood vessels in the shoulder region, sometimes causing numbness in the hand.

The injury can result from a traumatic event, such as a direct blow to or a fall on the shoulder, or from falling on an outstretched hand or arm. Susceptibility to shoulder dislocation may also be genetic, particularly if the shoulder pops out often or easily. Members of the same family are often affected. In some cases, the shoulder can dislocate during sleep. A shoulder dislocation is common in contact sports, especially football, and sports such as downhill skiing, lacrosse, hockey, volleyball, rugby, and soccer.

> Symptoms

A dislocated shoulder causes severe pain the moment the injury occurs. You may experience limited movement in the shoulder area, swelling, and bruising. The shoulder may look abnormal, with a large bump rising up under the skin on the front of the shoulder.

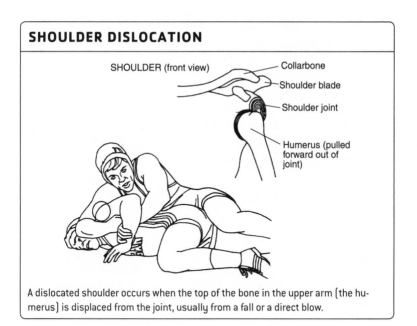

SHOULDER DISLOCATION

SHOULDER (front view)

Collarbone

Shoulder blade

Shoulder joint

Humerus (pulled forward out of joint)

A dislocated shoulder occurs when the top of the bone in the upper arm (the humerus) is displaced from the joint, usually from a fall or a direct blow.

> Immediate Treatment

Seek immediate medical treatment at a physician's office or hospital emergency department.

If possible, on your way to the doctor's office or hospital, apply an ice pack to the shoulder area. Cold treatments help stop internal bleeding and the accumulation of fluids in and around the injured area, thereby decreasing swelling. The shoulder may be put in a sling or wrapped to immobilize the area and aid recovery. (If you have a recurring dislocation, you may be able to pop the shoulder back into place yourself.) Your physician may recommend a nonsteroidal anti-inflammatory drug such as ibuprofen, naproxen, or ketoprofen to reduce swelling.

> Continued Care

Do not participate in sports until your shoulder has had time to heal, which may take 3 to 6 weeks, depending on the extent of the injury. With your physician's okay, work with a trainer or physical therapist to strengthen the muscles in the shoulder region. Take aspirin, ibuprofen, naproxen, or ketoprofen with food as directed to help reduce any pain and inflammation that may occur.

> Long-term Effects

With proper healing, the shoulder should regain its full range of motion. In some cases, especially after recurring dislocations, surgery may be recommended to help stabilize the shoulder.

> How to Prevent Recurring Injury

Avoid situations that could cause another shoulder injury. Wear layers of clothing or padding to help cushion a fall. Use weights and exercises recommended by a trainer or physical therapist to strengthen the muscles in the shoulder region. Muscle strengthening exercises also help strengthen ligaments and tendons. Use an ice pack to reduce any swelling. After the swelling subsides, use a heating pad.

SHOULDER SEPARATION

A shoulder separation occurs when ligaments that hold the collarbone to the shoulder blade are torn. The collarbone also may be pushed out of alignment. (For more information, see Collarbone Injury, p. 70.)

A shoulder separation usually results from an injury, such as a direct blow to or fall on the shoulder area. It can also result from falling on an outstretched hand or arm. The injury is very common in contact sports, especially football, and sports such as downhill skiing, lacrosse, hockey, volleyball, rugby, and soccer.

> Symptoms

A shoulder separation causes severe pain the moment the injury occurs. You may experience swelling, bruising, and limited movement in the shoulder area. The shoulder may have an abnormal shape.

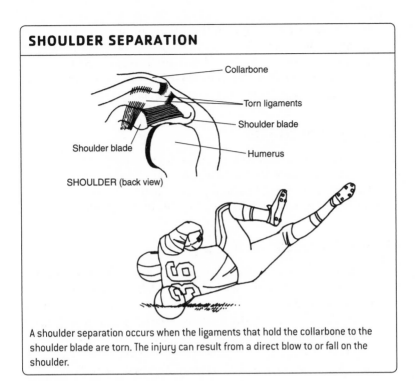

SHOULDER SEPARATION

Collarbone

Torn ligaments

Shoulder blade

Shoulder blade

Humerus

SHOULDER (back view)

A shoulder separation occurs when the ligaments that hold the collarbone to the shoulder blade are torn. The injury can result from a direct blow to or fall on the shoulder.

> Immediate Treatment

This injury always requires professional medical attention. Seek medical treatment at a doctor's office or hospital emergency department at once.

If possible, place an ice pack on the injury right after it occurs. Cold treatments help stop internal bleeding and the accumulation of fluids in and around the injured area, thereby decreasing swelling.

The doctor will put your shoulder in a sling or wrap it to immobilize the area and aid recovery. He or she may recommend a nonsteroidal anti-inflammatory drug such as ibuprofen, naproxen, or ketoprofen to reduce the pain and swelling.

> Continued Care

Do not participate in sports until the injury has healed, which may take 2 to 10 weeks, depending on the severity of the separation. With your physician's okay, work with a trainer or physical therapist to strengthen the muscles in the shoulder region. Take aspirin, ibuprofen, naproxen, or ketoprofen with food as directed to help reduce the pain and inflammation. See your physician if the pain and swelling reappear or if movement of the shoulder is limited.

> Long-term Effects

A shoulder separation usually has no lasting effects. Some people, however, may have pain, stiffness, or limitation of motion in their shoulder. In severe cases, surgery may be necessary; the surgery usually involves removing the outer ½-inch tip of the collarbone.

> How to Prevent Recurring Injury

Avoid situations that could cause another injury. Wear layers of clothing or padding to help cushion a fall. Use weights and exercises recommended by a trainer or physical therapist to strengthen the muscles in the shoulder region. Muscle-strengthening exercises also help strengthen ligaments and tendons. Once the swelling has subsided, apply a heating pad to aid recovery. Heat increases blood circulation in the area, providing vital nutrients to the injury and helping speed recovery.

SWIMMER'S SHOULDER

Swimmer's shoulder is a strain and, sometimes, a tiny tear, in the supraspinatus muscle on top of the shoulder between the neck and the top of the arm. Swimmer's shoulder can also result from a strain or tear in the rotator cuff, an intertwined unit of muscles and tendons that surrounds and gives stability to the shoulder at the ball-and-socket joint; this injury is called impingement syndrome.

Swimmer's shoulder is usually associated with a repetitive motion over time. It also can occur when a swimmer increases his or her distance or speed, or both, or uses an improper swimming stroke. Other sports that can cause swimmer's shoulder include baseball (pitching), football (passing), tennis (serving), racquetball, volleyball, basketball, golf, sailing, canoeing, kayaking, javelin throwing, shot putting, weight lifting, and rock climbing. Other activities that may cause swimmer's shoulder include those in which the arm is elevated above the head for a prolonged period, such as construction work, painting, plastering, or housework.

> Symptoms

Swimmer's shoulder causes pain on the top front part of the shoulder. You may experience pain from lying on your shoulder at night or pain and weakness when you extend the arm forward or upward. You may feel a painful "hitch" in the shoulder and have limited movement in the shoulder joint.

> Immediate Treatment

If you cannot extend your arm above your head or move your arm at all ("frozen shoulder"), or if there is a sharp pain and weakness where the arm connects to the trunk, see your doctor to determine proper treatment.

SWIMMER'S SHOULDER

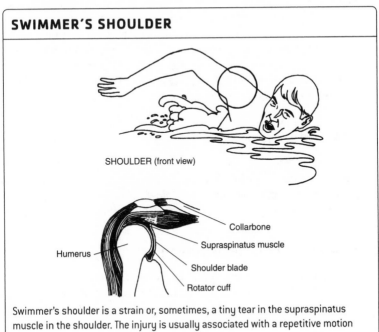

SHOULDER (front view)

Collarbone

Supraspinatus muscle

Humerus

Shoulder blade

Rotator cuff

Swimmer's shoulder is a strain or, sometimes, a tiny tear in the supraspinatus muscle in the shoulder. The injury is usually associated with a repetitive motion over time.

Stop the activity that is causing the pain. Place an ice pack on the shoulder intermittently (20 minutes every hour while you're awake) for the first 24 hours after the injury. Cold treatments help stop internal bleeding and the accumulation of fluids in and around the injured area, thereby decreasing swelling.

Unless your doctor has prescribed another medication, take aspirin, ibuprofen, naproxen, or ketoprofen with food as directed to relieve pain and inflammation. (Acetaminophen relieves pain but has no effect against inflammation; ask your doctor or pharmacist for guidance.) For severe inflammation or for a recurring case, your doctor may recommend an injection of a corticosteroid drug such as cortisone.

> Continued Care

Rest your arm for about 4 to 8 weeks. Do not engage in the activity that caused the injury until the pain has subsided. Ease into limited muscle workouts—for example, gradually swing your arm as if throwing a ball, work with light weights, and work with a trainer or physical therapist on light shoulder exercises that use and strengthen the injured muscle. Use an ice pack to help reduce any swelling that may recur, then apply a heating pad to help repair the injury. Take aspirin, ibuprofen, naproxen, or ketoprofen with food as directed to help reduce pain and inflammation. If the pain continues, is severe, or limits motion in your shoulder, see your physician.

> Long-term Effects

With proper treatment and rest, swimmer's shoulder seldom has any long-term effects, although some people experience recurring pain even with preventive measures (see below). In rare cases, surgery may be recommended to remove scar tissue from the rotator cuff area.

> How to Prevent Recurring Injury

Allow plenty of time for healing. Use weights and exercises recommended by a trainer or physical therapist to strengthen the shoulder muscle. Ask a swimming instructor or baseball or football coach about proper technique. You may need to continue to do these exercises throughout your life to avoid or reduce pain in your shoulder.

Part V

ENVIRONMENTAL INJURIES AND ILLNESSES

Environmental injuries and illnesses can occur at home or work, but are more likely to occur during camping, hiking, or other outdoor activities for which you may not be adequately prepared. Most injuries and illnesses can be prevented by considering the hazards (or dangers) that may be encountered and by planning for a possible delay in medical assistance. For example, if you are traveling to a desert climate, you will need to protect yourself from extreme sunlight, snakebites, scorpion stings, and the lack of water, among other things. Pre-travel preparation and planning must account for the situations and circumstances that will most likely be encountered. This includes having a portable first aid kit that includes basic supplies such as acetaminophen, naproxen or ibuprofen, diphenhydramine, bandages, splints, insect repellant, and sunscreen; being sure you have all appropriate vaccinations; and that you have an adequate supply of your prescription medications. Adequate food and water for the duration, as well as flashlights, batteries, and a cell phone are also necessary (see Part II). It is also important to stay fit and healthy. Always notify a family member or friend before any extended travel plans, particularly if you are traveling to potentially extreme or exotic environments.

ALTITUDE SICKNESS

Altitude sickness is caused by the reduced oxygen concentration in the air and decreased barometric pressure at high altitudes (above 7,000 feet).

> Symptoms

Altitude sickness can cause any or all of the following symptoms, usually within 12 to 24 hours after a person has arrived at a high altitude:

- Headache
- Extreme tiredness
- Light-headedness; fainting
- Feeling unable to catch one's breath (sometimes causing the person to try to breathe in more air, causing hyperventilation)

- Dry cough
- Pain in the chest; tightness in the throat
- Restlessness; inability to sleep
- Nausea; vomiting
- Fast heart rate
- Hallucinations
- Panic

> What to Do

If the person is not breathing:

1. Maintain an open airway; restore breathing and circulation, if necessary. (See CPR, pp. 33–49.)

2. Seek immediate medical attention.

If the person is breathing on his or her own:

1. Keep the person quiet and at rest until he or she can catch his or her breath. It is very important for you and others to remain calm so that the person will remain calm, which conserves oxygen and energy. Have the person breathe air from an auxiliary oxygen source, if available.

2. Do not continue climbing. The person may need to descend to a lower altitude. Do not send the person off alone. Stay with him or her.

3. Suggest that the person seek medical treatment, even after he or she has recovered and feels fine. Treatment with oxygen and medication may be necessary.

WARNING: LIFE-THREATENING SYMPTOMS

Seek immediate medical attention if a person experiences any of the following symptoms:

- Difficulty breathing
- Chest pain
- Confusion
- Decreased consciousness
- Loss of balance

> Preventing Altitude Sickness

If you have emphysema, heart disease, sickle cell anemia, epilepsy, or uncontrolled high blood pressure or have had a stroke, you may be at increased risk of altitude sickness and should talk to your doctor if you are planning to visit a high altitude. The following steps can help you avoid altitude sickness if you are traveling by air, mountain climbing, or visiting a place located at an altitude higher than you're used to:

- Ask your doctor about taking acetazolamide or asthma medication to prevent altitude sickness.

- Avoid alcohol, sedative drugs, and cigarettes for the first 2 days you are at an altitude higher than you're used to.

- Drink plenty of noncaffeinated fluids to avoid dehydration.

- Eat a diet high in carbohydrates (70 percent or more of total calories).

- Avoid strenuous exercise at high altitudes.

- If you are mountain climbing, gradually get your body acclimated to a higher altitude by climbing no more than 3,000 feet in 1 day and sleeping at the new altitude for two or three nights before continuing your ascent.

- If you are pregnant and not used to high altitudes, avoid altitudes over 10,000 feet. Check with your doctor.

- Symptoms of altitude sickness will improve by descending to a lower altitude.

ANIMAL AND INSECT BITES

ANIMAL BITES

Animal bites can result in serious infections—including rabies and tetanus—as well as in tissue damage. Bite wounds can become infected with bacteria or other organisms in the saliva or mouth of the biting animal. Bites can cause everything from mild, local infections to generalized serious and sometimes fatal illness.

Most animal bite wounds are minor and the victim never seeks medical attention. If you do not seek immediate attention after a bite has occurred, then watch closely for possible infection.

> General Symptoms

The following general signs and symptoms may signal a possible infection or that the bite wound may be contaminated (such as with teeth, clothes, or dirt):

- Redness at or around the bite site
- Swelling
- Pus (thick) drainage from the wound
- Increasing pain
- Localized warmth at the bite site
- Red streaks leading away from the bite site

■ RABIES

Rabies is a disease that humans may get from being bitten by an animal infected with the rabies virus. Despite medical advances in diagnosing and preventing this disease, rabies is almost always deadly in persons who do not receive treatment. Rabies can be totally prevented. It is important to recognize the possibility of exposure and get medical care promptly before symptoms develop.

ANIMALS THAT MAY CARRY RABIES

- Almost any wild or domestic animal can potentially get rabies (including dogs and cats) but it is very rare in small rodents (rats, squirrels, chipmunks). Large rodents (beavers, woodchucks/groundhogs) have been found to have rabies in some areas of the United States.

- Raccoons are the most common wild animals infected with rabies in the United States. Skunks, foxes, bats, and coyotes are also frequently affected. Of these animals, bats are the most likely to transmit rabies to humans in the United States.

- Cats are the most common domestic animals with rabies in the United States; dogs are the most common domestic rabid animals worldwide.

- Fish, reptiles, and birds are not known to carry the rabies virus.

> Rabies Symptoms

Signs and symptoms of rabies in animals:

- Animals infected with rabies may appear sick, crazed, or vicious. This is the origin of the phrase "mad dog." However, animals infected with rabies may also appear overly friendly or confused. They may even appear completely normal.

- Seeing a normally nocturnal wild animal during the day (for example, a bat or a fox) or seeing a normally shy wild animal that appears strange or even friendly should raise suspicion that the animal may have rabies.

Signs and symptoms of rabies in humans:

- The average incubation period (time from infection to time of development of symptoms) in humans is 30 to 60 days, but it may range from less than 10 days to several years.

- Most people first develop symptoms of pain, tingling, or itching shooting from the bite site (or site of virus entry).

- Nonspecific complaints of fevers, chills, fatigue, muscle aches, and irritability may accompany these complaints. Early on, these complaints may seem like any virus, except for the "shooting sensations" from the bite site.

- Gradually, the person will become extremely ill, developing a variety of symptoms, including high fever, confusion, agitation, and eventually seizures and coma.

- Typically, people with rabies develop irregular contractions and spasms of the breathing muscles when exposed to water (this is termed hydrophobia). They may demonstrate the same response to a puff of air directed at them (termed aerophobia). By this point, they are obviously extremely ill.

- Eventually, the various organs of the body are affected, and the person dies despite support with medication and respirator support.

> What to Do (For Any Animal Bite)

1. Immediately clean the wound thoroughly with a 1- to 5-percent solution of povidone-iodine or with soap and running water for 5 minutes or more to wash out contaminating organisms. Do not put medication, antiseptics, or home remedies on the wound.

2. Put a sterile bandage or clean, dry cloth over the wound. If it is bleeding, apply continuous pressure to the wound for 5 minutes or until the bleeding stops.

3. Seek medical attention promptly, particularly for a bite on the face, neck, or hands, which can develop into a serious infection. If some skin tissue, such as a part of an ear or a nose, is bitten off, bring it to the hospital emergency department or doctor's office with the person (see Amputations, p. 60).

4. Also seek medical attention if:

   > Swelling increases after the third day.

   > There is redness or streaking, or if there is excessive drainage from the bite wound.

   > You develop a fever greater than 101°F (38.3°C).

   > The wound is large and you can't stop the bleeding. Larger wounds may require stitches.

   > You have not had a tetanus shot in the past 5 years.

   > You were bitten by an unknown wild animal.

5. If you suspect that an animal has rabies, notify the local police, health department, or animal control authority immediately. It is very important to catch and confine any animal that has bitten someone so that it can be observed and evaluated for rabies. Do not attempt to catch the animal yourself.

> Avoiding Animal Bites

- Don't tease, provoke, or surprise an animal, especially when it is resting or eating.

- Don't keep wild animals as pets.

- Don't make any sudden moves or gestures toward a strange animal.

- If confronted by an animal, back away slowly and calmly.

- If an animal looks sick to you, don't touch it.

- Always wash your hands with soap and water after touching animals and before eating.

LIZARD BITES

The Gila monster and the Mexican beaded lizard are the only poisonous lizards found in North America, usually in southern Arizona and northwestern Mexico. Both of these lizards are longer than 1 foot and have heavy bodies with a beadlike surface, flat heads, short legs, and round, thick tails. The Gila monster's skin is patterned in pink or orange and black; the Mexican beaded lizard's skin is dark purple and black. Although poisonous, their bites are rarely fatal. The Gila monster hangs on tenaciously when it bites and must be removed carefully to prevent the teeth from remaining embedded in the skin.

> Symptoms

Bites from a Gila monster or Mexican beaded lizard can cause any or all of the following symptoms:

- Immediate, intense pain that shoots up from the site of the bite (usually the arm or leg)
- Swelling at the site of the bite
- Blueness of the skin at the site of the bite
- Nausea and/or vomiting
- Fainting
- Weakness

- Sweating
- Fever and chills
- High blood pressure

> What to Do

If you are being bitten by a Gila monster and it is holding on by its teeth:

Try to remove it without breaking its teeth by quickly and carefully submerging the affected area of your body (and the lizard) in cold water. If this doesn't release the lizard's hold, place a strong stick between the bitten area and the back of the lizard's mouth and push the stick against the rear of the lizard's jaw. Do not try to remove any teeth that are still embedded in the skin; a doctor will need to remove them. Once the lizard lets go, continue with steps 1 through 4 below.

For a bite by a Gila monster or a Mexican beaded lizard:

1. Wash the wound thoroughly with soap and water and rinse it under running water for 10 to 20 minutes.

2. Cover the wound with a clean dressing and apply pressure for 5 minutes if the wound is bleeding.

3. Immobilize the affected limb at heart level.

4. Seek medical attention immediately.

See also: Severe Allergic Reactions to Insect Stings (Anaphylactic Shock), p. 336; Unconsciousness, p. 233.

MOSQUITO BITES

Mosquito bites are annoying but rarely serious. Some mosquitoes, however, can transmit serious diseases such as West Nile encephalitis, malaria, and dengue fever.

> Symptoms

A "normal" reaction to a mosquito bite can vary. Some people will have only a small area of redness, swelling, and itching that typically goes away within 24 hours. Others may have a larger area of itching that can last for several days. Rarely, an individual may have a serious reaction to mosquito bites, which results in swelling in the throat, hives, and wheezing. This life-threatening condition (anaphylaxis) requires immediate medical attention.

> What to Do

1. Wash the infected area with soap and water as soon as you recognize that you've been bitten. Try to keep the site clean and dry until the irritation abates.

2. Avoid scratching. Although a mosquito bite should itch for only a few days, continual scratching may prolong the itching and may lead to infection.

3. Over-the-counter medications are usually enough to treat the itch and any swelling. You can use calamine lotion or a 1-percent hydrocortisone cream to relieve the itching. Use of aloe vera gel may reduce swelling and itching. If you have a large local reaction, consider taking an antihistamine, such as diphenhydramine (Benadryl) to see if it helps. Follow directions on these packages for safe use.

4. Consult your doctor if you're concerned about the severity of your reaction.

■ WEST NILE VIRUS

The West Nile virus is transmitted by mosquitoes. Most people who are infected experience no signs or symptoms. However, some people can develop a life-threatening illness that includes inflammation of the brain.

> Symptoms

Most people who are infected with West Nile virus will not develop any type of illness (an asymptomatic infection). Symptoms of mild disease include:

- Fever
- Headache
- Muscle aches

- Tiredness
- Lack of appetite
- A skin rash may be present (on the trunk of the body), as well as swollen lymph glands.

A small percentage (less than 1 percent) of infected people develop a more severe form of disease. Although serious illness can occur in people of any age, those over 50 and those whose immune system is not functioning optimally are at the highest risk for getting severely ill when infected with West Nile virus. The symptoms of severe disease (also called West Nile encephalitis or West Nile meningitis) include:

- Severe headache
- High fever
- Stiff neck
- Confusion
- Coma
- Seizures
- Muscle weakness

> What to Do

1. There is no specific medication for West Nile virus infection.

2. Fluids, rest, and acetaminophen are recommended for mild disease.

3. Seek immediate care for any symptoms of severe disease (high fever, severe headache, stiff neck, confusion, coma, seizures, weakness).

4. People with severe disease often need to be hospitalized to provide intravenous fluids and respiratory support.

> Avoiding Mosquito Bites

- Avoid exposure to mosquitoes and mosquito-breeding sites (such as pools of standing water and garbage dumps).
- Avoid unnecessary outdoor activity at dawn, dusk, and early evening, when mosquitoes are most active.

- Wear long-sleeved shirts and long pants when you go into mosquito-infested areas.

- Stay in screened or air-conditioned rooms or use an electric fan in your room.

- Consider covering your infant's stroller or playpen with mosquito netting when outside.

- Apply mosquito repellent with DEET (N, N diethylmetatoluamide) to your skin and clothing. The repellent is available in varying strengths up to 100 percent. Choose the concentration based on the hours of protection you need—the higher the percentage (concentration) of the active ingredient, the longer the repellent will work. Keep in mind that chemical repellants can be toxic, and use only the amount needed for the time you'll be outdoors. Don't use DEET on the hands of young children or on infants under 2 months of age. According to the Centers for Disease Control and Prevention, oil of lemon eucalyptus, a more natural product, offers the same protection as DEET when used in similar concentrations. Always follow the recommendations on the product label.

- If you have concerns about the use of DEET or other insect repellants, talk with your doctor.

SNAKE BITES

When you are bitten by a snake, it is important to know whether it is poisonous. Poisonous snakes in the United States include the rattlesnake, cottonmouth (water moccasin), copperhead, and coral snake. Rattlesnakes can be found all over the country and are responsible for two out of three poisonous snakebites in the United States. Cottonmouth and copperhead snakes are found primarily in the southeast and south central parts of the United States. Coral snakes are found primarily in the southeast. Snakebites are most common during the summer months and usually affect the arms or legs.

■ POISONOUS SNAKES

The rattlesnake, cottonmouth, and copperhead have a triangular-shaped head and deep pits (poison sacs) between the nostrils and the eyes. They also have slit-like eyes rather than the round eyes of non-

The rattlesnake (left), cottonmouth (center), and copperhead (right) have deep poison pits between their nostrils and eyes, slit-like eyes, and two long fangs. A unique feature of the rattlesnake is the set of rattles at the end of the tail. A distinctive feature of the cottonmouth (also called a water moccasin) is the white coloring inside the mouth. Unique features of the copperhead are a copper-colored head and a pinkish-gray body with a brown hourglass pattern.

poisonous snakes. The coral snake is an exception—instead of the slit-like eyes of the other poisonous snakes, it has round eyes. Poisonous snakes also have long fangs that leave distinctive marks followed by a row of tooth marks. Most nonpoisonous snakes, by contrast, have rounded heads and round eyes. They do not have pits between their eyes and nostrils and they do not have fangs.

The coral snake is a member of the cobra family. It has red, yellow, and black rings. The yellow rings are narrow and always separate the red rings from the black. A rhyme to remember that identifies the coral snake is "Red on yellow will kill a fellow, red on black won't hurt Jack." The coral snake is smaller than the pit vipers, has round eyes like nonpoisonous snakes, and always has a black nose. Its venom is highly toxic to humans. Unlike the other poisonous snakes, which usually bite once and let go, the coral snake hangs on and chews the person's flesh.

▪ RATTLESNAKE, COTTONMOUTH, OR COPPERHEAD BITES

If there is no swelling within 4 hours of a snakebite, the snake was probably not poisonous, but you should still seek medical attention. Bites from poisonous and nonpoisonous snakes can cause infection.

> Symptoms

Bites from a rattlesnake, cottonmouth, or copperhead can cause any or all of the following symptoms:

- Severe pain
- Rapid swelling
- Discoloration of the skin around the bite
- Weakness
- Nausea and vomiting
- Difficulty breathing
- Blurred vision
- Convulsions
- Numbness in arms or legs
- Redness at site of bite

> What to Do

If the person is not breathing:

1. Call 911 (or your local emergency medical dispatch number) or transport the person immediately to the nearest hospital emergency department.

2. Maintain an open airway. Restore breathing and circulation if necessary. (See CPR, pp. 33–49.)

If the person is breathing and a snakebite kit is available:

1. Place suction cups from the kit over the wound and draw out body fluids containing venom. This measure is most effective when used within minutes of the snakebite. Carefully follow the instructions in the kit.

2. Keep the person quiet to slow circulation, which will help stop the spread of the venom.

3. Remove rings, watches, and other jewelry.

4. Wash the bite area thoroughly with soap and water. Do not apply ice water or ice; it could damage the tissue.

5. Cover the wound with a sterile or clean bandage.

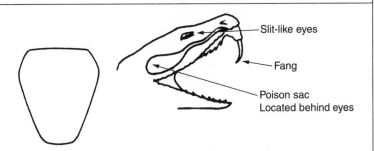

CHARACTERISTICS OF SOME POISONOUS SNAKES

Slit-like eyes

Fang

Poison sac
Located behind eyes

Most poisonous snakes have a triangular-shaped head (left), oval or slit-like eyes, deep pits (poison sacs) between their nostrils and eyes, and fangs (right). The rattlesnake, copperhead, and cottonmouth all share these characteristics. The coral snake is an exception because it has round eyes.

6. Immobilize a bitten arm or leg with a splint or other suitable device and keep it just below the level of the heart. Do not let the person walk unless absolutely necessary, and then slowly.

7. Give the person small sips of water if desired and if he or she has no difficulty swallowing. Do not give water if the person is nauseated, vomiting, having convulsions, or unconscious. Do not give the person alcoholic beverages.

8. Seek medical attention promptly, preferably at the nearest hospital emergency department. If possible, have someone telephone ahead to tell of the poisonous snakebite and type of snake so that anti-venom serum can be readied.

▪ CORAL SNAKE BITES

> Symptoms

Symptoms from a coral snake bite, which may not occur for up to 6 hours after the bite, may include any or all of the following:

- Slight pain and swelling at the site of the bite
- Blurred vision
- Drooping eyelids
- Difficulty speaking or swallowing

CORAL SNAKE

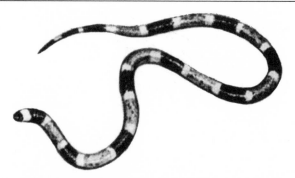

Unlike the rattlesnake, copperhead, and cottonmouth, the coral snake has round rather than slit-like eyes. It has fangs like the other poisonous snakes. Its markings consist of yellow, red, and black rings, with the narrow yellow rings always separating the red rings from the black. The coral snake always has a black nose and is about 2 to 4 feet long.

- Heavy drooling
- Drowsiness
- Heavy sweating
- Nausea and vomiting
- Difficulty breathing
- Paralysis
- Pain in joints
- Confusion
- Weakness
- Dizziness
- Slurred speech

> What to Do

If the person is not breathing:

1. Call 911 (or your local emergency medical dispatch number) or transport the person immediately to the nearest hospital emergency department.

2. Maintain an open airway. Restore breathing and circulation if necessary. (See CPR, pp. 33–49.)

If the person is breathing and a snakebite kit is available:

1. Place suction cups from the kit over the wound and draw out body fluids containing venom. This measure is most effective when used within minutes of the snakebite. Carefully follow the instructions in the kit. Do not try to mouth suction the bite.

2. Keep the person quiet to slow circulation, which will help stop the spread of the venom.

3. Remove rings, watches, and other jewelry.

4. Wash the bite area thoroughly with soap and water. Do not apply ice water or ice; it could damage the tissue.

5. Cover the wound with a sterile or clean bandage.

6. Immobilize a bitten arm or leg with a splint or other suitable device and keep it just below the level of the heart. Do not let the person walk unless absolutely necessary, and then slowly.

7. Give the person small sips of water if desired and if he or she has no difficulty swallowing. Do not give water if the person is nauseated, vomiting, having convulsions, or unconscious. Do not give the person alcoholic beverages.

8. Seek medical attention promptly, preferably at the nearest hospital emergency department. If possible, have someone telephone ahead to tell of the poisonous snakebite and type of snake so that anti-venom serum can be readied.

▪ NON-POISONOUS SNAKES

> Symptoms

Bites from non-poisonous snakes can cause any or all of the following symptoms:

- Pain
- Swelling
- Mild bleeding

> What to Do

1. Keep the affected area below the level of the person's heart.

2. Remove all rings, watches, and other jewelry.

3. Clean the area thoroughly with soap and water. Do not apply ice or ice water to the bite.

4. Put a bandage or clean cloth over the wound.

5. Seek medical attention. Medication or a tetanus shot may be necessary.

> Avoiding Snakebites

Some bites, such as those inflicted when you step on a snake in the woods, are nearly impossible to prevent. However, there are precautions that can reduce your chances of being bitten. These include:

- Leaving snakes alone. Many people are bitten because they try to kill a snake or get too close to it.

- Staying out of tall grass unless you wear thick leather boots, and remain on hiking paths as much as possible.

- Keeping hands and feet out of areas you cannot see. Do not pick up rocks or firewood unless you are out of a snake's striking distance.

- Being cautious and alert when climbing rocks.

SPIDER BITES

■ BLACK WIDOW SPIDER BITE

Black widow spider bites are particularly harmful to very young children, the elderly, and the chronically ill. The spiders appear most often during the summer months, usually in garages, barns, and garbage heaps. Their webs have an irregular shape, unlike most other spider webs.

BLACK WIDOW SPIDER

The black widow spider has a shiny black body less than 1 inch in length. Its unique feature is a red hourglass marking on the underside of its body.

> Symptoms

The bite of a black widow spider can cause any or all of the following symptoms:

- Slight redness and swelling around the bite
- Sharp pain around the bite
- Profuse sweating
- Nausea and vomiting
- Severe stomach cramps or hard, rigid abdomen within 1 hour of the bite
- Possible muscle cramps in other parts of the body
- Tightness in the chest and difficulty breathing and talking
- Weakness
- Swelling of the face

> What to Do

If the person is not breathing:

1. Call 911 (or your local emergency medical dispatch number) or take the person to the nearest hospital emergency department.

2. Maintain an open airway. Restore breathing and circulation if necessary. (See CPR, pp. 33–49.)

If the person is breathing:

1. Keep the bitten area lower than the person's heart. If the person was bitten on the arm or leg, immobilize the extremity with a splint.
2. Place ice wrapped in cloth or cold compresses on the bitten area.
3. Keep the person quiet.
4. Seek medical attention promptly, preferably at the nearest hospital emergency department.

▪ BROWN RECLUSE SPIDER BITE

Brown recluse spiders are found from spring to fall, usually in attics, closets, storage sheds, woodpiles, or vacant buildings, or under rocks. They are especially active at night and people often get bites while sleeping on sheets that have been in long-term storage. Brown recluse spider bites are particularly harmful to very young children and older people, causing severe, deep, irreversible tissue damage around the bite area. Immediate medical attention is required.

> Symptoms

The bite of a brown recluse spider can cause any or all of the following symptoms:

- A stinging sensation at the time of the bite
- Redness at the site of the bite, which later disappears as a blister forms

---

BROWN RECLUSE SPIDER

The brown recluse spider (also called the fiddleback or violin spider) is characterized by a dark brown violin-shaped marking on the top front portion of its body.

WARNING: LIFE-THREATENING SYMPTOMS

If a person who has been bitten by a brown recluse spider develops the following symptoms within 48 hours, take him or her immediately to the nearest hospital emergency department:

- Fever
- Blood in urine
- Rash
- Joint pain

- Pain that may become more severe over the next 8 hours
- Chills, fever, nausea, vomiting, joint pains, and rash over the next 48 hours
- Destruction of tissue that may form an open ulcer that could persist for months
- Blood in urine within 1 day of bite

> What to Do

Follow steps for "Black Widow Spider Bite," pp. 309–310.

■ TARANTULA BITE

Tarantula bites are not usually as serious as those of the black widow spider or the brown recluse spider. Tarantulas are usually between 1 and 3 inches long and tend to move more slowly than other spiders.

> Symptoms

The bite of a tarantula may cause any or all of the following symptoms:

- Severe itching
- Mild pain at the time of the bite
- A severe, painful wound a few days after the bite

> What to Do

1. Pull off spider hairs with adhesive or cellophane tape.
2. Wash the area with soap and water.

TARANTULA

The tarantula is a large spider with a very hairy body and legs.

3. Place ice wrapped in cloth or cold compresses on the bite area.

4. Elevate the affected part of the body above the level of the heart.

5. To relieve discomfort, take an antihistamine and/or a pain reliever such as ibuprofen, naproxen, or acetaminophen as directed.

6. If the person has shortness of breath, weakness, or chest pain, or if he or she faints, call 911 (or your local emergency medical dispatch number) or take him or her to the nearest hospital emergency department.

> Avoiding Spider Bites

- Pay attention. People who get bitten usually do not see the spider beforehand. Few spiders are truly aggressive; most are timid and will retreat if given a chance. Bites occur because someone invades the spider's space. Some bites occur, for example, when people put their hands in garden or household gloves that have been lying around, or when someone (particularly children) puts on clothes that have been lying on the floor or in a closet. Walking in bare feet, particularly at night, can lead to a bite as the spider lashes out as it is about to be crushed. Some recluse and widow bites occur because people unwittingly reach into or bump their webs and provoke an attack.

- Wear gloves if working in an area where spiders are likely to live.

- Avoid wood or rock piles and dark areas where spiders live.

- Look for spiders in low-lying webs in garages and barbecue grills, around swimming pools, and in woodpiles.

- Clear away old furniture, tires, junk, newspaper, and old clothes. This will eliminate places spider like to live.

- Plug openings and crevices into the house.
- Move your bed away from walls so spiders will be less likely to creep into bed with you.
- Shake out and check bedding for spiders before getting in the bed.
- Shake out and check clothing and shoes for spiders before putting them on.
- Do not leave your child's toys outside.
- Consider spraying insecticides on any high-risk areas, such as known black widow spider webs, indoor cracks and crevices, closets, attics, woodpiles, and under eaves and around baseboards and window areas. Repeat treatment is usually necessary.
- If a spider gets on you, brush it off. Do not crush it.

TICK BITES

Ticks are insects that thrive in wooded and grassy areas and feed on animals such as deer, mice, and rabbits. Ticks can transmit disease-causing organisms from animals to people. People who live near wooded and grassy areas or who camp or hike near them are most susceptible to tick bites. Family pets can transport ticks into the home. The worst time of the year for tick infestation is May through August. Because of the risk of developing a serious infection from a tick bite—especially Lyme disease (see p. 314) or Rocky Mountain spotted fever (see p. 316)—you should always see your doctor for an evaluation if you have been bitten by a tick or even suspect that you have been bitten by one. Your doctor will probably give you a blood test to determine if you have an infection. If the initial blood test is negative, as it often is in the early stages of infection, your doctor may ask you to return for additional blood tests. Both Lyme disease and Rocky Mountain spotted fever can be treated successfully with antibiotics in the early stages.

> What to Do

To remove a tick from the skin:

1. Do not touch the tick with your fingers; put on a pair of rubber gloves if you have them or protect your fingers with a tissue. Do

TICKS

Normal-size tick

Tick engorged with blood

Ticks are tiny, about ¹/₈ inch in length. When biting a person or animal, a tick attaches itself to the skin with its mouth and, engorged with blood, expands to five to seven times its original size.

not use a match or lighted cigarette on the tick because doing so could cause the tick to embed itself farther in the skin.

2. To remove a tick, use tweezers to grasp the tick's head and mouth as close to the skin as possible (but being careful not to crush or twist the tick's body). Pull the tick out gently but firmly and steadily in one piece. If the tick's head breaks off from the body, it could become embedded in the skin.

3. Dispose of the tick by flushing it down the toilet or placing it in a jar of alcohol.

4. Wash your hands thoroughly with soap and water.

5. Clean the wound with an antiseptic such as rubbing alcohol.

6. See a doctor to determine proper treatment and to make sure the tick's whole body has been removed.

If the tick becomes embedded in the skin:

1. Pinch the outer layer of skin that contains the embedded head and mouth of the tick and carefully scrape it (do not cut it) with a sharp, sterilized single-edge razor blade.

2. Clean the wound with an antiseptic such as rubbing alcohol.

3. If you don't want to remove the tick's head yourself, see a physician. You should see a physician anyway after removing a tick to make sure you have removed all of it.

▪ LYME DISEASE

Lyme disease, named for its discovery in Old Lyme, Connecticut, is a bacterial infection transmitted by the bite of a tick. The tick that can carry Lyme disease thrives in wooded and grassy areas throughout the United States and acquires the bacteria by feeding on infected deer and mice.

Although Lyme disease is not life threatening, it can be debilitating. In untreated cases, the disease can lead to heart irregularities, muscle weakness or numbness in the face and limbs, sensitivity to touch, arthritis, and meningitis (inflammation of the membranes that cover the brain and spinal cord).

> Symptoms

If you notice any or all of the following symptoms of Lyme disease (some of which may not appear for several days or months after the tick bite), seek medical attention immediately:

- A round, red, expanding rash or blotch at the site of the bite within 3 to 30 days after the bite (not everyone develops a rash). As the rash expands, the central part may appear pale and the border deep red, resembling a bull's-eye. The area is about 6 inches in diameter and usually appears at the site of the bite. The rash may persist for 3 to 5 weeks.

- Fever

- Chills

- Headache

- Stiff neck

- Fatigue

- Muscle and joint pain

- Dizziness

- Memory disturbance

- Red eyes

> What to Do

Most patients are cured with a few weeks of antibiotics taken by mouth. Patients with more severe forms of the illness may require intravenous treatment.

▪ ROCKY MOUNTAIN SPOTTED FEVER

Rocky Mountain spotted fever is a serious but rare infection transmitted by the bite of a tick. Although first recognized in the Rocky Mountains, the disease can occur anywhere in the United States and in Canada. The infection is caused by a parasitic microorganism called rickettsia. The tick feeds on small mammals, such as rabbits and rodents, and can then transmit the rickettsia from the animals to people. If you notice any of the symptoms listed below, seek medical attention immediately.

> Symptoms

Rocky Mountain spotted fever can cause any or all of the following symptoms, which may appear suddenly or not appear for several weeks after the bite:

- Headache
- Fever (usually high)
- Loss of appetite
- Nausea and/or vomiting
- Rash (pink to deep red spots) that appears first (within 2 to 5 days after the bite) on the wrists and ankles and then spreads to the palms of the hands, the soles of the feet, the forearms, and eventually the rest of the body
- Swelling of the inner eyelids and around the eyes
- Swelling of the feet and hands

> What To Do

Appropriate antibiotic treatment should be started immediately whenever Rocky Mountain spotted fever is suspected.

> Avoiding Tick Bites

The following steps can help you avoid tick bites when you're in an area that could be infested with ticks:

- Ticks prefer wooded and bushy areas with high grass and a lot of leaf litter. These are areas to avoid. At home, mow your lawn regularly; clear out brush and leaf litter; stack woodpiles neatly in a dry location, preferably off the ground; remove leaves and the remains of plants from the garden in the fall.

- Always wear shoes or boots and socks, long pants with socks over the bottom of the pants, and a long-sleeved shirt tucked into the pants when camping or hiking. Wear light-colored clothing with a tight weave so you can see the ticks more easily and avoid skin contact. Keep long hair pulled back; comb or brush your hair after hiking.

- Check all parts of your body and your clothes for ticks twice a day and brush yourself and your companions with a broom or towel after hiking. Inspect all parts of your body carefully. including your armpits, scalp, and groin. Remove ticks immediately using fine-tipped tweezers.

- Remove ticks from your clothes before going indoors. To kill ticks that you may have missed, wash your clothes with hot water and dry them using high heat for at least one hour.

- Shower and shampoo your hair after leaving a tick-infested area.

- Keep towels and clothing off the ground at camping areas and at the beach.

- Walk only on marked, clear, well-worn trails whenever possible.

- Use an insect repellent with chemicals specifically made to kill ticks (such as DEET [N, N-diethylmeta-toluamide] or permethrin).

- Check with your veterinarian for sprays or powders to use on pets.

- Ask your doctor or local health department and park or extension service about tick-infested areas to avoid.

COLD-RELATED PROBLEMS

FROSTBITE

Frostbite is freezing of parts of the body due to exposure to very low temperatures. Frostbite occurs when ice crystals form in the fluid in the cells of the skin and other tissues. The toes, fingers, nose, and ears are affected most often. A person is more susceptible to frostbite if he or she is in cold, windy weather after consuming alcohol or getting his or her skin wet.

> Symptoms

Frostbite can cause any or all of the following symptoms:

- Redness and stinging, burning pain (in early stages)
- White or grayish yellow, waxy-looking skin (in later stages)
- Swelling
- Throbbing
- Coldness and numbness
- Absence of pain (in later stages)
- Blisters

> What to Do

1. While outside, cover the frozen part with extra clothing or a warm cloth. If the hand or fingers are frostbitten, put the hand

> **WARNING: SEVERE FROSTBITE**
>
> If severe frostbite has occurred, the person may not have feeling in the frostbitten areas. The skin may be black, which indicates that skin tissue has died. In this case, cover the frostbitten areas with a dry dressing and take the person without delay to the nearest hospital emergency department for treatment. Take extreme care that frostbitten skin is not exposed to cold before it has thawed completely.

under the armpit for additional warmth. Do not rub the frostbitten part with snow or anything else.

2. Bring the person inside promptly and remove any wet, cold, or constricting clothing from the frostbitten area.

3. Seek medical attention promptly.

4. Rewarm the frostbitten area rapidly (which will probably cause some pain). Put the person's frostbitten part in warm (not hot) water that is between 104°F and 108°F. Test the water with a thermometer or by applying it to your forearm. Rewarming usually takes about half an hour.

5. If warm water is not available, gently wrap the frostbitten part in blankets or other warm, dry materials. Do not use heat lamps, hot water bottles, or heating pads. Do not allow the person to place the frostbitten part near a hot stove or radiator (parts could become burned because of the lack of pain sensation).

6. Put sterile gauze between frostbitten fingers or toes to keep them separated. Keep the frostbitten parts elevated, if possible.

7. Give the person warm drinks such as tea, coffee, or soup. Do not give alcoholic beverages (alcohol restricts blood flow).

8. Stop the warming process when the skin becomes its normal color and/or feeling begins to come back. Do not break blisters (blisters are a natural barrier against infection). Take extreme care that the frostbitten area is not exposed to cold until it has thawed completely. Ibuprofen may help relieve the pain.

9. Have the person move the fingers or toes as soon as they are warmed. Do not allow a person with frostbitten feet or toes to walk. This may cause further damage to the frostbitten part.

HYPOTHERMIA

Hypothermia is chilling of the entire body to 95°F. Hypothermia may result from immersion in very cold water, prolonged exposure to extremely cold weather, or wearing damp clothing in very cold conditions.

> Symptoms

Hypothermia can cause any or all of the following symptoms:

- Shivering
- Numbness

- Drowsiness or sleepiness

- Muscle weakness

- Dizziness

- Nausea

- Low body temperature

- Unconsciousness, if entire body is severely chilled or frozen

- Weak, slow pulse

- Large pupils

> What to Do

1. Call 911 (or your local emergency medical dispatch number). Maintain an open airway. Restore breathing and circulation, if necessary. (See CPR, pp. 33–49.)

2. Bring the person into a warm room as soon as possible.

3. Remove wet clothes.

4. Have the person lie down and wrap him or her in warm blankets, a sleeping bag, towels, additional clothing, or sheets. Do not massage the arms or legs because you could worsen any muscle damage.

5. If the person is conscious, give him or her comfortably warm drinks such as hot chocolate, soup, or warm gelatin (in liquid form). Do not give the person alcoholic beverages.

6. Check and treat for frostbite (p. 318), if necessary.

MILD CHILLING

For mild chilling, put the person in a warm room and wrap him or her in warm blankets. Give the person warm drinks such as coffee, tea, or soup. Do not give the person alcoholic beverages.

> Preventing Cold-related Problems

Here are some steps you can take to avoid frostbite and other problems during cold weather:

- Wear polyester (not cotton) underwear and several layers of loose-fitting clothing. Goose down, polypropylene, wool, and polyester are all good insulating materials.
- Do not wear tight, constricting socks or boots. Wear thin socks against your skin and one or two pairs of heavier outer socks.
- Try to keep your hands and feet dry and avoid sweating.
- Wear mittens instead of gloves; mittens should be loose.
- Never touch metal objects with your bare skin.
- Never travel or work alone out of doors in extremely cold weather.
- Avoid dehydration by drinking plenty of fluids.
- Avoid alcohol, barbiturates, and cigarettes.
- If you are an older person, set your indoor thermostat above 70°F. Consider using an electric blanket for sleeping.

See also: Unconsciousness, p. 233.

DECOMPRESSION SICKNESS

Decompression sickness, also known as the bends, occurs when an individual rises too quickly from a compressed atmosphere (such as very deep water) to a higher altitude. Doing so can cause air bubbles—mostly nitrogen—to form in the blood. An air bubble that travels to the brain can cause instant death. The condition occurs in varying degrees of severity, usually in inexperienced divers and, rarely, in miners.

> Symptoms

Decompression sickness may cause any or all of the following symptoms:

- Itchy rash, especially on the trunk, ears, wrists, or hands
- Blotchy purple rash near the waist
- Numbness and/or tingling, especially around the waist
- Dizziness or ringing in the ears
- Nausea or vomiting
- Pain that causes the person to bend over
- Difficulty breathing
- Paralysis
- Bleeding from the nose or ears
- Pain in the joints

> What to Do

If the person is not breathing:

1. Call 911 (or your local emergency medical dispatch number) or take the person to the nearest hospital emergency department. The person will need immediate medical attention (oxygen therapy).

2. Maintain an open airway. Restore breathing and circulation if necessary. (See CPR, pp. 33–49.)

If the person is breathing but unconscious:

1. Place him or her on his or her side to prevent choking on vomit.

2. Call 911 (or your local emergency medical dispatch number) or take the person to the nearest hospital emergency department. The person will need immediate medical attention (oxygen therapy).

> Preventing Decompression Sickness

If you have heart disease or a lung condition, do not dive without talking to your doctor first. Here are some steps you can take to avoid decompression sickness:

- Avoid dehydration by drinking plenty of fluids before diving.

- Do shallow dives.

- Ascend slowly (no faster than 16 to 23 feet per minute).

- Do not fly within 24 hours of diving.

- If you have had an episode of decompression sickness, do not dive again for at least 4 weeks.

DROWNING

In all emergencies involving a drowning person, remember first to be careful for your own safety. In deep water, a drowning person can drag a rescuer under water. Keep calm and do not overestimate your strength. If another person is with you, have that person call 911 or the local medical emergency dispatch number for help.

People who have been submerged in cold water (below 70°F) often can survive without brain damage. Some persons have been submerged for as long as 38 minutes and have lived. A reflex most prominent in young children slows the heartbeat and reserves the oxygen in the blood for the heart and brain. Rescue breathing and CPR must be started as soon as possible and continued, often for several hours, until the person's body has become warm and he or she begins breathing on his or her own. Further medical treatment at a hospital emergency department will also be necessary.

HOW TO RESCUE FROM WATER

Do not move a person with a suspected neck injury unless the person's life and yours are in danger. Any movement of the head, forward, backward, or side to side, can result in paralysis or death. If you must move the person, always keep the head, neck, and body in alignment. (See p. 35.)

If a drowning person is near a pier or the side of a swimming pool, lie down and give the person your hand or foot and pull him or her to safety. If the person is too far away, hold out a life preserver ring, pole, stick, board, rope, chair, tree limb, towel, or other object.

If the person is out from the shore, wade into the water and extend a pole, board, stick, or rope to the person and pull him or her to safety. It may be necessary to row a boat to the person. If so, hand the person an oar or other suitable object and pull him or her to the boat. If possible, the person should hold on to the back of the boat while being rowed to the shore. If this is not possible, pull the person carefully into the boat.

RESCUE FROM WATER

If a drowning person is near a pier, but too far away to reach your hand or foot, lie down and hold out a pole, paddle, or life preserver, and pull the person to safety.

> What to Do

If a neck or back injury is suspected (from a diving or surfing accident):

If trained medical personnel are not available to assist you, place a board (such as a surfboard or table leaf) under the person's head and back while he or she is still in the water. (The board should extend from the head to at least the buttocks.) This will keep the person from moving, thus preventing further damage to the neck or back. Lift the person out of the water on the board.

If the person is not breathing:

Artificial breathing must be started at once, before the person is completely out of the water, if possible. As soon as the person's body can be supported, either in a boat or in shallow water, start CPR (see pp. 33–49). Once the person is out of the water, lay him or her on his or her back on a firm surface and continue CPR if necessary.

If a board is not available:

If the person is facedown in the water, gently turn him or her over, keeping the head, neck, and body in alignment. Gently tow or push the person to shallow water and stay with him or her. Do not drag the person sideways. Pull him or her by the armpits or legs in the direction of the length of the body. Keep the head in line with the body. Call for help or have someone get help for you.

If the person is breathing:

1. Watch the person to ensure that he or she continues to breathe on his or her own. Do not give the person food or water.

2. Place the person on his or her side with the head extended backward so that fluids will drain.

3. Keep the person comfortably warm.

4. Reassure the person.

5. Seek medical attention promptly.

SHALLOW WATER BLACKOUT

Shallow water blackout is a condition that most often occurs when an individual—usually a child—hyperventilates on purpose in an effort to stay under water for a longer period of time. The process of hyperventilation, however, removes carbon dioxide from the blood, which at normal levels triggers the involuntary stimulus to breathe. Although the individual may actually be capable of staying longer under water, he or she may pass out because of the lack of oxygen.

The condition also results when young, inexperienced divers use 100 percent oxygen rebreather masks in training, usually at depths of 10 to 20 feet. In either situation, the person seldom has a warning before he or she loses consciousness. If not noticed in time, the individual may drown.

> Symptoms

- Has been under water, or facedown in the water, longer than usual
- Appears to be lifeless in the water

> What to Do

1. Remove the person at once from the water.

2. Maintain an open airway. Restore breathing and circulation, if necessary (see CPR, pp. 33–49).

3. Take the person to the nearest hospital emergency department for further evaluation.

> Preventing Drowning

Here are some steps you can take to prevent drowning:

- Learn to swim.
- Never swim alone.
- Don't drink alcohol while swimming or boating.
- Avoid swimming in very cold water (under 82°F).

See also: Head, Neck, and Back Problems, p. 138.

FISHHOOK INJURIES

A fishhook caught in the body is a common injury. If the fishhook goes deep enough so that the barb is embedded in the skin, it is best to have a doctor remove it because it may have penetrated bone. If a doctor is not readily available, the hook should be removed.

FISHHOOK IN THE EYE OR ON THE FACE

Never attempt to remove a fishhook caught in the eye or face. Seek medical help immediately. If a fishhook is in an eye, have the person hold a cup (preferably a metal one, which won't break or crush) over the eye until you reach the nearest hospital emergency department.

> What to Do

If only the point of the hook (and not the barb) entered the skin, remove the hook by carefully pulling it out.

If the hook is embedded in the skin:

1. Push the hook through the skin until the barb comes out.

2. Cut the hook with wire clippers or pliers at either the barb or the shank of the hook. Remove the remaining part. For either type of injury, clean the wound with soap and water, cover with a bandage, and seek medical attention as soon as possible. There is always the possibility of infection and the need for a tetanus shot.

REMOVING A FISHHOOK

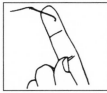

The fishhook is embedded beyond the barb in the tip of the finger.

To remove it, push the hook through the skin until the barb comes out.

Cut the hook with pliers or clippers at the barb or at the shank.

Carefully remove the remaining part of the hook.

HEAT-RELATED PROBLEMS

HEAT CRAMPS

Heat cramps are muscle pains and spasms caused by a loss of electrolytes (mainly sodium and potassium) from the body due to profuse sweating. Strenuous physical activity in hot temperatures can lead to heat cramps. Drinking large amounts of plain water while sweating profusely (without replacing the lost salt) can also contribute to heat cramps. Usually the muscles of the stomach and legs (calves) are affected first. Heat cramps may also be a symptom of heat exhaustion.

> Symptoms

Heat cramps may involve any or all of the following symptoms:

- Painful muscle cramping and spasms

- Heavy sweating

- Seizures

> What to Do

1. Have the person sit quietly in a cool place.

2. If the person is not vomiting, give him or her fluids to replace lost electrolytes. This can be a sports drink (check the label to make sure the carbohydrate content does not exceed 6 percent) or clear juice. Give the person half a glass of liquid every 15 minutes for 1 hour. Stop giving fluids if vomiting occurs.

3. Medical attention is needed because of possible complications.

HEAT EXHAUSTION

Heat exhaustion can occur after prolonged (about 3 to 5 days) exposure to high temperatures and high humidity.

> Symptoms

Heat exhaustion can cause any or all of the following symptoms:

- Slightly above normal body temperature
- Pale and clammy skin
- Heavy sweating
- Tiredness or weakness
- Dizziness
- Headache
- Nausea
- Muscle cramps
- Vomiting
- Fainting
- Fast heart rate
- Flu-like symptoms
- Abdominal cramping

> What to Do

1. Move the person into the shade or to a cooler area.
2. Stop activity or exercise.
3. Have the person lie down.
4. Raise the person's feet 8 to 12 inches.
5. Loosen the person's clothing.
6. If the person is not vomiting, give him or her a sports drink (check the label to make sure the carbohydrate content does not exceed 6 percent) or clear juice.
7. Place cool, wet cloths on the person's forehead and body.
8. Use a fan to cool the person while spraying him or her with water from a spray bottle, or place ice bags on the person's neck, armpits, and groin. If possible, remove the person to an air-conditioned room.
9. If symptoms are severe, become worse, or last longer than an hour, seek medical attention promptly.

HEATSTROKE (SUNSTROKE)

Heatstroke is a life-threatening emergency. It is a disturbance in the body's heat-regulating system caused by an extremely high body temperature resulting from exposure to heat and an inability of the body to cool itself.

> Symptoms

Heatstroke can cause any or all of the following symptoms:

- Extremely high body temperature (often 106°F or higher)
- Rapid and strong pulse
- Unconsciousness or confusion
- Fast breathing
- Vomiting and diarrhea
- Seizures
- Lack of coordination

> What to Do

If body temperature reaches 105°F:

1. Call 911 or your local emergency medical dispatcher.
2. Undress the person and put him or her into a tub of cool water, if possible. Otherwise, spray the person with a spray bottle or hose, sponge bare skin with cool water, or apply cold packs to the person's neck, armpits, and groin.
3. Continue treatment until body temperature is lowered to 101°F or 102°F.
4. Do not overchill; check the person's temperature constantly. If body temperature rises again, repeat the cooling process.
5. Do not give the person aspirin, acetaminophen, or other pain relievers; alcoholic beverages; or stimulants (such as coffee or tea).
6. Dry off the person once temperature is lowered. Place the person in front of a fan or an air conditioner.
7. Seek medical attention promptly, preferably at the nearest hospital emergency department.

> Preventing Heat-related Problems

Infants, older people, and those who are overweight or have an endocrine disease (such as diabetes) or a skin disease (such as psoriasis) are most susceptible to heat-related problems. Here are some steps you can take to avoid problems from overexposure to heat:

- Until your body is accustomed to hot weather (about a week for adults and 2 weeks for children), limit outdoor activities to 90 minutes a day. It's best to exercise before 8 AM or after 6 PM.

- Wear loose, lightweight clothing that is light colored to reflect the sunlight.

- Drink 8 ounces of fluid 15 minutes before engaging in a vigorous outdoor activity and drink 8 to 12 ounces of fluid every 30 minutes during the activity.

- Avoid alcohol, caffeine, nicotine, amphetamines, or antihistamines when exercising in hot weather.

See also: Dehydration, p. 101; Sunburn, p. 351.

INSECT AND MARINE LIFE STINGS

INSECT STINGS

Though most insect stings cause only local reactions (redness, swelling), some can be life-threatening if the person is allergic to the insect's venom. Insect stings cause more deaths per year than snakebites. The most common stinging insects are honeybees, hornets, wasps, yellow jackets, bumblebees, and fire ants. (See Severe Allergic Reactions to Insect Stings, p. 336.)

> Symptoms

Insect stings can cause any or all of the following symptoms, which occur at the bite area and may last 48 to 72 hours:

- Pain
- Swelling
- Redness
- Itching
- Burning

> What to Do

1. If the insect has left its stinger behind, carefully remove it by gently scraping the skin with a dull knife blade or card edge. Do not squeeze it with tweezers, as this may cause more venom to enter the body.

2. Wash the area with soap and water. Do not break blisters caused by fire ants. Doing so could cause an infection.

3. Place ice wrapped in cloth or cold compresses on the sting area to decrease the absorption and spread of the venom.

4. Take an oral antihistamine to help ease the symptoms.

> Avoiding Bee Stings

Here are some steps you can take to avoid bee stings:

- Don't disturb nests.
- Clean up food spills and remove garbage frequently.
- Eliminate beehives by spraying insecticide in them at night when it's dark and the bees are inside the hives and quiet.
- Check open soda cans for bees, wasps, and other insects before drinking out of them.

■ MULTIPLE INSECT STINGS

Sometimes, when a person receives several insect stings, he or she may have a reaction that is not necessarily life threatening, but still requires an evaluation by a doctor.

> Symptoms

Multiple insect stings can cause any or all of the following symptoms:

- Rapid onset of swelling
- Headache
- Muscle cramps
- Fever
- Drowsiness

> What to Do

1. If the insects have left stingers behind, carefully remove them by gently scraping the skin with a dull knife blade or a credit card edge. Do not squeeze the stingers with tweezers because this can cause more venom to enter the body.
2. Wash the sting sites with soap and water.
3. Place ice wrapped in cloth or cold compresses on sting sites.
4. Take an oral antihistamine to help ease symptoms.
5. Seek medical attention because other medication may be needed.

▪ SEVERE ALLERGIC REACTIONS TO INSECT STINGS

An allergic reaction to insect stings can be life threatening and can result from one or more bites or stings. Allergic reactions often occur in people who have been bitten or stung previously and have become sensitized to the particular venom.

Anaphylactic shock, which can occur from such stings, is a total body allergic reaction. Anyone who knows he or she is allergic to bee venom should always carry an anaphylaxis emergency kit and wear a medical identification tag.

> Symptoms

Anaphylactic shock can cause any or all of the following symptoms:

- Swelling in other parts of the body such as the eyes, lips, and tongue, as well as at the bite site
- Hives or hive-like rash on the body
- Coughing or wheezing
- Severe itching
- Difficulty breathing
- Stomach cramps
- Nausea and vomiting
- Anxiety
- Weakness
- Dizziness
- Bluish tinge to the skin
- Collapse
- Unconsciousness

> What to Do

If an emergency kit for insect stings is not available:

1. Call 911 (or your local emergency medical dispatch number) or take the person to the nearest hospital emergency department immediately.

2. If the person is not breathing, maintain an open airway. Restore breathing and circulation, if necessary. (See CPR, pp. 33–49.)

If an emergency kit for insect stings is available:

1. If the person is unable to administer an injection of epinephrine (see p. 58), give the injection, carefully following the instructions in the emergency kit.

2. Seek medical attention immediately. Call 911 (or your local emergency medical dispatch number) or take the person to the nearest hospital emergency department.

See also: Severe Allergic Reaction, p. 57.

MARINE LIFE STINGS

Stings from certain types of marine life are poisonous. Four of the most common offenders are the Portuguese man-of-war, the jellyfish, the scorpionfish, and the stingray.

■ PORTUGUESE MAN-OF-WAR AND JELLYFISH

Jellyfish can be poisonous even when they're dead because they still contain active stinging cells. The Portuguese man-of-war is usually found in the Gulf of Mexico in late summer; the jellyfish can be found in the Florida area, the Chesapeake Bay area, and in the South Pacific.

> Symptoms

Stings from the Portuguese man-of-war and the jellyfish can cause any or all of the following symptoms:

- Intense burning pain
- Reddening of the skin
- Skin rash
- Muscle cramps
- Nausea and vomiting
- Difficulty breathing

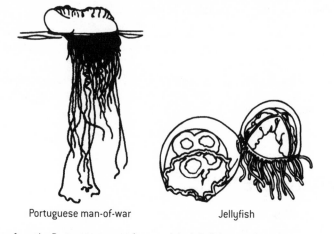

PORTUGUESE MAN-OF-WAR AND JELLYFISH

Portuguese man-of-war

Jellyfish

Stings from the Portuguese man-of-war and the jellyfish are poisonous.

■ SEVERE MARINE LIFE STINGS

If a sting affects more than half of an arm or leg or if the person is unconscious, call 911 (or your local emergency medical dispatch number) or transport the person immediately to the nearest hospital emergency department.

> What to Do

If stung by a Portuguese man-of-war:

Wrap cloth around your hands (or use tweezers, pliers, or forceps) and carefully remove any attached tentacles. *Note that an unattached tentacle can still sting.* Then continue with steps 1 through 4 below.

If stung by a Portuguese man-of-war or a jellyfish:

1. Wash the affected area with seawater or vinegar (3- to 5-percent acetic acid) to deactivate the stinging cells. Do not use fresh water (or tap water) because fresh water can stimulate the stinging cells to release venom.

2. To help remove the stinging cells that are still attached to the skin, apply shaving cream and gently shave the area or rub with a paste of sand or mud and seawater.

3. To relieve discomfort, apply a mild hydrocortisone cream to the area or take an oral antihistamine.

4. If the person has shortness of breath, weakness, or chest pain, or becomes unconscious, call 911 (or your local emergency medical dispatch number) or take the person to the nearest hospital emergency department.

▪ STINGRAYS AND SCORPIONFISH

Stingrays (also called devilfish) are flat fish that inhabit the bottom of shallow tropical waters. Scorpionfish, which also inhabit the bottom of shallow tropical waters, are colorful fish that are found throughout the world. Scorpionfish include lionfish, butterfly cod, bullroot, and stonefish.

> Symptoms

Stings from the stingray or scorpionfish can cause any or all of the following symptoms:

- Intense pain in the area of the sting
- Nausea, vomiting, and/or abdominal cramps

STINGRAYS AND SCORPIONFISH

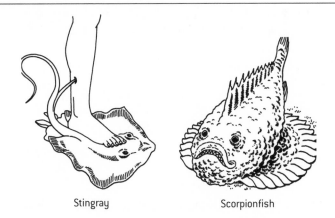

Stingray   Scorpionfish

When disturbed, which usually means being stepped on, a stingray will whip its tail to inject venom, usually into the person's leg. The spine on a stingray's tail can penetrate a rubber or leather boot or wet suit. Scorpionfish use the spines on their back as stinging agents. Scorpionfish can appear to be dead when they are not.

- Fast heart rate
- Dizziness
- Muscle cramps or spasms

> What to Do

1. Have the person immerse the affected area in a container of hot but not scalding (113°F) water and take him or her to the nearest hospital emergency department. The person should keep the area immersed in water during transport because it takes about 30 to 90 minutes to deactivate the fish venom.

2. If possible, keep the affected area immobilized.

3. If you cannot get the person to a hospital emergency department immediately, have him or her immerse the affected area in hot water for at least 90 minutes and seek medical attention as soon as possible.

SCORPION STINGS

Some species of scorpions are more poisonous than others. Scorpion stings are particularly harmful to very young children. Scorpions, which tend to hide under wood or in crevices, are usually found in desert areas of the southwestern United States, Mexico, and Brazil. They are most active during hot weather and at night.

> Symptoms

A scorpion sting may cause any or all of the following symptoms:

- Severe burning pain at the site of the sting
- Nausea and vomiting
- Stomach pain
- Numbness and tingling in the affected area
- Spasm of jaw muscles, making opening the mouth difficult
- Fast heart rate
- Blurred vision
- Twitching and spasm of affected muscles

SCORPION

The scorpion looks like a 2-inch-long lobster or crab. It has a set of pincers and a stinger located in the tail, which arches over its back.

- Convulsions
- Coma

> What to Do

If the person is not breathing:

1. Call 911 (or your local emergency medical dispatch number).

2. Maintain an open airway. Restore breathing and circulation, if necessary. (See CPR, pp. 33–49.)

If the person is breathing:

1. Keep the bitten area lower than the person's heart.

2. Place ice wrapped in cloth or cold compresses on the bitten area.

3. Keep the person quiet.

4. Seek medical attention promptly, preferably at the nearest hospital emergency department.

> Avoiding Scorpion Stings

Here are some steps you can take to avoid scorpion stings:

- Remove all wood debris, including dead wood and firewood, from around your home.
- Set up your campsite away from wood debris.
- Always wear footwear in scorpion-infested areas.
- When camping, shake out clothing, sheets, and sleeping bags before you use them.

LICE INFESTATION

Lice are small (about 1/8 inch), wingless insects that can infest any part of the body, but are usually found on children's heads. Lice are parasites that feed off of small amounts of your blood. They are very contagious and spread easily among children in school, especially from the ages of 3 to 12. Female lice lay a daily batch of tiny, white eggs (nits) that attach firmly to the sides of hairs, usually close to the scalp.

> Symptoms

A lice infestation can cause any or all of the following symptoms:

- Intense itching at the site of infestation
- Redness of the skin
- Enlarged lymph nodes in the neck

> What to Do

If you know for sure it is a lice infestation on the scalp:

1. Use shampoo with the active ingredient permethrin (check the label); carefully follow the instructions on the container. These shampoos are available without a prescription.

2. After shampooing, comb through the hair using a special fine-toothed comb to remove any nits. You should comb through each section of hair every 3 days for 2 weeks until all the nits are gone. Use the comb to check for persistent lice or eggs and to determine if the treatment has been successful.

3. Spray any furniture and bedding that have been used in the previous 3 days with permethrin.

4. Dry clean or machine wash at the hottest setting all exposed towels, sheets, and clothing. Iron them if possible.

5. Place small, potentially contaminated objects in plastic bags for 2 weeks, or until the lice are no longer visible.

6. Throw out all exposed combs and brushes.

7. If your child is infested, report it immediately to his or her school.

8. If the lice reappear within a week after using the shampoo, see a doctor.

9. Do not get this shampoo in your eyes. If you have lice in your eyebrows contact a doctor immediately.

If the infestation is in another area of the body, such as the genitals:

1. See a physician; he or she may recommend a special shampoo or lotion.

2. Inform your sexual partner and anyone with whom you have had close physical contact so that they can also seek treatment.

> Preventing Lice Infestations

- Avoid head-to-head (hair-to-hair) contact during play and other activities at home, school, and elsewhere (sports activities, playground, slumber parties, camp).

- Do not share clothing such as hats, scarves, coats, sports uniforms, hair ribbons, or barrettes.

- Do not share combs, brushes, or towels.

- Do not lie on beds, couches, pillows, carpets, or stuffed animals that have recently been in contact with an infested person.

- Vacuum the floor and furniture, particularly where the infested person sat or lay. However, spending much time and money on housecleaning activities is not necessary to avoid reinfestation by lice or nits that may have fallen off the head or crawled onto furniture or clothing.

- Do not use fumigant sprays or fogs; they are not necessary to control head lice and can be toxic if inhaled or absorbed through the skin.

- Teach children how to avoid activities that may spread head lice.

See also: Scabies Infestation, p. 349.

LIGHTNING STRIKE

Being struck by lightning is a serious incident. Electricity generated by lightning disrupts the electrical activity in the brain that controls breathing and heartbeat and can make the person's heart stop beating. Heat generated by the lightning can cause severe burns and internal injuries. Broken bones can occur from sudden, strenuous muscle contractions. The person may also be injured if he or she is thrown into the air from the force of the lightning strike. You can immediately touch a person who has been struck by lightning because the source of the electricity is no longer present. Most lightning injuries occur between noon and 6 PM.

> Symptoms

A lightning strike can cause any or all of the following symptoms:

- Disorientation, confusion, or dizziness
- Inability to speak
- Unconsciousness or seizures
- Absence of breathing
- Burn marks
- Bleeding
- Temporary or permanent blindness
- Ruptured eardrum
- Amnesia that lasts for hours or even days
- Internal or external injuries

> What to Do

1. Call 911 (or your local emergency medical dispatch number). Maintain an open airway. Restore breathing and circulation, if necessary. (See CPR, pp. 33–49.)

2. While waiting for medical help to arrive, provide first aid for any problems such as bleeding (see p. 52) or broken bones (see p. 79).

3. Calm and reassure the person.

> Preventing Lightning Injuries

Here are some steps you can take to avoid a lightning injury:

- Be aware of violent, fast-moving storms in your area. Lightning can strike before a storm is overhead.

- If planning outdoor activities, know the weather forecast and have a plan if bad weather presents itself.

- When undergoing outdoor activities, always note the sound of thunder and seek shelter immediately.

- Seek shelter in a large, substantial building; shelters such as tents or sheds offer little protection.

- Remain in an all-metal vehicle with rubber tires; a cloth-top convertible offers less protection.

- Outdoors, stay away from metal objects such as power lines, ski lifts, and fences. Do not open your umbrella if you can hear thunder or see lightning.

- Do not stand near tall trees. If you are in a wooded area, seek shelter in a thick growth of young trees or saplings.

- If you are in an open area, seek shelter in a dry cave or ditch (make sure there is no water around it). Crouch there rolled up like a ball.

- If you are swimming or boating, get to shore as quickly as possible or stay underneath a bridge.

- If you are indoors, try not to use the telephone or computer modem. Stay away from fireplaces and open doors and windows.

PLANT IRRITATIONS

Poison ivy, poison oak, and poison sumac are three plants that can cause a reaction on the skin of sensitive people. An oily substance on the plants causes the irritation. You can be exposed to the plant toxins indirectly by touching pets or clothing that have come in contact with the plants. Burning the leaves of the plants can cause breathing problems in sensitive people.

> Symptoms

Contact with poison ivy, poison oak, and poison sumac can cause any or all of the following symptoms:

- Redness of the skin
- Blisters
- Itching
- Headache
- Fever

POISON OAK

Poison oak may grow as a bush or vine. The leaf has three leaflets.

POISON IVY

Poison ivy may grow as a plant, bush, or vine. The leaf has three shiny leaflets.

> What to Do

1. Wear gloves if you are helping someone who has been exposed to any of these plants. As soon as possible, remove clothes and thoroughly wash the affected area with soap and water.

2. Apply calamine lotion to help relieve itching. A colloid oatmeal bath (available in most drugstores) can also help relieve itching.

3. You may take over-the-counter antihistamines such as diphenhydramine and loritadine as directed.

4. Seek medical attention if the symptoms are severe or don't improve in 2 to 3 days.

> Preventing Reactions To Plants

The best way of preventing reactions is education. Be sure that you read about and are familiar with the appearance of these plants. If you know you are allergic to poison ivy, poison oak, or poison sumac, or you know you will be in an area where you might come in contact with the plants, ask your doctor about using a protective lotion containing the active ingredient bentoquatum to block a reaction. The over-the-counter lotion is available in drugstores. Apply the lotion to exposed skin 15 minutes before possible contact with the plants and every 4 hours thereafter for continued protection. To be extra safe, you should also wear protective clothing to avoid exposure to the plants. You can

POISON SUMAC

Poison sumac may grow as a bush or tree. The leaf consists of rows of two leaflets opposite each other plus a leaflet at the top. Leaflets are pointed at both ends.

remove the lotion from your skin later with soap and water. Do not use bentoquatum if you have already developed a rash. **Do not** apply in or around the eyes, nose, or mouth.

If you are unsure what type of plant you have come in contact with or are unsure what type of reaction you may be having to plant exposure, contact your poison control center or seek medical attention.

SCABIES INFESTATION

Scabies is an infestation by a mite that burrows into the skin. Scabies infestations are very contagious—spreading from person to person and from furniture, clothing, or pets. Common sites of infestation include areas between the fingers and toes, the inside of the elbow or wrist, under the armpits, or on the genitals. Scabies spreads rapidly under crowded conditions where there is frequent skin-to-skin contact between people, such as in hospitals, institutions, child-care facilities, and nursing homes.

> Symptoms

A scabies infestation can cause any or all of the following symptoms, which usually develop about 3 to 4 weeks after the initial contact:

- Intense itching that is usually worse at night and after bathing

- Red, pimple-like irritations of the skin (especially between the fingers; the skin folds on the wrist, elbow, or knee; the penis, the breast, or shoulder blades).

- Sores on the body caused by scratching. These sores can sometimes become infected with bacteria.

> What to Do

1. Successful treatment of scabies requires killing the scabies mites, treating any family members who have been in close contact with the infected person, and preventing the scabies from returning.

2. There is no home remedy for scabies. People should see their doctor so that treatment for scabies can be prescribed to kill the mites and eggs. See a doctor; he or she may prescribe a special cream or lotions to kill the mites.

3. Spray your furniture with gamma benzene hexachloride spray. Do not spray your skin with this product.

4. Wash all contaminated clothing, bedding, and towels in very hot water the morning after you begin treatment. Clothes should then be dried in a hot dyer. Iron everything, if possible, to help kill the mites. For those items that can't be washed, use dry cleaning. Personal items (such as belts, purses, and shoes) should also be properly cleaned.

5. Have all of your family members treated because it is very contagious.

> Preventing Scabies Infestations

Avoiding contact with infected individuals and practicing good personal hygiene are the most important ways to prevent scabies.

SUNBURN

Sunburn is usually a first-degree burn of the skin resulting from over-exposure to the sun. Prolonged exposure can lead to a second-degree burn. The peak hours for sunburn, when the ultraviolet (UV) rays from the sun are most harmful, are between 10 AM and 4 PM.

> Symptoms

Sunburn can cause any or all of the following symptoms, which usually subside in 2 or 3 days:

- Redness
- Pain
- Mild swelling
- Blisters and swelling in severe cases
- Itching

> What to Do

1. Put cold water on the sunburned area.

2. If sunburn is severe, submerge the sunburned area under cold water until pain is relieved. It is also helpful to place cold, wet cloths on the burned area. Do not rub the skin. Taking aspirin, ibuprofen, or naproxen with food as soon as possible after the burn may help reduce pain and redness.

3. If possible, put a dry, sterile bandage on a severely sunburned area.

4. Seek medical attention for severe sunburn. Do not break blisters or put ointments, sprays, antiseptic medications, or home remedies on severe sunburns.

> Preventing Sunburn

Here are some steps you can take to avoid sunburn:

- Wear protective clothing such as long sleeves and a wide-brim hat.
- Use UVA and UVB ray sunscreen protection.
- Apply the sunscreen 30 minutes before going out into the sun to allow for skin absorption.

- If you have light skin, wear a sunscreen with a sun protection factor (SPF) of at least 30 for routine or prolonged outdoor activity. If your skin is darker, wear a sunscreen with an SPF of 15 for routine or prolonged outdoor activity. Blocking agents such as zinc and iron oxide are also effective at blocking radiation. In children, use an SPF of 45 to 50. Be sure to bring protection from the sun such as an umbrella or sun tent.

- When first getting out into the sun, limit your sun exposure to 20 minutes at a time.

- If you have blue eyes, red or blond hair, or lots of freckles, you are at risk for sunburn.

- Especially protect your eyes, nose, shoulders, and lips from the sun.

- A high-altitude area increases your sun exposure, so be extra careful.

See also: Dehydration, p. 101; Fever, p. 208; Seizures, p. 150.

SUNBURN OF THE EYE

The eyes—especially the protective, transparent coating over the front of the eye (the cornea)—are extremely sensitive to damage from ultraviolet rays from the sun. These burns, often referred to as snow blindness, are most likely to occur at high altitudes when a thick coating of snow is on the ground (skiers and mountain climbers are especially susceptible). People who use tanning salons are also at risk of eye burns. The best way to prevent burns of the eyes or the eyelids is to wear sunglasses that have attached side panels and to apply sunscreen to the eyelids before going out in the sun.

> Symptoms

Sunburn of the eyes can cause any or all of the following symptoms, which usually occur within 12 hours of exposure:

- Redness of the eye

- Severe pain, especially in light (but vision is usually not affected)

- Spasm of the eyelids

> What to Do

1. Avoid sunlight.

2. Seek medical attention promptly.

Part VI

DISASTER PREPAREDNESS

Disasters such as the World Trade Center attacks on September 11, 2001, and Hurricane Katrina in 2005, as well as the emergence of infectious diseases such as severe acute respiratory syndrome (SARS) and the arrival of West Nile virus in the Western hemisphere, have awakened all of us to the importance of disaster preparedness.

In a disaster, local citizens can play very important roles in local response efforts. The U.S. Department of Homeland Security (DHS) recognizes the importance of citizen participation in community disaster preparedness and is working to make sure everyone in the United States is fully aware, trained, and practiced on how to prevent, prepare for, respond to, and recover from disasters and other public health emergencies. Training programs are being developed to:

- Improve individual and family public health and medical preparedness;
- Give citizens opportunities to contribute to local, regional, and national preparedness and response efforts; and
- Increase personal and community resilience to disasters and other public health emergencies.

2008 IOWA FLOODS

An American Red Cross worker surveys the damage from a boat after the Cedar River flooded its banks and inundated much of Cedar Rapids, Iowa. This flood was much worse than the Great Flood of 1993.

Talia Frenkel/American Red Cross

WHEN DISASTER STRIKES

A disaster exists when response needs exceed available resources. Disasters can strike quickly and without warning, forcing people to evacuate their neighborhoods or stay at home for days. Everyone should think about what to do in a disaster, particularly if water, gas, electricity, or telephones are cut off for a long period of time.

In a disaster, individuals and communities will likely have to deal with an increased demand for medical resources, especially in rural areas and when local emergency medical services and hospitals are overwhelmed. The first minutes or hours are the most critical for seriously injured persons. During this time, doctors and other skilled emergency responders will probably not be available at the disaster scene. Even when they arrive, emergency responders and relief workers cannot reach everyone right away. In such situations, citizens can help give immediate assistance at a time when rapid intervention may be essential for survival.

Until help arrives, citizens will be the "first responders" to care for injured victims. In such situations, citizens must be able to:

- Recognize and protect themselves from potential hazards
- Know how and when to call for help
- Be willing and able to help without interfering with organized response efforts
- Know how to provide critical life support

Local and state governments are responsible for protecting citizens and helping them to recover when a disaster strikes. When a disaster

In any disaster, early detection, rapid reporting, and immediate action are important to reduce casualties. Any suspicious or confirmed emergency situation should be reported immediately by calling 911 or other local emergency medical dispatch number. If you believe that someone has been exposed deliberately to a biological, chemical, or radioactive agent, or if you believe a terrorist threat will occur or is occurring, contact your local health department, your local police or other law enforcement agency, and/or the Centers for Disease Control and Prevention (see *www.bt.cdc.gov/emcontact*).

situation is beyond the capabilities of the state and local government to respond, the state governor can ask for federal assistance. Following receipt of a request for federal support by a governor and the subsequent declaration of an emergency by the president of the United States, the federal government provides local and state governments with personnel, technical experts, equipment, and other resources. The Federal Emergency Management Agency (FEMA), which is part of the DHS, organizes this assistance. FEMA has 10 regional offices and 2 area offices. Each region serves several states, and regional staff works directly with the states to plan for disasters and relief programs and meet the needs of affected citizens.

Disaster relief focuses on meeting people's immediate survival needs. Disaster relief workers provide shelter, food, and medical and mental health services. Disaster relief organizations, such as the American Red Cross and the Salvation Army, help individuals and families return to normal daily activities. In addition, relief workers may feed emergency workers, handle questions from family members outside the disaster area, provide blood and blood products to disaster victims, and help those affected by disaster to get other available resources.

WEATHER-RELATED AND OTHER NATURAL DISASTERS

Without question, a natural disaster will occur somewhere in the United States every year. Intensive monitoring by governmental agencies such as the U.S. Geological Survey, National Weather Service, and National Oceanic and Atmospheric Administration can provide early warning for some of these events. This allows for the early implementation of emergency communication and evacuation plans. Although some natural disasters are predictable according to season and geographical location and by using tracking systems, many others (for example, wildfires, flash floods) can occur with little or no warning. After a disaster occurs, local authorities will watch the situation and decide what protective actions citizens should take. The most appropriate action will depend on the situation.

> Types of Natural Disasters

EARTHQUAKES

An earthquake results from the sudden, rapid shaking of the earth caused by the breaking and shifting of rock beneath the earth's surface. This shaking can cause buildings and bridges to collapse; disrupt gas, electric, and phone service; and sometimes trigger landslides, avalanches, flash floods, fires, and huge, destructive ocean waves (tsunamis). Earthquakes strike suddenly, without warning; they can occur at any time of the year and at any time of the day or night. Each year, 70 to 75 damaging earthquakes occur throughout the world. The keys to surviving an earthquake and reducing your risk of injury are planning, preparing, and practicing what you and your family will do if it happens.

FLOODS

Ninety percent of all natural disasters in the United States involve flooding. Each year, about 100 people lose their lives in floods, with damage averaging more than $2 billion. Flash floods are the leading weather-related killer in the United States. They can occur within a few minutes or hours of excessive rainfall, a dam or levee failure, or a sudden release of water held by an ice jam.

HEAT WAVES

Heat is one of the most underrated and least understood of the deadly weather events. Unlike other natural disasters, such as floods and tornadoes, a heat wave can be a "silent killer." The worst heat disasters, in terms of loss of life, occur in large cities when a combination of high daytime temperatures, high humidity, warm nighttime temperatures, and an abundance of sunshine occurs for several days. Large urban areas become "heat islands." Brick buildings, asphalt streets, and tar roofs store heat and radiate it like a slow burning furnace. Heat builds up in a city during the day and cities are slower than rural areas to cool down at night.

HURRICANES/TROPICAL STORMS

A hurricane is a severe tropical storm that forms in the southern Atlantic Ocean, Caribbean Sea, Gulf of Mexico, or in the eastern and central Pacific Ocean. Hurricanes need warm tropical oceans, moisture, and light winds above them. Under the right conditions, a hurricane can produce violent winds, enormous waves, torrential rains, and floods.

LANDSLIDES

Landslides are typically associated with periods of heavy rainfall or rapid snow melt and tend to worsen the effects of flooding that often accompanies these events. In areas burned by forest and brush fires, less rain or snowfall may be needed to cause landslides. Debris flows, sometimes referred to as mudslides, mudflows, lahars, or debris avalanches are common types of fast-moving landslides.

THUNDERSTORMS

A thunderstorm is formed from a combination of moisture to form clouds and rain; rapidly rising warm air; and lift from cold or warm fronts, sea breezes, or mountains. Some of the most severe weather occurs when a single thunderstorm affects one location for a long time, bringing heavy rains (which can cause flash flooding), strong winds, hail, lightning, and tornadoes. Lightning is a major threat during a thunderstorm. In the United States, between 75 to 100 people are killed each year by lightning. While thunderstorms and lightning are found throughout this country, they happen most often in the central and southern states.

TORNADOES

Tornadoes are among the most violent storms. Every year, an average of 1,200 tornadoes kill about 55 Americans, injure 1,500 people, and cause more than $400 million in damage. A tornado is a violently rotating column of air extending from a thunderstorm to the ground. The most violent tornadoes are capable of tremendous destruction, with wind speeds of 250 miles per hour or more. Damage paths can be in excess of 1 mile wide and 50 miles long. Tornadoes can occur anywhere in the United States at any time of the year. In the south-

THE MOST VIOLENT STORMS

A tornado is a rotating column of air that extends from a thunderstorm to the ground. Tornadoes can reach wind speeds of over 250 miles per hour.

OAR/ERL/National Severe Storms Laboratory

ern states, peak tornado season is March through May, while peak months in the northern states are during the summer.

TSUNAMIS

Tsunamis are a series of very long waves created by any rapid, large-scale disturbance of the sea. Most are generated by sea floor displacements from large undersea earthquakes. Tsunamis can cause great destruction and loss of life within minutes on shores near their source; some tsunamis can cause destruction within hours across an entire ocean basin. Most tsunamis occur in the Pacific Ocean but can occur in every ocean and sea.

VOLCANOES

Explosive volcanoes spew hot solid and molten rock fragments and gases into the air. As a result, ash flows can occur on all sides of a volcano and ash can fall hundreds of miles downwind. Dangerous mudflows and floods also can occur in valleys leading away from volcanoes. If you live near a known volcano, active or dormant, be prepared to follow instructions from your local emergency officials.

WILDFIRES

In many areas, wild lands have become overgrown with trees and other plant life. When coupled with drought conditions and a fire source, this buildup of plants can provide the fuel for a potentially disastrous fire. Wildfires often begin unnoticed and can spread quickly, igniting brush, trees, and homes.

WINTER STORMS

Severe winter storms can cause widespread damage and disruption. Heavy snow often results in paralyzed transportation systems, highway crashes, and stranded motorists. When accompanied by intense winds, ice, and extreme cold, winter storms can isolate individuals and entire communities.

KEY ACTION STEPS IN THE EVENT OF A NATURAL DISASTER

- Stay tuned to the local emergency response network or news station for up-to-date information and instructions.

- If you were evacuated, return home only after local officials tell you it is safe.

- Stay away from floodwaters.

- Check yourself and family members for injuries. Help those who may need special assistance and give first aid where appropriate.

- Avoid loose or dangling power lines and report them to the power company, police, or fire department.

- Enter your home or any building with caution. Do not enter if there is water around the building.

- Use flashlights to examine walls, floors, doors, staircases, and windows. Consider calling a qualified person to inspect foundations for cracks and make sure the building is not in danger of collapsing.

- Look for fire hazards such as flooded electrical circuits or submerged furnaces and appliances.

- Check for gas leaks. If you smell gas or hear a "hissing" noise, open a window, and leave quickly. Turn off the gas at the outside main valve and call the gas company from a neighbor's home.

- Look for electrical system damage. If you see sparks or frayed wires, turn off the electricity at the main fuse box or circuit breaker. Do not step in water to get to the fuse box or circuit breaker before calling an electrician for advice.

- Check for sewage and water line damage. If you think sewage lines are damaged, don't use toilets and call a plumber. If water pipes are damaged, don't use tap water and call the water company.

- Watch out for animals, especially poisonous snakes that may have entered the building with floodwaters.

- Take pictures of the damage for insurance claims.

- Avoid drinking or preparing food with tap water until local officials tell you it is not contaminated.

- Open windows and doors to ventilate and dry out your home.

- Telephone systems may be jammed. Use the telephone for emergency calls only.

THE THREAT OF TERRORISM

Terrorism is the use of force or violence against people or property in violation of the criminal laws of the United States. Terrorist threats can come from many sources and take many forms. Recent attention has focused on terrorist use of toxic or poisonous chemicals, infectious disease organisms, radioactive materials, and explosives. Government response plans have focused on developing resources in local, state, and federal government agencies including health departments, emergency responders (for example, police and fire departments, hazardous materials (hazmat) units, and emergency medical systems), and federal and military response units. Education and training efforts also have been directed to better prepare the civilian community.

To address the rising threat of terrorism in this country, the federal government established the Homeland Security Advisory System involving 5 color-coded threat conditions for possible terrorist attack:

Low (green): low risk of terrorist attacks

Guarded (blue): general risk of terrorist attacks

Elevated (yellow): significant risk of terrorist attacks

High (orange): high risk of terrorist attacks

Severe (red): severe risk of terrorist attacks

> Biological Emergencies

Biological emergencies include naturally occurring diseases and epidemics, and the use of biological warfare agents (for example, by terrorists). Biological agents are bacterial, viral, fungal, and parasitic organisms that cause disease in humans, plants, and animals. People may be exposed to these agents through inhalation (breathing in), skin exposure, or swallowing contaminated food or water.

In recent years, concern has increased about the deliberate use of certain biological agents by terrorists to cause diseases such as anthrax, pneumonic plague, tularemia, smallpox, and botulism. Potential targets include human beings, food crops, livestock, and other resources essential for national security, economy, and defense. The most likely biological weapon agents are bacteria, viruses, and biotoxins (which are poisonous chemicals produced by bacteria). Concern also exists for the spread of naturally occurring diseases such as malaria, tuberculosis, and influenza.

Responding to an infectious disease outbreak (natural or intended) depends on quickly identifying the cause and diagnosing the related illness. For some of these agents, delay in medical response could result in a large number of casualties. Any suspicion about exposure to a biological weapons agent should be reported to national, state, and local authorities.

KEY POINTS ABOUT BIOLOGICAL EMERGENCIES

- Some biological agents (for example, anthrax spores) remain in the environment for long periods, creating a long-term hazard.

- The onset of a biological emergency may be difficult to detect. For some infectious agents, disease transmission may continue for weeks before it is detected.

- You may not know right away if you were exposed to the germs or poisons that caused the emergency. Symptoms depend on the type of germ or poison. Some common signs include trouble breathing and flu-like symptoms (fever, headache, chills).

- Be suspicious of any symptoms you notice, but do not assume that any illness is related to a biological emergency. Use common sense and practice good hygiene.

- In case of a biological emergency, public health officials may not immediately be able to provide information on what you should do. It will take time to determine what the illness is, how it should be treated, and who is in danger.

- Local or state health officials will monitor the situation and recommend protective action. They will let you know what symptoms to look for, areas in danger, if medications or vaccinations are being distributed, and where you should seek medical attention if you become ill. The most appropriate action will depend on the situation.

- Listen to a television, radio, or emergency alert system for up-to-date information and instructions. Have a battery-powered radio available, if needed. Officials will tell you whether to stay inside or leave your home. They will tell you where to go if you need to leave your home.

- Some biological agents may be spread easily from infected patients to others. Health officials will provide clearly defined instructions for dealing with exposed or infected persons. This includes measures for protecting yourself first (for example, by using masks and gloves) before trying to help others.

- If you suspect that something unusual is occurring, report that information to your local public health or law enforcement agency.

> Bombings

Across the globe, the threat of terrorism involving the use of explosive agents in urban or otherwise crowded environments has become reality. Despite widespread concern for biological and chemical attacks, conventional explosives (such as bombs) are by far the most commonly used terrorist weapons because they are the easiest to create, obtain, and use.

IMPORTANT CLUES THAT MAY SIGNAL A BIOLOGICAL EMERGENCY

- Unusual number or pattern of commonly occurring illness among animals or humans
- A single suspected case of an uncommon disease
- Single or multiple cases of a suspected common disease that does not respond to treatment as expected
- Clusters of a similar illness occurring in the same time frame in different communities
- Unusual clinical, geographical, or seasonal presentation of a disease and/or unusual route of transmission

- Sudden increase in the following nonspecific illnesses:
  - pneumonia, flu-like illness, or fever with unusual features
  - Bleeding disorders
  - unexplained rashes and mucus membrane or skin irritation, particularly in adults
  - neuromuscular illness, such as muscle weakness and paralysis diarrhea

After an explosive event, the health system must be prepared to treat hundreds of casualties. The response, however, may be complicated by the loss of utilities (e.g., electricity, water), difficulty in transporting victims, lack of trained personnel, and damage to the surrounding infrastructure. Similar effects can be encountered in natural disasters such as tornadoes, earthquakes, and industrial or gas main explosions.

KEY POINTS ABOUT BOMBINGS

- Bombs and explosions can cause unique patterns of injury, involving multiple organs. In the United States, such injuries are seldom seen outside of military combat.

- The effects of an explosion depend on the amount of explosive materials used and how the device was made, the surrounding environment, the delivery method, and the distance and barriers between the victim and the blast.

- Most injuries from an explosion involve penetrating injuries and blunt trauma.

- Explosions in confined spaces (buildings, large vehicles, mines) and/or building collapse cause the most serious injuries and more deaths.

- People who were near an explosion should receive follow-up medical examinations. Some health effects may be delayed.

- All bomb events may result in chemical and/or radiological contamination of people and surrounding environments. Medical help should never be delayed because of the possibility of radioactive contamination of the person. The use of standard protective measures is effective in protecting first responders and other caregivers against contamination with radioactive materials.

- Victims may require hepatitis B immunization and age-appropriate tetanus toxoid vaccine.

> Chemical Emergencies

Toxic chemical agents are gases, liquids, or solids that have harmful effects on people, animals, or plants. These materials come in the form of explosives, flammable and combustible substances, corrosive agents, and poisons and are shipped daily on the nation's highways, railroads, waterways, and pipelines. Many products containing hazardous chemicals, such as pesticides and drain cleaners, are also used and stored routinely in homes.

Chemical agents can be released by unintended or deliberate means, such as through a spill from a damaged railroad tank car or explosion at an industrial facility with contamination of surrounding air, food, water, and other resources.

Health effects of toxic chemical agents range from irritation and burning of eyes, skin, and mucous membranes to rapid collapse of the heart and lungs, resulting in death. Such effects may be immediate (a few seconds) or delayed (several hours to days). Immediate symptoms may include blurred vision, eye irritation, difficulty breath-

For help in dealing with health effects from chemical exposures, contact a Regional Poison Control Center at 800-222-1222.

ing, and nausea. People who are exposed may require urgent medical attention. To minimize exposure, strict precautions must be used until thorough decontamination has been performed or the specific chemical agent is identified.

Many communities have a local emergency planning committee (LEPC) that identifies industrial hazardous materials and keeps the community informed of the potential risks. Contact your local emergency management office to find out if your community has an LEPC and how you can participate.

KEY POINTS ABOUT CHEMICAL EMERGENCIES

- Evaluate the risks to your household using information from your LEPC and local emergency management office. Determine how close you are to factories, highways, or railroads that may produce or transport potentially hazardous chemicals.

- Learn about your community's plans for responding to a hazardous materials incident at a plant or other facility or a transportation incident involving hazardous materials. Talk to your LEPC or emergency management office.

- Primary detection of exposure to chemical agents is based on the signs and symptoms of the potential victim.

- Confirmation of a chemical agent, using detection equipment or laboratory analyses, will take considerable time and will not likely contribute to the early management of affected victims.

- The release of a chemical agent may be difficult to identify easily:

  > Symptoms of exposure to some chemical agents can be similar to those of common diseases, such as gastroenteritis (stomach flu).

  > Immediate symptoms of certain chemical exposures might be nonexistent or mild despite the risk for long-term effects.

  > Health care professionals might be less familiar with clinical presentations suggesting exposure to chemical agents than with illnesses they treat more frequently.

- After the release of a chemical agent, local authorities will monitor the situation and recommend protective action. The most appropriate action will depend on the situation. Stay tuned to the local emergency response network or news station for up-to-date information and instructions. You may be advised to "shelter in place," which means to stay in your home or office, or you may be advised to move to another location.

- If you are instructed to remain in your home or office building, you should:

  > Close doors and windows and turn off all ventilation, including furnaces, air conditioners, vents, and fans.

  > Seek shelter in an internal room and take your disaster supplies kit.

  > Listen to your radio for instructions from authorities.

- If you are caught outside during a chemical incident, try to stay uphill and upwind of the scene. Hazardous gases and mists are generally heavier than air and can be transported quickly by the wind.

IMPORTANT CLUES THAT MAY SIGNAL A CHEMICAL RELEASE

- An unusual increase in the number of persons with rapid onset of symptoms after exposure to a potentially contaminated source (for example, diarrhea and vomiting within minutes of eating a meal)

- Rapid onset of illness with little or no warning

- Unexplained illness or death among young or previously healthy persons

- Presence of an unexplained odor, low level clouds, or vapors at the scene

- Clusters of people who have common exposure characteristics, such as drinking water from the same source

- Unexplained death of plants, fish, or animals (domestic or wild)

- Clusters of people with clinical signs and symptoms suggestive of known chemical exposures:

  > Sudden unexplained weakness, collapse, or convulsions in previously healthy persons

  > Dimmed or blurred vision

  > Excessive tearing, drooling, diarrhea

  > Irritation of eyes, nose, throat, chest

  > Shortness of breath

  > Redness, burning, blistering, itching, peeling of skin

- Effects from exposure to chemical agents will vary depending on the:
  - > Type of agent
  - > Route of exposure (skin, inhaled, ingested)
  - > Amount and strength of the chemical
  - > Length of exposure
  - > Pre-existing medical conditions (for example, people with heart or respiratory diseases)
- Professional emergency responders will need to use personal protective gear and determine appropriate decontamination procedures to avoid contamination of themselves and others, as well as transport vehicles and treatment facilities.
- Removal of clothing and washing with soap and large amounts of water should be used to remove external chemical contamination.
- If you suspect that something unusual is occurring, report that information to your local public health or law enforcement agency.

> Radiation Emergencies

In a radiation emergency, dangerous radioactive materials are released into the environment. The type of radiation that is most dangerous is called ionizing radiation. Ionizing radiation is produced by devices such as x-ray machines. Radiation can be easily detected with equipment carried by many emergency responders.

For many people, radiation provokes a special fear, which can be alleviated through appropriate education and preparation. In a radiation emergency, the health threat to response personnel is low and can be minimized by using standard safety precautions. People who are contaminated with radioactive materials may expose or contaminate others with whom they come in close contact and should avoid such contact until they are appropriately decontaminated. Treatment for people exposed to radioactive materials may need to be started quickly to be effective.

A radiation emergency might be a single nuclear detonation or an incident involving unintentional or deliberate radiological contamination (such as a leak at a nuclear power plant). The most likely deliberate radiation emergency involves direct placement of a radioactive source in a public place or detonation of a high-yield explosive contaminated with radioactive material (a "dirty bomb").

A "dirty bomb" can result in:

- Extensive spread of radioactive material in the environment
- Blast injuries, burns, and trauma, with some persons being trapped after the blast
- Injuries due to radioactive material blown onto skin or embedded in wounds
- Internal contamination of victims if radioactive material is vaporized or dispersed in fine particles
- Acute radiation syndrome is not likely unless persons are trapped near sources of penetrating gamma radiation (such as iridium-192, cesium-137, cobalt-60)
- Vaporization/aerosolization of radioactive materials and subsequent dispersal by wind and weather, which could cause contamination of the environment and economic disruption
- Widespread fear and anxiety

Explosive destruction of a nuclear reactor can result in:

- Blast injuries to people in the vicinity
- Radiation exposure and contamination to those people in or near the reactor and in surrounding areas
- Airborne spread of radioactive materials that could cause contamination of the environment and economic disruption
- Release of radioactive iodine, which requires administration of thyroid-blocking potassium iodide (KI) to children, pregnant women, and others
- Widespread fear and anxiety

Detonation of a nuclear weapon can result in:

- Massive widespread destruction with catastrophic consequences from the blast, heat, and radiation
- Hundreds to thousands of immediate deaths
- Hundreds to thousands of victims with burns, blast injuries and trauma, radiation exposure, contamination, flash blindness, and other injuries

- Destruction of medical facilities, fire, emergency medical services, and emergency management capabilities in the involved area with loss of personnel

- Widespread environmental contamination

- Nationwide psychological trauma

- Computer, electrical equipment, and phone system malfunction due to electromagnetic interference that can occur with a nuclear detonation

KEY POINTS ABOUT RADIATION EMERGENCIES

- The primary risk of a dirty bomb or other isolated radiation incident is the psychological effect on citizens rather than sickness caused by radiation.

- After a release of radioactive materials, local authorities will monitor the levels of radiation and determine what protective actions to take.

- The most appropriate action will depend on the situation. Stay tuned to the local emergency response network or news station for up-to-date information and instructions.

- If a radiation emergency involves the release of large amounts of radioactive materials, you may be advised to "shelter in place," which means to stay in your home or office, or you may be advised to move to another location.

- The longer a person is exposed to radiation, the greater the dose; victims should be removed from the disaster scene as quickly as possible.

- The farther away you are from a radiation source, the lower the radiation dose.

- Emergency responders should wear protective gloves, protective clothing, and radiation dosimeters (devices that measure amounts of radiation exposure); respirators or protective masks can prevent breathing in radioactive particles.

- Removal of clothing and washing with soap and large amounts of water are sufficient to remove most external radiation contamination.

- The health effects of radiation exposure are directly related to the amount of radiation absorbed by the body (radiation dose) and are determined by the:

> Radiation type (alpha, beta, x-ray, or gamma radiation);

> Means of exposure, internal or external (absorbed by the skin, inhaled, or ingested); and

> Length of time exposed.

- People being examined for potential radiation exposure may not show obvious symptoms when first examined (even if they received a large radiation dose) due to the delayed onset of symptoms following exposure. Follow-up medical examination is needed to establish the true nature and extent of exposure.

- For exposure to radioactive iodine (for example, a nuclear power plant incident), potassium iodide (KI) is given to protect the thyroid gland. KI will not protect a person from other radioactive materials or protect other parts of the body from radiation exposure.

MENTALLY COPING WITH DISASTER

Experiencing a disaster can be one of the most difficult events a person can endure and can have both short- and long-term effects. Most people who experience a disaster, whether as a victim or responder, will have some type of psychological, physical, and/or emotional response to the event. Common symptoms include:

- Fear

- Helplessness

- Shock

- Worry

- Anger

- Confusion

- Difficulty concentrating

- Changes in sleep

- Loss of appetite

- Post-traumatic stress disorder (PTSD)

- Depression

HURRICANE DOLLY

Representatives from FEMA and the U.S. Small Business Administration document damage to a multifamily building in South Padre Island, Texas. Hurricane Dolly struck the island in July of 2008 with winds of 100 miles per hour.

Patricia Brach/FEMA

KEY POINTS TO HELP COPE WITH DISASTER

- Educate yourself about the potential danger. Keep informed about breaking news and developments. If television or other news reports greatly increase your feelings of anxiety and helplessness, avoid them; you don't need every graphic detail.

- Avoid overexposure to news rebroadcasts of the events. Television news of traumatic events can be particularly frightening to children, especially when it is viewed repeatedly.

- Try to take control of your situation as best you can. If possible, avoid places that will cause you unnecessary stress and anxiety. If you feel anxious, angry, or depressed, realize that others are experiencing similar emotions.

- Avoid being alone. Talk about your feelings with family or friends.

- If you have contact with children, let them know that you are there for them to talk about the disaster and their feelings.

- Avoid becoming preoccupied with the disaster. Take some time to get away from your "normal" routine. Find ways to distract yourself from thinking about the event and the potential for further harm. Get involved in an activity that you can control (work in the house or garden, do volunteer work, go see a movie or play).

- Maintain healthy behaviors. Eat a well-balanced diet. Avoid or at least minimize alcohol intake. Get regular exercise. If you smoke, don't increase your tobacco consumption. Although it may seem to ease anxiety in the short term, smoking has significant health risks.

- Remember that feelings of anxiety and depression following a traumatic event are natural. If these symptoms continue for several weeks after the event has passed, or if these feelings begin to overwhelm you to the extent that you cannot continue your daily activities, you should consider talking to your doctor or a mental health professional. Symptoms that indicate a need for a medical evaluation include but are not limited to:

  > Changes in eating and sleeping habits

  > Physical problems such as stomach upset, back and neck aches, and headaches

  > Inability to focus or concentrate on routine tasks or work

  > Lack of interest in previously enjoyable activities

  > Extreme fear of leaving your home

  > Irritability and significant mood swings

  > Having flashbacks or nightmares or playing the events over and over in your mind

  > Taking extreme measures to avoid the memories through the use of alcohol or other drugs

  > Feeling hopeless, helpless, or that life is not worth living

  > Feeling suicidal

  > Having extreme anxiety such as panic attacks

PREPARE BEFORE DISASTER STRIKES

The best way to make homes and communities safer is to be prepared before disaster strikes. This can be done through thoughtful planning and can ensure that if a disaster occurs, people are ready to get through it safely and respond to it effectively.

CRITICAL DISASTER PREPAREDNESS STEPS FOR CITIZENS

- Understand the disaster risks in your community. Ask local authorities about possible hazards that may affect your community and what the risks might be for you and your family.

- Prepare and practice an emergency plan with your family.

- Prepare a disaster kit (more on this later in the chapter).

- Be aware of your surroundings. Move or leave if you feel uncomfortable or if something does not seem right.

- Take precautions when traveling. Be aware of conspicuous or unusual behavior. Do not accept packages from strangers. Do not leave luggage unattended. Learn where emergency exits are located in buildings you frequent.

- Promptly report unusual behavior, suspicious or unattended packages, and strange devices to the police or security personnel.

- Learn about emergency preparedness and response plans for your community, schools, and place of employment.

- Know how to contact local medical, public health, and law enforcement authorities.

- Be aware of available medical and mental health information and resources and how to access them immediately and in various ways.

- Be prepared emotionally; understand how to deal with stress.

- Be prepared physically; maintain a healthy lifestyle (eat a well-balanced diet, be physically active; get adequate sleep; avoid tobacco, alcohol, and other drugs).

- Learn immediate actions to protect the health and safety of yourself, your family, and your neighbors.

- Take measures to protect your home and personal belongings.

- Learn first aid and basic life support procedures; participate in additional education and training programs to improve your knowledge, ability, and willingness to respond to an emergency or mass casualty situation.

- Learn about your community's emergency warning system and emergency communications plan.

- Learn about local disaster relief services that can provide assistance. Contact local agencies and organizations about volunteer opportunities.

> Create and Practice a Family Disaster Plan

It is important for all family members to know how to react in a disaster or other emergency. Talk with your family about disasters that are likely to happen in your area and how to prepare for each type. Practice your family disaster plan at least twice each year so that everyone will remember what to do when in an emergency. In any disaster, the best protection is knowing what to do.

A family disaster plan is simple to create. You can begin by gathering family members and making sure each person is well-informed on potential hazards and community action plans. Discuss with them what you would do if family members are not home when an emergency alert or other warning is given. In addition, think about:

ESCAPE ROUTES

Talk about and decide on escape routes in the home for all family members. Know the fastest way out of your home and how not to become trapped.

PLACES TO MEET

Decide on a place for family members to meet if an emergency happens. Agree on a meeting place away from your home (a neighbor or relative's house or even a street corner) where you would get together if you were separated in an emergency. Give each family member an emergency list with the name, address, and phone number of the meeting place. For children who are old enough, help them to memorize the person's name, address, and phone number.

EVACUATION ROUTES

The amount of time you have to leave the area will depend on the type of disaster. If the event is weather-related, such as a hurricane that can be monitored, you might have a day or two to get ready. Many other disasters allow no time for family members to gather even the most basic necessities. In such situations, it is essential to plan ahead.

FAMILY COMMUNICATIONS

Your family may not be together when a disaster strikes, so plan in advance on how you will contact each other. Think about how you will communicate in different situations. Keep emergency phone numbers where family members can find them. Pick an out-of-state family contact person whom family members can "check-in" with if you are separated during an emergency or if your home is damaged or you cannot get to it.

UTILITY SHUT-OFF AND SAFETY

In the event of a disaster, you may be instructed to shut off the utility service (water, electricity, natural gas) at your home. Learn the location of utility shut-off valves and how to close them.

INSURANCE AND IMPORTANT DOCUMENTS

Make special arrangements to back up or otherwise secure important records, documents, and files.

SPECIAL NEEDS

If you or someone close to you has a disability or other special need (for example, children, the elderly, pregnant women, and disabled persons), you may have to take additional steps to protect yourself and your family in an emergency:

- Have extra eyeglasses and hearing-aid batteries.
- Have extra wheelchair batteries.

- Keep a list of the style and serial number of medical equipment required by you and your family members.

- Know where to find your family's medical insurance cards.

- Have a list of doctors, relatives, or friends who should be notified in an emergency.

- Have an emergency supply of prescription medications. Carry a current list of your prescription medications with you at all times (this includes why you are taking the medicine, the doses, and your doctor's and pharmacist's contact information). With your doctor, discuss ways you can be sure to have a large enough supply of prescription medications for an emergency situation.

CARE FOR PETS

If you have to leave your home, do not leave your pets behind. Pets most likely cannot survive on their own, and if they do, you may not be able to find them when you return. Because pets are not allowed in many emergency shelters, find out in advance whether the motels and hotels to which you plan to evacuate will allow pets.

CARE FOR LIVESTOCK

Evacuate animals whenever possible. Ensure all animals have some form of identification that will allow you to identify them later. Arrangements for evacuation, including routes and places to take the animals, should be made in advance. If evacuation is not possible, a decision must be made whether to move large animals to available shelter or move them outside. This decision should be determined based on the type of disaster and the condition and location of the animal shelter.

LEARN FIRST AID AND SAFETY SKILLS

It is important that family members know how to administer first aid and CPR and how to use an AED and a fire extinguisher.

> Assemble a Disaster Supplies Kit

After a disaster, you and your family may be on your own for hours or days before outside help is available. There also may be times, such as during a flood or a heavy winter storm, when you can't leave your home for days. In other situations, you may be asked to leave at a moment's notice with very little time to pack personal belongings.

A disaster supplies kit is a collection of basic items that family members may need in a disaster (this includes items already mentioned on page 18 of this handbook). Every household should have adequate food, water, and other supplies to last for at least 3 days, and if possible, for up to 2 weeks. Keep the items that you would most likely need while away from home in an easy-to-carry container (possible containers include a large, covered trash can; camping backpack; large suitcase; or duffle bag). Basic items that should be considered in a family disaster kit include:

WATER

You should have at least a 3-day supply of water and you should store at least 1 gallon of water per person per day.

FOOD

Store at least a 3-day supply of food that doesn't need refrigeration, preparation, or cooking and requires little or no water. Select food items that are compact and lightweight. Avoid foods that will make you thirsty. Choose salt-free items, whole grain cereals, and canned foods with high liquid content.

FIRST AID KIT

A list of suggested supplies is provided in Part II of this handbook (see p. 18).

CLOTHING AND BEDDING

Include at least one complete change of clothing and shoes per person. Provide sleeping bags or blankets to keep warm.

SANITATION SUPPLIES

Includes toilet paper; soap; liquid detergent; feminine hygiene products (such as tampons and sanitary pads); personal hygiene items (deodorant, toothpaste, toothbrushes, comb and brush, etc.); lip balm; sunscreen; plastic garbage bags and ties (for personal sanitation uses); a plastic bucket with tight lid; disinfectant; and household chlorine bleach.

OTHER SUPPLIES AND EQUIPMENT

- Portable, battery-operated radio and extra batteries; preferably this should be a battery-operated National Oceanic and Atmospheric Administration (NOAA) all-hazard alert radio. You will pick up the frequency of the NOAA, which will include instructions on whether to stay in your home, when to evacuate, and the status of the emergency event. You can purchase such a radio at a local electronics store.

- Flashlight and extra batteries

- Cash or traveler's checks, credit and ATM cards

- Extra set of house and car keys

- Manual can opener, utility knife

- Fire extinguisher (small canister, ABC type)

- Small tent

- Mess kits, or paper cups and plates and plastic utensils

- Basic tools (such as hammer, pliers, screwdrivers, shovel, wrench to turn off household utilities)

- Compass

- Matches in a waterproof container

- Aluminum foil

- Plastic storage containers

- Signal flares

- Needles, thread

- Medicine dropper (this can be used to sanitize water by using 16 drops of unscented liquid chlorine bleach to a gallon of water)

- Whistle
- Plastic sheeting and duct tape
- Regional maps
- Portable generator

SPECIAL ITEMS FOR INFANTS

Include formula, diapers, bottles, pacifiers, powdered milk, and medications.

SPECIAL ITEMS FOR OTHER FAMILY MEMBERS

Include prescription and nonprescription medications, insulin, denture needs, contact lenses and supplies, extra eyeglasses, hearing aid batteries.

IMPORTANT FAMILY DOCUMENTS

Be sure to include copies of wills; insurance policies, contracts, deeds, stocks and bonds; photo IDs, passports, and Social Security cards; immunization and other health records; bank account numbers; birth, marriage, and death certificates; mortgage records; motor vehicle records; and photocopies of credit and identification cards (keep these records in a waterproof, portable container).

IMPORTANT TELEPHONE NUMBERS AND ADDRESSES

Keep a list of contact information for physicians, pharmacists, special needs service providers, and caregivers, as well as contact and meeting place information for family members.

> Protect Your Assets

If you are unsure whether your property or business is at risk in a disaster, check with your local building official, city engineer, or planning and zoning administrator. They can tell you whether you are in

THE NORTHRIDGE EARTHQUAKE

During the California Northridge earthquake (January 1994), 72 people died and the final material cost was estimated at $25 billion. Approximately 114,000 residential and commercial structures were damaged.

FEMA News Photo

a disaster-prone area and can usually tell you how to protect yourself, your house, business, and property from different hazards. In addition to seeking such guidance, you should:

BUY INSURANCE

Obtain property, health, and life insurance if you do not have them. Review existing policies for the amount and extent of coverage to be sure you have what is required for you and your family for all possible hazards. If you live in a flood-prone area, consider purchasing flood insurance to reduce your risk of flood loss. Buying flood insurance to cover the value of a building and its contents will not only provide greater peace of mind but will also speed the recovery if a flood occurs.

INVENTORY HOME POSSESSIONS

Make a record of your personal property for insurance purposes. Take photos or a video of the interior and exterior of your home. Include personal belongings in your inventory.

PROTECT IMPORTANT DOCUMENTS

Store important documents such as insurance policies, deeds, property records, and other important papers in a safe place, such as a safety deposit box away from your home. Make copies of important documents for your disaster supplies kit.

STOW AWAY SOME MONEY

Consider saving money in an emergency savings account that could be used in any crisis. It is a good idea to keep a small amount of cash or traveler's checks at home in a safe place where you can find them quickly.

> Get Trained, Get Involved

The need for trained citizens is vital in the first minutes, hours, and even days after an event, when survivors may have no alternative to treating and caring for themselves, their families, coworkers, and neighbors. At times, citizens may be required to act independently for many hours after a disaster event until outside help arrives. To improve personal and community preparedness, all citizens should have the education and training to make sure they can:

- Recognize potential life-threatening situations and act appropriately, while protecting personal health and safety

- Know how to contact and work with local emergency medical and public health systems

- Make decisions with limited resources and limited information

- Understand and use reliable disaster health information and resources

- Know about medical, social, and mental health resources that can give assistance in a disaster

- Know about opportunities to become more involved in local preparedness and response efforts through participation in local volunteer efforts

In many communities, disaster education and training is available through chapters of the American Red Cross, through Citizen Corps Councils, Medical Reserve Corps units, and Community Emergency Response Teams.

KNOW WHERE TO FIND MORE INFORMATION

The following agencies, organizations, and Internet sites can provide helpful information for your disaster planning needs:

> Government Agencies

Centers for Disease Control and Prevention
www.bt.cdc.gov

Citizen Corps Program
www.citizencorps.gov

Community Emergency Response Team (CERT) Program
www.citizencorps.gov/cert/

Federal Emergency Management Agency
www.fema.gov
www.fema.gov/kids
www.disasterhelp.gov

Medical Reserve Corps (MRC) Program
www.medicalreservecorps.gov/HomePage

National Hurricane Center
www.nhc.noaa.gov

National Oceanic and Atmospheric Administration
www.noaa.gov

National Weather Service
www.nws.noaa.gov

Substance Abuse and Mental Health Services Administration
www.mentalhealth.samhsa.gov/cmhs/EmergencyServices/default.asp

U.S. Department of Health and Human Services
www.hhs.gov/disasters/index.shtml
www.pandemicflu.gov
www.remm.nlm.gov

U.S. Department of Homeland Security
www.dhs.gov/index.shtm
www.ready.gov

U.S. Geological Survey
www.usgs.gov

World Health Organization
www.who.int/en

> Professional Associations and Volunteer Organizations

American Academy of Pediatrics
www.aap.org/disaster

American Association of Poison Control Centers
www.aapcc.org/DNN

American Medical Association
www.ama-assn.org/go/disasterpreparedness

American Psychiatric Association
www.psych.org

American Public Health Association
www.getreadyforflu.org/newsite.htm

American Red Cross
www.redcross.org

National Voluntary Organizations Active in Disaster
www.nvoad.org

> ## State and Local Directories

Federal Bureau of Investigation (FBI) Field Offices
www.fbi.gov/contact/fo/fo.htm

Local Public Health Agencies
www.naccho.org

State Emergency Management Offices
www.fema.gov

MEDICAL CHART

Family Members (Names)	Allergies	Major Medical Problems (Date)	Medications (Date)	Tetanus Booster (Date)	Influenza (Date)

Pneumonococcal Pneumonia [Date]	Haemophilus Influenzae [Date]	Hepatitis B [Date]	Polio [Date]	Diptheria Tetanus Pertussis [DPT] [Date]	Measles Mumps Rubella [Date]	Other Medical Information

INDEX

●●

n=note

on drowning victims, 324, 325
glossary of terms, 42
hands-only, 39
on infants, 40–42
knowing, 8
medical personnel and, 23
on newborn, 228
cramps, 173–74, 282–83, 330
cranberry juice, and medication, 137
croup, 165–66
Cushing's syndrome, 5
cuts, 185–87
in eyes, 128

D

dark tarry stool, 100
date rape drugs, 195–96
decompression sickness, 322–23
defibrillators. *See* AEDs
dehydration, 101–2, 114, 174, 197. *See also* diarrhea; heat-related problems; seizures; vomiting
delusions, 215
dental problems, 92–93
depressants, 201–3
depression, 7, 214
diabetes, 3, 5, 6, 7
diabetes-related emergencies, 94–95
diabetic coma, 94–95. *See also* unconsciousness; vomiting
diaper rash, 180
diarrhea, 102–4, 109–10. *See also* dehydration; enteric food poisoning; vomiting
diet, role of, 2, 3–4, 8
digestive problems, 96–115. *See also* pregnancy; shock
   abdominal pain, 96–98
   bloody stool, 98–99
   constipation, 99–100
   dark tarry stool, 100
dirty bombs, 369
disaster preparedness, 353–85
   asset protection, 380–82
   critical steps, 374–75
   disaster supplies kits, 377–80
   family disaster plan, 375–77
   first response, 355–56
   government agencies, 383–84
   importance of, 354
   mental coping mechanisms, 371–73
   natural and weather-related disasters, 356–61
   terrorist threats, 361–71
   training and involvement, 382–83
disaster supplies kits, 377–80
dislocations, 82–83. *See also* bone injuries

elbow, 70–72
   kneecap, 66–67
   shoulder, 75–76, 284–86
diuretics, fainting and, 156
dizziness, 197–98. *See also* stroke; transient ischemic attack
dressings, 26, 52–53
   for burns, 85
drinking, excessive, 2
drowning, 324–27
drug abuse, 198–99
drug and alcohol problems, 198–207
drugs. *See also* medications
   alcohol, 200–201
   date rape, 195–96
   depressants, 201–3
   hallucinogens, 203–4, 215
   inhalants, 204–5
   stimulants, 206–7
dust allergies, 56–57

E

E. coli poisoning, 106, 107–8
ear, amputated, 61
ear, nose, and throat problems, 116. *See also* cold-related problems
   choking, 116
   common cold, 117
   dizziness and, 197
   ear injuries, 120–21
   earaches, 118–20
   epiglottitis, 121–22
   foreign objects inside the ear, 122
   mononucleosis, 123
   nosebleeds, 123–24
   snoring, 233
   sore throat, 124–25
ear injuries, 120–21
earaches, 118–20
early warning signs, recognizing, 3
earthquakes, 357
ECG tracings, 23
elbow injuries, 70–72, 245–51. *See also* bone injuries
   bursitis, 245–46
   dislocation, 70–72
   golfer's elbow, 247–49
   sprain, 176
   tennis elbow, 249–51
elderly
   abuse of, 190–92
   brown recluse spider bite to, 310–11
   falls in the, 207–8
   nosebleeds in the, 123
electrical burns, 89–91